# Corporate Governance, Ownership Structure and Firm Performance



The relationship between ownership structure and firm performance has been studied extensively in corporate finance and corporate governance literature. Nevertheless, the mediation (path) analysis to examine the issue can be adopted as a new approach to explain why and how ownership structure is related to firm performance and vice versa. This approach calls for full recognition of the roles of agency costs and corporate risk-taking as essential mediating variables in the bi-directional and mediated relationship between ownership structure and firm performance.

Based on the agency theory, corporate risk management theory and accounting for the dynamic endogeneity in the ownership–performance relationship, this book develops two-mediator mediation models, including recursive and non-recursive mediation models, to investigate the ownership structure–firm performance relationship. It is demonstrated that agency costs and corporate risk-taking are the 'missing links' in the ownership structure–firm performance relationship. Hence, this book brings into attention the mediation and dynamic approach to this issue and enhances the knowledge of the mechanisms for improving firm's financial performance.

This book will be of interest to corporate finance, management and economics researchers and policy makers. Post-graduate research students in corporate governance and corporate finance will also find this book beneficial to the application of econometrics into multi-dimensional and complex issues of the firm, including ownership structure, agency problems, corporate risk management and financial performance.

**Dr. Hoang N. Pham** is a research associate at Decision Sciences and Modelling Program at Victoria University, Australia.

**Prof. Sardar M. N. Islam** is a professor at the Institute of Sustainable Industries and Liveable Cities at Victoria University, Australia.

## Routledge Studies in Corporate Governance

**Resource Security and Governance**
The Globalisation of China's Natural Resources Companies
*Edited by Xinting Jia and Roman Tomasic*

**Corporate Governance in Action**
Regulators, Market Actors and Scrutinizers
*Edited by Lars Engwall*

**Enhancing Board Effectiveness**
Institutional, Regulatory and Functional Perspectives for Developing and Emerging Markets
*Edited by Franklin N. Ngwu, Onyeka Osuji, Chris Ogbechie, and David Williamson*

**Corporate Governance and Effectiveness**
Why Companies Win or Lose
*Dipak R. Basu and Victoria Miroshnik*

**Corporate Governance in India**
*Arindam Das*

**Corporate Governance and Whistleblowing**
Corporate Culture and Employee Behaviour
*Moeen Umar Cheema, Rahat Munir and Sophia Su*

For more information about this series, please visit www.routledge.com/Routledge-Studies-in-Corporate-Governance/book-series/RSCG

# Corporate Governance, Ownership Structure and Firm Performance

## Mediation Models and Dynamic Approaches

Hoang N. Pham and
Sardar M. N. Islam

Routledge
Taylor & Francis Group
NEW YORK AND LONDON

First published 2022
by Routledge
605 Third Avenue, New York, NY 10158

and by Routledge
2 Park Square, Milton Park, Abingdon, Oxon, OX14 4RN

Routledge is an imprint of the Taylor & Francis Group, an informa business



*Library of Congress Cataloguing-in-Publication Data*
Names: Pham, Hoang N., 1977- author. | Islam, Sardar M. N., 1950- author.
Title: Corporate governance, ownership structure and firm performance: mediation models and dynamic approaches / Hoang N. Pham and Sardar M. N. Islam.
Description: 1 Edition. | New York, NY: Routledge, 2022. | Series: Routledge studies in corporate governance | Includes bibliographical references and index.
Identifiers: LCCN 2021042383 (print) | LCCN 2021042384 (ebook) | ISBN 9781032186849 (hardback) | ISBN 9781032186900 (paperback) | ISBN 9781003255741 (ebook)
Subjects: LCSH: Corporate governance. | Corporations--Finance. | Risk management. | Organizational behavior. | Organizational effectiveness.
Classification: LCC HD2741.P523 2022 (print) | LCC HD2741 (ebook) | DDC 658.4--dc23
LC record available at https://lccn.loc.gov/2021042383
LC ebook record available at https://lccn.loc.gov/2021042384

ISBN: 978-1-032-18684-9 (hbk)
ISBN: 978-1-032-18690-0 (pbk)
ISBN: 978-1-003-25574-1 (ebk)

DOI: 10.4324/9781003255741

Typeset in Sabon
by MPS Limited, Dehradun

# Contents

# Figures

# Tables

# Appendices

# Book Summary

## Introduction

The relationship between ownership structure and firm performance is an important issue in corporate finance and governance literature. A range of mixed findings on the issue has been produced in the literature. However, a mediation approach that accounts for the indirect effect (or mediated effect) of ownership structure on firm performance has received little attention in prior studies. Additionally, most prior studies examine this relationship from a static perspective; that is, ownership structure and firm performance are contemporaneously correlated. Thus, addressing these gaps is essential in order to obtain an improved understanding of how and why ownership structure is related to firm performance and vice versa.

## Critical Literature Review

The conventional approach to the ownership–performance relationship is that they are directly related. Therefore, the 'missing links' between ownership structure and firm performance are not studied (Le and Buck, 2011). Under this approach, the estimated effects of ownership structure indicate only the total effects of ownership structure on firm performance. Meanwhile, agency theory and corporate risk management theory suggest that the mediating roles of agency costs and corporate risk-taking are potentially significant in the ownership–performance relationship. However, these theories have not yet been collectively applied to the mediation context to explain this relationship.

In addition, prior literature primarily focuses on the contemporaneous (or static) relationship between ownership structure and firm performance. A dynamic interrelationship between them is possible and it can be specified in a non-contemporaneous model (Hu and Izumida, 2008, Wintoki et al., 2012). In general, there are no prior studies that have sought to adopt both mediation and dynamic approaches in order to explore the ownership structure–firm performance relationship.

## Objectives

The broad goal of this book is to adopt both the mediation and dynamic approaches in order to examine the relationship between ownership structure and firm performance. To this end, there are two main objectives of this research: (1) testing the mediating role of both agency costs and corporate risk-taking in the ownership–performance relationship; and (2) examining the non-contemporaneous interrelationship between ownership structure and firm performance in the mediation context.

## Methodology

The main variables of interest in this book consist of three types of equity ownership (government ownership, insider ownership and foreign ownership), two mediating variables (agency costs and corporate risk-taking) and two measures of financial performance of listed firms (return on assets and Tobin's Q).

Two mediation models are developed in this book, namely: a recursive model and a non-recursive model; which are respectively used for the first and the second objectives of the research mentioned above. In the recursive model, Baron and Kenny (1986) causal-steps approach, which includes the generalised method of moments and fixed-effects estimation, is adopted to model the relationship from past ownership structure via current agency costs and current corporate risk-taking to current firm performance. In the non-recursive model, maximum likelihood estimation is used, and all paths in the model are estimated simultaneously. This method is also employed to re-estimate the recursive model when the mediators are treated differently. This book uses a sample of 475 observations of 95 listed firms on the Vietnamese stock market over a five-year period (2008–2012).

## Findings, Implications and Contributions

This book finds a mediating role for agency costs and corporate risk-taking in the relationship between ownership structure and firm performance. Precisely, the mediating role of agency costs is significant in the relationship between previous-year government ownership and current-year firm performance, while the mediating role of corporate risk-taking is significant in the relation between previous-year insider ownership and current-year performance. These results demonstrate that agency costs and corporate risk-taking are the 'missing links' in the ownership–performance relationship.

In addition, it is found that there are significant effects of previous-year firm performance on government ownership and foreign ownership in the current year. In the case of a developing and transition economy like Vietnam's, this implies that decisions on changing government ownership and foreign ownership in listed firms are influenced by prior firm performance. However, changes in the level of current insider shareholdings are independent of prior firm performance.

Furthermore, this study finds that previous-year insider ownership, but not previous-year government ownership, ultimately contributes to improving current-year firm performance, and this positive effect is significantly driven by corporate risk-taking channels. This finding supports the positive view of private ownership, rather than government ownership, in transition economies. In contrast, the contribution of previous-year foreign ownership to current-year firm performance is negative, perhaps because foreign ownership is not concentrated in Vietnam's listed firms.

Based on agency theory and corporate risk management theory, and accounting for the dynamic endogeneity in the ownership–performance relationship, this book makes an original contribution to the literature by developing a two-mediator mediation model to explain the ownership structure–firm performance relationship. Additionally, this book provides empirical evidence on how and why government ownership, insider ownership and foreign ownership contribute differently to firm performance. Useful implications for the privatisation of SOEs in transition economies can also be obtained from this study. Moreover, this is the first study of the mediated and dynamic interrelationship between ownership structure and performance in Vietnamese listed firms.

# 1 Corporate Governance, Ownership Structure and Firm Performance

## An Introduction

### 1.1 Background of the Research

The relationship between ownership structure and firm performance has been studied extensively in corporate finance and governance literature. The adoption of mediation (path) analysis to examine the issue has emerged recently as a new approach to explain why and how ownership structure is related to firm performance. In addition to the work of Le and Buck (2011) on the mediating role of agency costs on the relationship between government ownership and firm performance, there is some other relevant literature on the issue (to be introduced in Chapter 2). Some more recent research that uses the mediation approach to consider the associations between ownership structure and firm performance is that of Wahba and Elsayed (2015). However, firm performance is considered in Wahba and Elsayed (2015) as the mediating variable for the effect of corporate social responsibility on institutional ownership. In the context of Bangladesh, Rashid (2020) examines the mediating role of board characteristics on the relationship between ownership structure and firm performance; the authors find that the impact of ownership structure on firm performance is partially mediated by board size and board independence. Further research in this direction is essential in order to understand the associations between ownership structure and firm performance. Thus, this book studies this relationship through a new mediation approach integrated with a dynamic approach.

It is well established in the literature that ownership structure does matter and that ownership structure and firm performance affect each other. The ownership structure of firms is one of the core internal characteristics of an effective corporate governance framework, making noticeable distinctions in governance systems across countries (Denis, 2010, Liang and Lin, 2011). The performance of a firm can be influenced by its ownership structure for several reasons:

DOI: 10.4324/9781003255741-1

1 owners have different levels of power, incentives and ability to monitor managers due to differences in their identities, concentration and resource endowments; and
2 owners have varying goals for their involvement in firms, resulting in different effects on firm performance (Douma et al., 2006). In turn, ownership structure is also affected by firm performance because they are endogenous, as claimed in many recent works such as those of Bhagat and Jefferis (2002), Bhagat et al. (2010) and Firth and Rui (2012), among others.

However, there is still limited knowledge on two aspects of this relationship in the literature. First, there is still little attention in the literature on the mediation channels between ownership structure and firm performance. It is implicitly assumed in many studies that firm performance is directly affected by ownership structure. Consequently, it is questionable whether there are underlying forces that intervene the impact of ownership structure on firm performance.[1] Moreover, when the mediation approach is not applied, the estimated coefficients on ownership structure only indicate the total effects of ownership structure on firm performance. In contrast, the other types of effects, such as indirect and direct effects, are not identified. Therefore, this book adopts a mediation approach in order to examine the relationship between ownership structure and firm performance.

Secondly, there is little literature on the non-contemporaneous or dynamic interrelationship between ownership structure and firm performance. It is likely that the current-year ownership structure can be affected by previous-year firm performance, while firm performance in this year can also be affected by ownership structure in the last year. This is termed the 'lead–lag' relationship between ownership structure and firm performance (Hu and Izumida, 2008). The dynamic relationship between current governance and past firm performance is an aspect of endogeneity that is often ignored in the literature, which may result in biased estimates (Wintoki et al., 2012). It is thus plausible to argue that there is still a large gap in the literature that investigates the co-deterministic relationship between ownership structure and firm performance from a dynamic perspective.

Consistent with Le and Buck (2011), this book firstly argues that agency cost is a 'missing link' in the relationship between ownership structure and firm performance. Agency theory suggests that the relationship between firm performance and ownership structure is closely associated with agency costs. Different forms of ownership may have different agency costs. In turn, agency costs can adversely affect firm performance (Brown et al., 2011).

Agency theory also suggests a link between equity owners and corporate risk-taking. Shareholders have different risk preferences; for example, managers are commonly regarded as risk-averse shareholders, since their human capital invested in the firm is not diversified (Himmelberg et al., 1999). It can be argued that these differences influence the risk-taking behaviours of the firm. In addition, it is well documented in corporate risk management theory that risks are closely associated with firm performance. For example, 'high risk–high return' is a hypothesis in this connection. As a result, an issue of concern is whether there is a continual connection between ownership structure, corporate risk-taking and firm performance. It is thus argued in this book that corporate risk-taking is another 'missing link' between ownership structure and firm performance.

Furthermore, this book attempts to examine the mediated relationship between ownership structure and firm performance in the framework of the non-contemporaneous interdependence between them. Thus, the direct effect of previous-year firm performance on current-year ownership structure is also examined, in addition to the mediated effects of previous-year ownership structure on current-year firm performance. While prior studies focus mainly on the contemporaneous relationship between ownership structure and firm performance from a static perspective (Hu and Izumida, 2008), this study uses a combination of the mediation approach with a dynamic perspective to produce new insights into the nature of the ownership–performance relationship.

On this basis, this book focuses on

1 the indirect effects of three equity ownership identities (government ownership, insider ownership and foreign ownership), through two mediating variables (agency costs and corporate risk-taking), on firm performance (return on assets or Tobin's Q);
2 the non-contemporaneous feedback effect of firm performance on ownership structure; and
3 the total effect of ownership structure on firm performance.

This book examines the issue from the context of the stock market in the developing and transition economy of Vietnam. Vietnam has been chosen as the case study for several reasons, namely,

1 no prior research has been undertaken on the mediated relationship between ownership structure and performance of Vietnamese listed firms;
2 the relationship between equity ownership and firm performance is still an issue of great concern and heated debate in this country during the process of the privatisation of state-owned enterprises; and, more importantly,

3 Vietnam is unique in having a young stock market associated with the privatisation programs of the state-owned enterprises. Under such circumstances, it provides all the variables of interest needed to develop the empirical models used in this study (see Section 1.3 for the details of the country-specific characteristics).

## 1.2 Research Problems and Motivation for Further Study

There remained opposing views about this association between ownership structure and firm performance until recently. For instance, the impact of ownership structure on firm performance has a long tradition of academic research, at least since Berle and Means (1932) emphasised managerial ownership and the separation of ownership and control. Under the 'alignment of interest effect' hypothesis (Jensen and Meckling, 1976), the higher the level of managerial ownership, the better firm performance is. On the contrary, the 'entrenchment effect' hypothesis postulates that the impact of managerial ownership becomes negative when managerial ownership reaches a certain level because managers will then become involved in non-maximising profit activities (Shleifer and Vishny, 2008). While many authors such as Megginson et al. (2012) and Djankov and Murrell (2002) argue that government ownership is inefficient and negative for firm performance, other authors, such as Tian and Estrin (2008) and Vaaler and Schrage (2009), claim that government ownership at certain levels helps improve firm performance.

Moreover, most empirical research on the issue has applied the direct approach, that is, ownership structure directly affects firm performance. As already mentioned, it can be argued that the direct approach yields a limited understanding of this relationship because the indirect effects of ownership structure via potential mediating variables are not considered. Hence, the empirical models developed in previous studies may not be suitable if the indirect channels of the effect of ownership structure exist in reality.

In this connection, it can be inferred from agency theory that the relation between firm performance and ownership structure is closely associated with agency costs because different forms of ownership may have different levels of agency costs. In turn, agency costs can adversely affect firm performance (Brown et al., 2011). The out-of-equilibrium model of the relationship between corporate governance and firm performance also suggests that corporate governance has a causal effect on firm performance indirectly through its impacts on the agency conflict of the firm, which is embodied by the incentives and monitoring of the management (Tan, 2009). However, few discussions have been had about the role of agency costs as a mediating variable in the ownership–performance relationship. Such a mediation approach is adopted to examine the relationship between firm performance and government ownership only in Le and Buck (2011). This leaves a large knowledge gap in the literature in terms of the mediated effect of ownership structure on firm performance via agency costs. Therefore, this study primarily attempts to examine the indirect association via agency costs between a set of ownership structures and firm performances.

Agency theory also suggests a link between equity owners and corporate risk-taking. Accordingly, shareholders have different risk preferences, such as risk-averse, risk-neutral and risk-seeking attitudes. For example, it is often argued in corporate governance literature that managers/insiders prefer a lower level of risk in comparison with the owners of a firm; hence they are commonly regarded as risk-averse shareholders (Himmelberg et al., 1999, Downs and Sommer, 1999). It is thus suggested that these differences can determine the types of risk-taking behaviours of equity owners. In addition, corporate risk management theory implies a close association between corporate risk-taking and firm performance under the assumption of 'high risk–high return' (Drever et al., 2007). Thus, corporate risk-taking can be considered another potential link between ownership structure and firm performance. Nevertheless, there is limited understanding in the literature about this channel of ownership–performance relationship. Taken together, it can be argued that a new mediation approach that considers both agency costs and corporate risk-taking as mediating variables could be adopted on the basis of agency theory and corporate risk management theory in order to explain the ownership structure–firm performance relationship.

In addition to the mediated associations, endogenously determined associations are potential in the relationship between ownership structure and firm performance. Much empirical evidence has shown that ownership structure and firm performance have a co-deterministic relationship, and they are interrelated (Farooque et al., 2010, Bhagat and Jefferis, 2002, Firth and Rui, 2012). Ownership structure and firm performance may be endogenous variables, and hence, the connection between them should not be treated as a uni-directional relationship. Ownership structure can affect firm performance, and simultaneously firm performance can have feedback effects on ownership structure.

In this regard, Wintoki et al. (2012) imply that a non-contemporaneous or dynamic relationship is another aspect of endogeneity that is often neglected in the ownership–performance relationship. Controlling for this dynamic endogeneity problem is, therefore, necessary for corporate finance and governance research because any potential endogeneity issues in the ownership–performance relationship should be investigated and resolved (Brown et al., 2011).

However, most prior studies control for endogeneity only in the framework of the contemporaneous and direct bidirectional relationships, such as those of Bhagat and Bolton (2008), Firth and Rui (2012) and Tian and Estrin (2008). Even with a mediation approach, Le and Buck (2011) do not consider the feedback effects of firm performance. This leaves a significant gap in the literature that investigates the non-contemporaneous or dynamic endogeneity between ownership structure and firm performance in a mediation framework. The issue becomes more complicated if both mediation effects and non-contemporaneous interdependence are taken into account, but a further understanding of the ownership structure–firm performance relationship can thereby be obtained.

Furthermore, there are fundamental differences in corporate governance systems across countries. Most of the influential studies in the field of corporate governance have been conducted in developed markets such as the USA, Europe and Japan. However, each country has its own set of country-specific conditions, such as history, culture, politics and legal origin, that affect the corporate governance framework of a firm. Typical ownership structures range from widely held to concentrated ownership (Denis, 2010, IFC, 2010). Thus, the impact of ownership structure on firm performance is likely to be different in developing countries in comparison with developed ones (Douma et al., 2006). Therefore, a study on the issue that uses a different context of a developing country like Vietnam will provide new evidence to the literature.

## 1.3 The Vietnamese Context

As aforementioned, Vietnam provides a unique sample for this type of research. This section highlights this country's specific characteristics, including the privatisation process and the issues related to equity ownership pattern, agency costs and corporate risk-taking behaviours.

### *1.3.1 Privatisation of the State-Owned Enterprises*[2]

The privatisation of the public sector has been rigorously pursued since the early 1990s, leading to a great volume of government shares being wholly or partially sold to the public and many former state-owned enterprises (SOEs) becoming joint-stock companies owned by different types of shareholders. In the first stage of privatisation from 1989 to 1992, the number of SOEs in Vietnam dropped from 12,300 to about 6500 (Pham and Carlin, 2008).

Before the Enterprise Law 2014, an SOE is defined as a corporation with more than 50% equity owned by the government. SOEs are regarded as the main driving force of the national economy and have the largest influence on the economy. The state sector in general and SOEs, in particular, maintain a 'strategic economic role' in Vietnam (Martin, 2003). The public sector (including the state and collectives) contributes three times more to the national GDP than the private sector (37.57% versus 11.13%) (General Statistics Office of Vietnam, 2012). The Vietnamese government still holds either the whole or the majority of interest in numerous important sectors of Vietnam's economy (IFC, 2010) (illustrated in Figure 1.1).

However, the contributions to the nation's GDP by different types of ownership have changed significantly over the last two decades in favour of the private sector, partly due to the transformation of the SOEs' equity ownership structure. For example, the composition of the non-state sector and foreign direct investment sector increased from 47.22% and 15.16% in 2005 to 49.34% and 18.09% in 2012, respectively. The achievements of privatisation have helped Vietnam gradually transform from a centrally planned economy to a market-based economy with growing economic power which is projected to become the 17th largest economy in the world by 2025 (Wilson and Stupnytska, cited in Vu et al., 2011).

In addition, the privatisation of SOEs and expansion of private firms in Vietnam have been supported by the operation of two national stock exchanges in Ho Chi Minh City (since 2000) and in Hanoi (since 2005). The two national stock exchanges in Vietnam have been the main marketplace for ownership restructuring of SOEs (Vu et al., 2011). By the end of 2020, the total shares market capitalisation of both exchanges is recorded at more than 87.6% of GDP.[3] It should be noted that most of the listed firms on the stock market are privatised SOEs. Having a young stock market that is closely associated with the privatisation programs of the SOEs is also a remarkable feature of the modern Vietnamese economy. Outside the national stock exchanges, there are thousands of other joint-stock companies which have not been listed as yet to meet listing requirements or their own decision not to be exchange-traded. The non-listed companies also include about a dozen SOEs wholly owned by government, which are the largest corporations in terms of capital and influence on the national economy.

In terms of post-privatisation economic efficiency, the sales of state shares to the public in Vietnam does represent a step forward because it creates new incentives for firms (Gainsborough, 2009). The privatisation of SOEs in Vietnam marks the retreat of government ownership and the state share of economic activity will continue declining (Vietnam Development Report 2004). Vietnam is, therefore, an economy in transition, with many government-controlled companies under privatisation (Hidenobu and Lai Thi Phuong, 2012).

Nevertheless, the role of the state in the Vietnamese economy is still particularly strong. Under the single-party political system, Kerkvliet (2018) interprets this fact as the 'dominating state', where rules and programs governing this country are made by and within the state. Some prior researchers argue that Vietnam could be a laboratory for replicating a research on China; and these two countries are similar in terms of reforming economically but not politically (Le and Buck, 2011, Wright and Nguyen, 2000). However, the two countries are far different in terms of the size of the national economy and related issues such as the policy towards foreign investors on the national stock markets. Until recently, the state sector maintains a dominant role while the private sector is under-developed in the Vietnamese economy, regardless of the impressive progress of the privatisation of the SOEs. It is also believed that the state sector in Vietnam is provided with greater access to resources such as land and finance (Nguyen and Van Dijk, 2012).

### *1.3.2 Patterns of Ownership Structure of Listed Firms*

Ownership concentration is a typical ownership pattern in non-Anglo-Saxon countries (Tirole, 2006). Therefore, the overall pattern of ownership structure of listed firms in Vietnam is the concentration of ownership; more precisely, this is government ownership concentration. Most of Vietnam's listed firms as of June 2014 are privatised SOEs, and the Vietnamese Government still retains a large proportion of total common equity in many of these firms. In the data sample for this research, for example, the number of privatised SOEs is 77 out of 95 firms (over 80%); while majority government ownership (25% or above of total common equity of a firm) is recognised in 270 out of 475 observations (more than 56%).

In comparison with other countries, prior studies, such as those of Le and Buck (2011) and Preacher and Hayes (2008), argue that the ownership structure in China is unique because government ownership is still dominant and the government has a strong influence on the economy regardless of the first steps of transformation towards a market economy. However, it is quite similar to the context of Vietnam with respect to the role and influence of the SOEs and government ownership in the national economy, as mentioned above. In contrast, this pattern is different from other East Asian countries like Indonesia, where control of firms is typically concentrated within families (Kumala & Siregar, 2020). In the USA, the dominant shareholders are households and institutional investors (Tirole, 2006). On the Vietnamese stock market as a whole, the government is a large shareholder (owning more than 5% of total equity) in almost all industries, as illustrated in Figure 1.1.

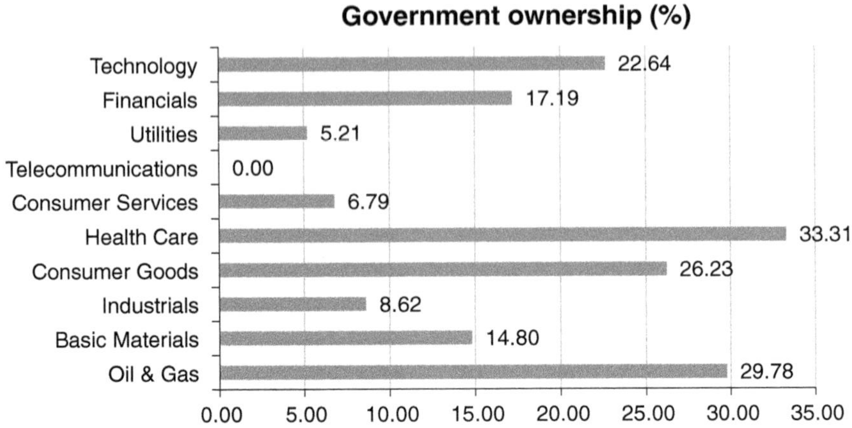


*Figure 1.1* Government ownership by industry on Vietnam's stock market.

Notes: This figure presents the ratios of government ownership by industry on the Vietnamese stock market. Data is as of June 2014 and has been sourced from the FiinGroup.[4]

In terms of private ownership, private companies in Vietnam are also characterised by a concentrated pattern of ownership. Numerous private companies in this country are controlled by a single person or a small group of family members or shareholders, and there has been no change in the controlling shareholders of many firms regardless of their significant expansion (IFC, 2010). There is little separation of ownership and control in Vietnamese firms. It is quite common that there is a dual role of chief executive officer (CEO) and chairman of the board of directors. In other words, most controlling shareholders assume the functions of managers and directors at the same time.

Another common type of private ownership in Vietnam's listed firms is foreign ownership. It is not uncommon that listed companies have some ownership stakes of foreign investors, but the maximum level of foreign ownership in a listed company is restricted by law to 49% of total common equity.[5] Like Korea, where foreign ownership is another type of institutional ownership (Kim, 2011), foreign investors in Vietnam are in many cases also institutional investors. As for market structure, while foreign investors can only buy and sell shares in a separated board (the B-share market) in China (Li et al., 2009), Vietnam offers a single platform of trading for both domestic and foreign investors.

It is also worth mentioning that among the above three types of ownership structure, not only is foreign ownership restricted as mentioned but there are also some trading limitations applicable to government ownership and insider ownership on Vietnam's stock market. Typically, government ownership is not tradable in the secondary market and insider ownership is not allowed to be exchanged in the first year of listing.

The public opinion on Vietnam's stock market called for a decrease in government ownership in listed companies, which should arguably be replaced by foreign ownership in order to improve firm performance.[6] As policy measures in response, the Vietnamese Government has required SOEs to reduce shareholdings in joint-stock companies not belonging to the SOEs' main business lines (see the next section for a list of policy and regulatory documents on this issue). On the other hand, the maximum level of shareholding by foreigners will be raised from the current threshold of 49% as mentioned earlier. However, it appears that the underlying justifications for adjusting the abovementioned levels have not been provided in any academic research so far.

### *1.3.3 Potential Agency and Corporate Risk-Taking Problems in Relation to Firm Performance*

As a code law country, the overall pattern of ownership concentration in Vietnam, as discussed above, is in conformity with the argument that ownership structure is more concentrated and complex in a code law country, while there is less effective legal protection for investors (Brown et al., 2011). As indicated by Vu et al. (2011), one of several problems facing Vietnam's stock market is weak shareholder protection. Under these circumstances, concentrated government ownership can serve as a means of protection. According to Brown et al. (2011), while a concentrated ownership structure is usually concerned with agency problems, it may be an alternative mechanism to protect small investors.

Another potential agency problem in Vietnamese listed firms is the limited separation of ownership and control between board members (directors) and managers (IFC, 2010). Typically, managers are also members of the board of directors, which is often referred to as 'duality' in corporate governance literature. According to IFC (2010), a typical consequence of this fact is a weak accountability and control structure for managers, which may adversely influence their corporate risk-taking appetite and incentives to work towards firm performance. In this context, an appropriate form of private ownership to be considered is insider ownership, which consists of the equity ownership of both managers and directors.[7] It is plausible to assume that the interest of managers and directors are homogenous in this case.

Furthermore, it is necessary to make a clear distinction between insider ownership and government ownership in government-controlled firms. This is because some directors may be assigned the role of a representative owner of government ownership in such firms, i.e. they are nominal owners of government stakes. Hence, the total proportion of insider ownership in many firms covers both the shareholding of managers and representative shareholding for the government. Under such a circumstance, there might be another duality problem in addition to the duality of director and manager roles, as aforementioned. Precisely, this is the dual task of directors, who should work for profit maximisation as expected by other principals (shareholders), while at the same time they are agents of government shareholders, who have to meet a certain number of social targets mandated by the government. There is thus a potential conflict between the social objective of the government and the profit objective of the firm (Sun et al., 2002). In theory, the government shareholder may focus on the 'social service assignment principle' rather than purely on 'shareholder value interests' (Kankaanpää et al., 2014). Therefore, a study of ownership structure in Vietnam needs to distinguish between directors' nominal ownership for government (i.e. government ownership) and their own shareholding.

In terms of corporate risk-taking, it can be observed that financial investments[8] were quite common in Vietnam's listed firms, in particular listed SOEs, during the period of study (2008–2012). Many listed firms engaged actively in trading stocks for short-term profits such as dividends and capital gains. For instance, in the data sample for this study, the number of observations with non-zero values for short-term financial investment (i.e. significant amounts of financial investment) accounts for nearly 58% (275/475) of firm-year observations. With respect to long-term financial investment, a large number of listed SOEs sought to expand capital into new businesses, mostly in the form of capital contribution or cross-shareholdings in other companies. As parent companies, they held a part or majority of common shares of the newly established ones. The problem was that many of the new businesses did not operate in the SOEs' main business lines. For example, a firm belonging to the oil and gas industry could invest in setting up new firms in the financial or basic materials industries. When Vietnam's stock market experienced a serious downturn during the period 2008–2010, it was observed that such financial investments suffered huge losses in market value. As a result, sharp reductions in profit were recognised in these firms' balance sheets as provisions because they had to spend a considerable amount of net income on provisions against potential financial losses. As policy measures against such inefficient long-term financial investments of SOEs, the Vietnamese Government enacted a series of policy and regulatory documents which require that SOEs retreat capital invested in non-core business lines.[9]

From the corporate governance viewpoint, financial investment in the form of cross-shareholding between parent companies and subsidiary ones is associated with a range of problems, such as a lack of transparency in ownership structure, difficulty for shareholders and investors in understanding the company, poor consolidated accounting and the ability to expropriate and ignore the rights of small individual shareholders (IFC, 2010).

Hence, it can be argued that there are inherent problems facing Vietnamese listed companies, which emphasises the need to properly consider the agency problems and risk-taking behaviours of these firms. This consideration relates to both the ownership structure and financial performance of listed firms.

## 1.4 Objectives of the Study and Research Questions

The first objective of this research is to test for the mediating roles of agency costs and corporate risk-taking in the ownership–performance relationship using a *recursive mediation model*. As such, only the direction of influence from ownership structure via agency costs and corporate risk-taking towards firm performance is considered (i.e. the feedback effect of firm performance is not yet accounted for). As the mediating roles of agency costs and corporate risk-taking are vital in order for this mediation mechanism to occur, agency costs and corporate risk-taking will be examined comprehensively and thoroughly by two different treatments, namely exogenous and endogenous treatments. The estimated results will then be compared to each other. The following research questions are raised for this purpose:

> ***Research question 1***: Do agency costs and corporate risk-taking mediate the effect of ownership structure on the performance of listed firms, assuming that agency costs and corporate risk-taking are exogenous?

> ***Research question 2***: Is there any variation in the mediating roles of agency costs and corporate risk-taking in the ownership structure–firm performance relationship, assuming that agency costs and corporate risk-taking are endogenous covariates?

As for Research question 1, agency costs and corporate risk-taking are assumed to be exogenous because each path of the hypothesised mediation mechanism in the recursive model is estimated separately. As such, the disturbances of the two mediators are not correlated. This is an application of the causal-steps approach of Baron and Kenny (1986), which is the most commonly used method in mediation analysis (Preacher and Hayes, 2008). Le and Buck (2011) also adopt this strategy to investigate the intervening role of agency costs in the relationship between government ownership and firm performance. Therefore, this book starts the mediation analysis by following the causal-steps approach in order to investigate the mediated relationship between ownership structure and firm performance. The findings obtained at this step are then compared with those for the next research question.

In terms of Research question 2, the two mediators are treated as endogenous; that is, agency costs and corporate risk-taking are no longer tested separately, but are estimated within a system of simultaneous equations, and the disturbances of the two mediators are allowed to be correlated. It is recommended in the mediation literature that the error terms of two mediating variables in a two-mediator mediation model should be set to be correlated because they mutually depend on predictor variables so that any non-modelled sources of covariance between the mediators are accounted for (Preacher and Hayes, 2008). According to Acock (2013), in a two-mediator model where the two mediating variables do not necessarily have a direct causal link, it is usually important to allow the residuals of the mediators to co-vary, on the assumption that the unexplained variance of the first mediator is correlated with some of the unexplained variances of the second mediator. Otherwise, it would have to be assumed that all of the covariances of the two variables is completely explained by their independent variables.

If there are significant variations in the mediation effects of agency costs and corporate risk-taking when these two mediators are permitted to co-vary, then it is plausible to argue that agency costs and corporate risk-taking are not exogenous. Hence, the estimated results obtained from the causal-steps method of Baron and Kenny (1986) are potentially biased for estimating a simultaneous equation system (Antonakis et al., 2010). In this case, the estimated paths in the recursive model with endogenous mediators will be regarded as more reliable.

The second objective of this book is to examine the non-contemporaneous interrelationship between ownership structure and firm performance in *a non-recursive model* that takes into account the feedback effects of firm performance on ownership structure and also allows the covariance of disturbances of different equations. This is an attempt to extend mediation analysis from a recursive to a non-recursive model. The following research questions are explored for this purpose:

> ***Research question 3***: Is there any non-contemporaneous feedback effect of ownership structure on firm performance in the mediation context?
>
> ***Research question 4***:
>
> i What is the total effect of ownership structure on firm performance when the non-contemporaneous interrelationship is accounted for?
>
> ii Which mediation channel is more important in determining the improvement in performance of Vietnamese listed firms?

With respect to Research question 3, the literature on this issue suggests that there is interdependence among corporate governance elements such as ownership structure and firm performance, as already mentioned. Hence, there is a potential feedback effect of firm performance on ownership structure. While prior works have often utilised a static view in order to investigate this effect, this book examines this interrelationship from a dynamic perspective, that is, that ownership structure and firm performance are non-contemporaneously co-deterministic. Time lags are recommended to be applied in mediation analysis because the mediation effect takes time to occur (MacKinnon, 2012). Also, the indirect effect of government ownership on firm performance may be spurious if the feedback effect of firm performance on ownership structure is not taken into consideration. It is believed in this book that correlating the disturbances of the mediators (i.e. treating them as endogenous) is not enough because we also need to account for the two-way relationship between ownership structure and firm performance in order to obtain more accurate and comprehensive results of the mediated/indirect and total effect of ownership structure on firm performance.

Regarding Research question 4, the first part of this question seeks insights into the total effect of ownership structure on firm performance, which is equal to the sum of the direct effects of ownership structure on firm performance plus the indirect effects of ownership structure through both agency costs and corporate risk-taking. It is plausible to argue that research on the ownership–performance relationship would have considerable practical significance if an understanding of how ownership structure ultimately affects firm performance is obtained. Moreover, the findings of the total effect of ownership structure on firm performance are to be compared with those obtained in prior literature. This is because most previous studies on the ownership–performance relationship have come up with the total effect only as a result of the direct approach, as aforementioned.

The second part of Research question 4 is to identify the more important mediation channel (either via agency costs or via corporate risk-taking) that determines the positive total effect of ownership structure on performance of Vietnam's listed firms when the non-contemporaneous interdependence between ownership structure and firm performance is accounted for. The implications for agency theory and corporate risk management theory can also be drawn on that basis.

## 1.5 Research Design, Methodology and Data

As mentioned earlier, the mediated relationship between ownership structure and firm performance is being investigated from a dynamic perspective. Hence, the main conceptual framework of this study first depicts the indirect links from previous-year (hereafter referred as lagged, past or last year) ownership structure to current-year (hereafter referred to as current or this-year) firm performance via two channels, namely: current-year agency costs and current-year corporate risk-taking. In addition, the direct feedback effects from previous-year firm performance to current-year ownership structure are also modelled.

For that conceptual framework, two mediation models are used in this study, namely, a recursive model and a non-recursive model. The difference between them is that the former model deals with the uni-directional relationship, while the latter model accounts for the bidirectional relationship. While the former model is aimed at addressing research questions 1 and 2, the latter model is to answer research questions 3 and 4.

In terms of the estimation method, the Baron and Kenny (1986) causal-steps approach, which consists of a generalised method of moments estimation and fixed-effects estimation with Driscoll–Kraay standard errors, is employed for the recursive model. The product-of-coefficient approach using full-information maximum likelihood estimation is used for the non-recursive model. The maximum likelihood estimation is also employed to address Research question 2 of the recursive model, where the correlation of cross-equation error terms is allowed. All econometrics techniques and estimations for the above models are conducted in Stata 13.1.

This research employs a panel dataset consisting of 95 listed companies on the Vietnamese stock market during five consecutive years from 2008 to 2012, resulting in 475 firm-year observations in total. Specific entries for the financial data were extracted from audited financial statements sourced from DataStream. The ownership data was taken from company annual reports and market stock prices from the websites of the stock exchanges (www.hsx.vn; www.hnx.vn).

## 1.6 Contributions of the Study

This book contributes to the theory by undertaking a new approach in order to investigate the relationship between ownership structure and firm performance. Most prior studies on this issue have adopted the direct and contemporaneous approach, that is, ownership structure directly and contemporaneously affects firm performance and vice versa. In contrast, this book combines the mediation and dynamic approaches on the assumption that there are 'missing links' in this relationship and that there is potential for a dynamic endogeneity or 'lead–lag' interrelationship between ownership structure and firm performance (Wintoki et al., 2012, Hu and Izumida, 2008).

On that basis, this book makes an original contribution to the literature by innovating a two-mediator mediation model for the relationship between ownership structure and firm performance. In this model, agency costs and corporate risk-taking are conceptualised as the two main mediating variables that transmit the indirect effect of ownership structure on firm performance. It is demonstrated that agency theory and corporate risk management theory can complement each other to properly explain the ownership–performance relationship.

In relation to the methodological aspects, this book contributes to the corporate governance literature by arguing against the use of the asset utilisation ratio as a proxy for agency costs. While this is one of the most commonly used measures of agency costs in the literature, this study casts doubts on the validity of this ratio. In addition, this book provides evidence that the full-information maximum likelihood method is an equivalent estimator of fixed-effects estimation with Driscroll–Kraay standard errors, which are of course conditional on the appropriate use of techniques to account for the violation of the normal assumptions of error terms.

With respect to practical contributions, this study enhances the current understanding of how insider ownership, government ownership and foreign ownership can ultimately contribute to improving firm performance in Vietnamese listed firms. This book extends the argument in Le and Buck (2011) that government ownership can be used as an effective internal governance mechanism to reduce agency problems. From the dynamic perspective for Vietnamese listed firms, it finds that the total effect of government ownership on firm performance is positive but relatively small. Intuitively, the impact of government ownership via agency costs channel does not strongly improve firm performance. Accordingly, corporate risk-taking might be the driver for the positive effect of insider ownership on accounting/financial firm performance, but this channel is detrimental to the market value of the firm. Additionally, this book provides empirical evidence that foreign ownership contributes negatively to firm performance. This has been probably caused by errors in the data for this variable.

Also, the empirical findings of the positive impact of both government and private forms of equity ownership on the performance of Vietnam's listed firms provide useful implications for reforms. Finally, this is the first study on the mediated and dynamic interrelationship between ownership structure and performance of Vietnamese listed firms. Future studies of Vietnam's stock market can obtain useful information from this book.

More in-depth, comprehensive theoretical and empirical studies are necessary to reach definite conclusions regarding SOE and corporate governance reforms.

## 1.7 Structure of the Book

The first chapter of the book provides background information and the major elements of the book, including the motivation for the research and the country-specific context of this study. The other important elements of the research are presented in short summaries.

Chapter 2 focuses on a review of the most relevant literature on the issue of the ownership structure–firm performance relationship. In addition to a section on theoretical mediation models, the contents of this chapter are organised mainly by the type of effect in mediation analysis, including the mediated effect of ownership structure on firm performance, feedback effect of firm performance and the total effect of ownership structure on firm performance. The literature on the issue in the Vietnamese context is also presented.

Chapter 3 discusses the theoretical foundations of the research, including the theoretical perspectives underlying the paths among all the main variables employed in this study, and also the development of the conceptual framework and theoretical models for the mediated and non-contemporaneous interrelationship between equity ownership structure and firm performance. Next, this chapter describes the measurement of all variables and specifies two empirical models, namely, a recursive model and a non-recursive model.

Chapter 4 presents the dataset of this study and describes the data sample, including summary statistics. The main focus of this chapter is on the justifications of what and how estimation methods and econometrics techniques are employed to solve the two empirical models.

Chapter 5 makes an in-depth analysis of the empirical results of the research. The results are presented in two major sections, where each covers the results of one of the empirical mediation models introduced in previous chapters.

Chapter 6 discusses the implications of the above results. The contents are grouped according to the relevant answers to the research questions of this book, which include the mediating roles of agency costs and corporate risk-taking, the non-contemporaneous interrelationship between ownership structure and firm performance, and the total effect of ownership structure on firm performance.

Chapter 7 concludes the book and provides a synthesis of the main findings and key contributions. The limitations of the book and recommendations for future research on the issue are also included in this chapter.

## Notes

1 An interesting statement about the need for attention on a mediation approach is that 'In the absence of a concern for such mediating or intervening mechanisms, one ends up with facts, but with incomplete understanding' (Morris Rosenberg, cited in MacKinnon, 2012, p. 23).
2 The term 'privatisation' is not officially used in legal documents and media in Vietnam, while the term 'equitisation' is used instead. In China, likewise, the privatisation of state-owned enterprises is termed 'share ownership scheme', 'corporatisation' or the 'shareholding system' (Wei et al., 2005, Sun et al., 2002).
3 The market capitalisation statistics can be retrieved from the official website of Vietnam's securities market regulator: www.ssc.gov.vn
4 www.fiingroup.vn
5 In June 2015, the Vietnamese Government issued Decree 60/2015/NĐ-CP, in which the 49% threshold for foreign ownership in Vietnam's stock market is removed, except for some industries. This decree is effective from 1 September 2015.
6 http://kinhdoanh.vnexpress.net/tin-tuc/doanh-nghiep/doanh-nghiep-muon-co-dong-nha-nuoc-nam-it-von-hon-2984767.html
7 In this study, insider ownership is basically defined as the proportion of common shares owned by the board of directors, including managers (see Section 3.2.1.1 for the definition in detail).

8 Financial investments are recognised in a firm's balance sheet, which consists of short-term and long-term financial investments, including marketable securities.
9 For example, (1) Decision 929/QĐ-TTg of the Prime Minister dated 17 July 2012 regarding the restructuring of SOEs; (2) Decree 71/2013/NĐ-CP of the government dated 11 July 2013 regarding state capital investment in businesses and financial management of enterprises wholly owned by the state; (3) Decree 15/NQ-CP of the government dated 6 March 2014 regarding some measures to speed up equalisation and retreat state capital in businesses; and (4) Decision 51/2014/QĐ-TTg of the Prime Minister dated 15 September 2014 regarding the retreat, sales of and registration of trading and listing on stock markets of SOEs.

## References

Acock, A. C. 2013. *Discovering structural equation modeling using stata*, College Station, Texas: Stata Press.

Antonakis, J., Bendahan, S., Jacquart, P. & Lalive, R. 2010. On making causal claims: A review and recommendations. *The Leadership Quarterly*, 21, 1086–1120.

Baron, R. M. & Kenny, D. A. 1986. The moderator-mediator variable distinction in social psychological research: Conceptual, strategic, and statistical considerations. *Journal of Personality and Social Psychology*, 51, 1173–1182.

Berle, A. A. & Means, G. C. 1932. *The modern corporation and private property*. New York: The Macmillan Company.

Bhagat, S. & Bolton, B. 2008. Corporate governance and firm performance. *Journal of Corporate Finance*, 14, 257–273.

Bhagat, S., Bolton, B. & Romano, R. 2010. The effect of corporate governance on performance. *In:* Kent, B. H. & Ronald, A. (eds.) *Corporate governance: A synthesis of theory, research, and practice*. Chichester: Wiley.

Bhagat, S. & Jefferis, R. H. 2002. *The econometrics of corporate governance studies*, Cambridge, Mass: MIT.

Brown, P., Beekes, W. & Verhoeven, P. 2011. Corporate governance, accounting and finance: A review. *Accounting and Finance*, 51, 96–172.

Denis, D. K. 2010. International corporate governance research. *In:* Kent, B. H. & Ronald, A. (eds.) *Corporate governance: A synthesis of theory, research, and practice*. Chichester: Wiley.

Djankov, S. & Murrell, P. 2002. Enterprise restructuring in transition: A quantitative survey. *Journal of Economic Literature*, 40, 739–792.

Douma, S., George, R. & Kabir, R. 2006. Foreign and domestic ownership, business groups, and firm performance: Evidence from a large emerging market. *Strategic Management Journal*, 27, 637–657.

Downs, D. H. & Sommer, D. W. 1999. Monitoring, ownership, and risk-taking: The impact of guaranty funds. *The Journal of Risk and Insurance*, 66, 477–479.

Drever, M., Stanton, P. A. & Mcgowan, S. 2007. *Contemporary issues in accounting*, Milton, Qld: John Wiley & Sons Australia.

Farooque, O. A., Zijl, T. V., Dunstan, K. & Karim, A. W. 2010. Co-deterministic relationship between ownership concentration and corporate performance: Evidence from an emerging economy. *Accounting Research Journal*, 23, 172–189.

Firth, M. A. & Rui, O. M. 2012. Does one size fit all? A study of the simultaneous relations among ownership, corporate governance mechanisms, and the financial performance of firms in China. *In:* Boubaker, S., Nguyen, B. D. & Nguyen, D. K. (eds.) *Corporate governance: Recent developments and new trends*. Berlin Heidelberg: Springer-Verlag.

Gainsborough, M. 2009. Privatisation as state advance: Private indirect government in Vietnam. *New Political Economy*, 14, 257–274.

General Statistics Office of Vietnam 2012. *Statistical Handbook of Vietnam*. Hanoi, Vietnam: Statistical Publishing House.

Hidenobu, O. & Lai Thi Phuong, N. 2012. Capital structure and investment behavior of listed companies in Vietnam: An estimation of the influence of government ownership. *International Journal of Business and Information*, 7, 137.

Himmelberg, C. P., Hubbard, R. G. & Palia, D. 1999. Understanding the determinants of managerial ownership and the link between ownership and performance. *Journal of Financial Economics*, 53, 353–384.

Hu, Y. & Izumida, S. 2008. Ownership concentration and corporate performance: A causal analysis with Japanese panel data. *Corporate governance: An international review*, 16, 342–358.

IFC 2010. *Corporate Governance Manual*, 2nd edn, IFC advisory services in East Asia and the Pacific. Hanoi, Vietnam: International Finance Corporation.

Jensen, M. C. & Meckling, W. H. 1976. Theory of the firm: Managerial behavior, agency costs and ownership structure. *Journal of Financial Economics*, 3, 305–360.

Kankaanpää, J., Oulasvirta, L. & Wacker, J. 2014. Steering and monitoring model of state-owned enterprises. *International Journal of Public Administration*, 37, 409–423.

Kerkvliet, B. J. T. 2018. An approach for analysing state-society relations in Vietnam. *SOJOURN: Journal of Social Issues in Southeast Asia*, 33, S156–S198.

Kim, B. 2011. Do foreign investors encourage value-enhancing corporate risk taking? *Emerging markets finance & trade*, 47, 88–110.

Kumala, R., & Siregar, S.V. (2020). Corporate social responsibility, family ownership and earnings management: the case of Indonesia. *Social Responsibility Journal*, 17, 69–86. doi:10.1108/srj-09-2016-0156.

Le, T. V. & Buck, T. 2011. State ownership and listed firm performance: A universally negative governance relationship? *Journal of Management and Governance*, 15, 227–248.

Li, T., Sun, L. & Zou, L. 2009. State ownership and corporate performance: A quantile regression analysis of Chinese listed companies. *China Economic Review*, 20, 703–716.

Liang, C.-J. & Lin, Y.-L. 2011. Does endogenously determined ownership matter on performance? Dynamic evidence from the emerging Taiwan market. *Emerging Markets Finance & Trade*, 47, 120–133.

MacKinnon, D. 2012. *Introduction to statistical mediation analysis*, Hoboken: Taylor and Francis.

Martin, P. 2003. The politics of economic restructuring in Vietnam: The case of state-owned enterprise "Reform". *Contemporary Southeast Asia: A journal of international and strategic affairs*, 25, 20–43.

Megginson, W. L., Nash, R. C. & Randenborgh, M. 2012. The financial and operating performance of newly privatised firms: An international empirical analysis. *The Journal of Finance*, 49, 403–452.

Nguyen, T. T. & Van Dijk, M. A. 2012. Corruption, growth, and governance: Private vs. state-owned firms in Vietnam. *Journal of Banking & Finance*, 36, 2935–2948.

Pham, C. D. & Carlin, T. M. 2008. Financial performance of privatised state-owned enterprises (SOEs) in Vietnam. *Journal of International Business Research*, 7, 105.

Preacher, K. J. & Hayes, A. F. 2008. Asymptotic and resampling strategies for assessing and comparing indirect effects in multiple mediator models. *Behavior Research Methods*, 40, 879–891.

Rashid, M. M. 2020. Ownership structure and firm performance: The mediating role of board characteristics. *Corporate Governance: The International Journal of Business in Society*, 20, 719–737.

Shleifer, A. & Vishny, R. W. 2008. Large shareholders and corporate control. *In*: Ricketts, M. (ed.) *The economics of modern business enterprise*. Elgar Reference Collection. International Library of Critical Writings in Economics, vol. 214. Cheltenham, U.K. and Northampton, Mass.: Elgar.

Sun, Q., Tong, W. H. S. & Tong, J. 2002. How does government ownership affect firm performance? Evidence from China's privatisation experience. *Journal of Business Finance & Accounting*, 29, 1–27.

Tan, D. T. 2009. *Corporate governance and firm outcomes: Causation or spurious correlations?* PhD, University of New South Wales.

Tian, L. & Estrin, S. 2008. Retained state shareholding in Chinese PLCs: Does government ownership always reduce corporate value? *Journal of Comparative Economics*, 36, 74–89.

Tirole, J. 2006. *The theory of corporate finance*, Princeton, NJ: Princeton University Press.

Vaaler, P. M. & Schrage, B. N. 2009. Residual state ownership, policy stability and financial performance following strategic decisions by privatising telecoms. *Journal of International Business Studies*, 40, 621–641.

Vu, K. A., Tower, G. & Scully, G. 2011. Corporate communication for Vietnamese listed firms. *Asian Review of Accounting*, 19, 125–146.

Wahba, H. & Elsayed, K. 2015. The mediating effect of financial performance on the relationship between social responsibility and ownership structure. *Future Business Journal*, 1, 1–12.

Wei, Z., Xie, F. & Zhang, S. 2005. Ownership structure and firm value in China's privatised firms: 1991–2001. *Journal of Financial & Quantitative Analysis*, 40, 87–108.

Wintoki, M. B., Linck, J. S. & Netter, J. M. 2012. Endogeneity and the dynamics of internal corporate governance. *Journal of Financial Economics*, 105, 581–606.

Wright, P. C. & Nguyen, V. 2000. State-owned enterprises (SOEs) in Vietnam–perceptions of strategic direction for a society in transition. *International Journal of Public Sector Management*, 13, 169–177.

# 2 The Ownership Structure and Firm Performance Relationship

## A Literature Review

## 2.1 Mediation Mechanisms and the Methods of Testing Two-Mediator Mediation Models

### 2.1.1 *Single-Mediator Mediation Model*

The traditional approach to mediation is the use of a three-variable model consisting of an exogenous independent variable, an endogenous mediating variable and an endogenous outcome variable (Acock, 2013). Such a design is termed a 'simple mediation' model (Preacher and Hayes, 2008), which is illustrated in Figure 2.1.

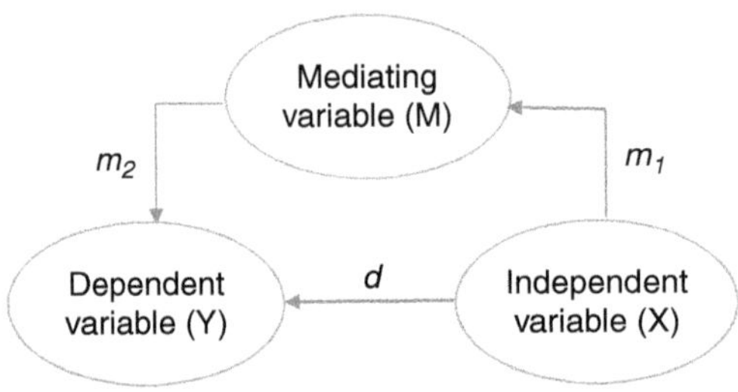


*Figure 2.1* The decomposition of effects in a simple mediation model.

Source: Adapted from Figure 1 in Preacher and Hayes (2008).

The product of $m_1$ and $m_2$ is the indirect effect (or mediated effect) of X on Y through M. $d$ is the direct effect of X on Y controlling for M. If $t$ is denoted as the total effect of independent variable X on outcome variable Y, the total effect of X on Y is the sum of the direct effect and indirect effect ($t = d + m_1m_2$). As Acock (2013) summarises, M fully mediates the effect of X on Y if $d$ is small and insignificant, and M partially mediates the effect of X on Y if $d$ is significant but smaller than $t$.

In econometrics modelling, Figure 2.1 can be specified by the following two equations:

DOI: 10.4324/9781003255741-2

$$M = \beta_{0m} + \beta_{xm}X + \varepsilon_m$$
$$Y = \beta_{0y} + \beta_{xy}X + \beta_{my}M + \varepsilon_y$$

where $M$ is the intervening variable that transmits the effect of independent variable $X$ to dependent variable $Y$. The direct effect of $X$ on $Y$ is represented by the coefficient $\beta_{xy}$. The indirect effect is the product of two coefficients $\beta_{xm}$ and $\beta_{my}$. A full mediation mechanism occurs if the direct effect $\beta_{xy}$ of $X$ on $Y$ is no longer significant in comparison with the total effect, and partial mediation is valid if the direct effect $\beta_{xy}$ is reduced when the mediating variable is included in the second equation.

An important task in mediation analysis is the calculation of indirect effect. The above method of multiplying two regression coefficients to obtain indirect effect is actually the Sobel (1982) 'product-of-coefficients' approach (Preacher and Hayes, 2008). Another approach is the 'difference-of-coefficients' approach proposed by Judd and Kenny (1981), in which the indirect effect is the difference between the total effect and the direct effect of $X$ on $Y$, respectively.

A single-mediator model can be estimated by the causal-steps approach of Baron and Kenny (1986), in which several regression analyses are undertaken for the related paths among the abovementioned three variables. An important condition is that every step of the regression must show a significant relationship in order for the mediation to be possible. Two assumptions underlying the use of multiple regression equations to test the mediation effect are that

1 there is no measurement error in the mediator and
2 the mediator is not caused by the dependent variable.

However, the application of the above stepwise regression proposed by Baron and Kenny (1986) is problematic in cases where there are multiple independent and mediating variables. Here, several equity ownership variables mediated by two or three mediators are to be estimated. That is problematic because each variable will then be regressed individually and separately, causing difficulty in obtaining a proper understanding of how these variables collectively affect the outcome/independent variables. More importantly, in a multiple-mediator model where the mediators are endogenous (i.e. they are influenced by unobservable common causes), then the estimates will not be robust if each mediator is considered separately, as under the causal-steps approach (Vanderweele and Vansteelandt, 2014).

### *2.1.2 Two-Mediator Mediation Model*

In a mediation model, if the flow of impacts runs in a single direction, that is, there is no feedback effect, the model is termed a *recursive* mediation model, while if there is a feedback effect or reciprocal influence, it is termed a *non-recursive* mediation model (Acock, 2013).

Following MacKinnon (2012), Figure 2.2 shows how all paths of a two-mediator recursive model can be depicted.

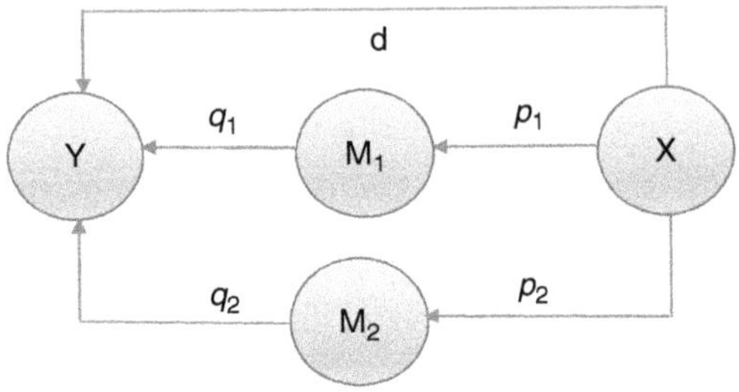


*Figure 2.2* Path diagram for a two-mediator recursive mediation model.

Source: Adapted from Figure 5.1 in MacKinnon (2012).

To measure the relationships among the variables in Figure 2.2, MacKinnon (2012) proposes a system of four equations, which is restated as below:

$$Y = i_1 + tX + e_1 \tag{2.1}$$

$$Y = i_2 + dX + q_1M_1 + q_2M_2 + e_2 \tag{2.2}$$

$$M_1 = i_3 + p_1X + e_3 \tag{2.3}$$

$$M_2 = i_4 + p_2X + e_4 \tag{2.4}$$

Where $X$ is the independent variable; $Y$ is the dependent variable; $M_1$ is the first mediator; $M_2$ is the second mediator; $p_1$ and $p_2$ are the parameters relating the independent variable to the first and second mediators, respectively; $q_1$ represents the effect of the first mediator on the dependent variable adjusted for the independent variable and the second mediator; $q_2$ represents the effect of the second mediator on the dependent variable adjusted for the independent variable and the first mediator; $t$ represents the total effect of X on Y, while $d$ is the direct effect of X on Y; $e_1$, $e_2$, $e_3$ and $e_4$ are error terms; and $i_1$, $i_2$, $i_3$ and $i_4$ are intercepts.

In the above two-mediator model, the first mediated effect by $M_1$ is the product of $p_1$ and $q_1$. Similarly, the second mediated effect by $M_2$ is the product of $p_2$ and $q_2$. Hence, the total mediated effect of both $M_1$ and$_2$ is the sum of $p_1q_1$ and $p_2q_2$, which is equal to the difference between the total effect and the direct effect of $X$ on $Y$; that is, $p_1q_1 + p_2 q_2 = t - d$. The individual mediated effect ($p_1q_1$ or $p_2q_2$) can be termed the 'specific indirect effect' to distinguish it from the total indirect effect (Bollen, cited in MacKinnon, 2012, p. 106). MacKinnon also claims that the parameters in the four equations presented earlier can be estimated by using ordinary least squares regression.

It can be seen from the above model specification that it is not always necessary to include Equation 2.1 in a two-mediator model because the total effect of $X$ on can be calculated from the regression results of Equations 2.2, 2.3 and 2.4. Precisely, once each specific indirect effect and the direct effect are obtained, the total effect $t$ can be estimated using the equation $t = p_1q_1 + p_2q_2 + d$. Furthermore, if the objective of the study is not to find the total effect of an independent variable on the dependent one, it is clear that Equation 2.1 can be omitted from the system. In addition, as pointed out in MacKinnon (2012), the requirement that the total effect must be significant for mediation analysis to proceed is a limitation of the causal-steps approach. The total effect can be equal to zero but the mediation effects may still be present if some of the mediated effects and direct effects have opposite signs. Thus, according to Preacher and Hayes (2008), the condition that 'the total effect of predictor variable on outcome variables must be significant' is not always necessary for mediation to occur.

With respect to the estimation method, a two-mediator mediation model can be tested using a number of different regression techniques. Baron and Kenny (1986) propose the use of structural equation models or two-stage least squares to deal with the problems associated with mediation testing, such as measurement error, correlated measurement error and the feedback effect of the dependent variable on the mediator. MacKinnon (2012) suggests that the parameters in the four equations of the two-mediator model can be estimated using ordinary least squares regression or maximum likelihood estimation. Preacher and Hayes (2008) review various strategies to test the mediation effect and show how a multiple-mediator model should be dealt with using the bootstrapping method.

Nevertheless, the literature in the field also indicates that the above equations can be solved by other regression methods, depending on whether a different method is needed to suit an empirical issue. For instance, Chen (2011) addresses a two-mediator recursive model by applying a multiple regression approach for a system of three simultaneous equations. Specifically, the mediation mechanism is tested for the relationship between ownership structure and research and development investment (expenditure to total sales), and the two mediating variables are financial slack (operation cash to total sales) and financial leverage (total debt to total assets). Fixed-effects estimation is selected to estimate the effect of these mediators on ownership structure and other controlling variables. The direct effects of the mediators and ownership structure on research and development investment are then estimated in a separate equation using the generalised method of moment. At this step, an instrumental variable for ownership structure is used, which is the predicted value of ownership structure uncorrelated with both mediators. The author argues that this technique dismantles the direct and indirect effects of ownership structure on research and development investment. Overall, the suspected mediation effects of the two mediating variables mentioned above are confirmed in this research. However, the standard errors and significance level of the specific indirect effects and the total mediation effects of financial leverage and financial slack are not estimated. In particular, the potential covariance of the two mediators is not controlled for in this research.

## 2.2 Ownership Structure, Agency Costs and Firm Performance

Many studies have been undertaken to examine the impact of agency costs in a range of finance-related elements such as 'capital structure, maturity structure, dividend policy, and executive compensation' (Ang et al., 2000). However, few studies have sought to discover the intervening role of agency costs in the equity ownership–performance relationship.

Instead, most previous studies merely investigated the association either between ownership structure and agency costs or between agency costs and firm performance. For example, Ang et al. (2000) argue that agency costs (the expense ratio and the asset utilisation ratio) are closely associated with the agency conflict between shareholders and managers within a firm. They eventually find that agency costs are inversely related to managerial ownership in the U.S. market. In the context of a developing country, Sabur et al. (2012) argue that there exists a large agency problem and that agency conflict lies with shareholdings by sponsors, government, institutions and foreigners, as indicated by the negative effects of such identities on firm performance. Nevertheless, the mediating role of agency costs in the ownership–performance relationship is not examined by the above authors.

It is also common that previous studies investigate only the direct channels of impacts of ownership identities or ownership concentration on firm performance. For example, in the context of Jordan, Alabdullah (2018) find that managerial ownership is positively associated with firm performance, and foreign ownership has no impact on firm performance. In contrast, Kao et al. (2019) show that foreign ownership, family ownership, institutional ownership and block ownership have positive impacts on firm performance in Taiwan.

In terms of the mediating role of agency costs in the ownership–performance relationship, some authors such as Thomsen and Pedersen

(2000) state that ownership structure may affect agency costs, and consequently a firm's financial performance and investment opportunities. Denis (2010) and Jensen and Meckling (1976) indicate that concentrated ownership may reduce agency costs because large shareholders have more incentive and ability to influence managers, thus increasing firm value when there is a concentration of cash flow rights.

Wei et al. (2005) study the relationship between ownership structure and firm value in Chinese stock markets. This research utilises a panel data sample of 5284 firm-year observations of partially privatised former SOEs in China during the period 1991–2001. After controlling for simultaneous endogeneity by adopting two-stage least squares estimation for both cross-sectional and pooled data panels, one of the main findings of this study is that agency problems play a role in the negative relationship between government ownership and firm performance (Tobin's Q). Accordingly, a conflict of interest among different block shareholders in firms with high retained ownership by the government may reduce firm value. When government ownership levels are higher, the agency problem in the firm is more serious because the personal ownership of top managers who are perhaps appointed by the government is not meaningful. While pointing out agency conflict as the rationale for the negative impact of government ownership on firm value, this study does not make any empirical model specifications for testing a possible intervening role of agency costs.

In contrast, Le and Buck (2011) also examine the effect of government ownership on the performance of Chinese listed firms, but their empirical findings are opposite to those of Wei et al. (2005). The causal-steps regression technique proposed by Baron and Kenny (1986) is used to find that government ownership has a positive impact on firm performance via the mediating role of agency costs (the expense ratio and the asset utilisation ratio). Specifically, there is no direct effect of government ownership on firm performance in the Chinese stock market. Instead, agency costs play the role of a 'missing link' between these two variables and a full mediation mechanism occurs whereby agency costs transmit the positive effect of government ownership on firm performance (return on assets and return on equity). The work of Le and Buck (2011) is the most relevant literature on the mediated effect of ownership structure on firm performance reviewed in this book. However, there are several limitations of this study, namely,

- the authors do not consider the feedback effect of firm performance on government ownership;
- the composition of ownership structure is confined to government ownership only; and
- agency costs are treated as exogenous since each path of mediation is estimated separately.

In general, it can be argued that research on the mediated relationship between ownership structure and firm performance is not extensive in existing corporate governance and finance literature. Apart from the finding for government ownership in Le and Buck (2011) and some arguments of other authors for the potential mediating role of agency costs, little empirical evidence has been provided in the literature for the mediation effect of agency costs associated with other forms of ownership, such as insider ownership and foreign ownership.

## 2.3 Ownership Structure, Corporate Risk-Taking and Firm Performance

Similar to the case of agency costs, there is limited knowledge about the mediating role of corporate risk-taking in the association between ownership structure and firm performance. The literature shows that only isolated paths have been tested in this regard, such as the relationship between ownership structure and corporate risk-taking, and the relationship between corporate risk-taking and firm performance.

Using a sample of Turkish data with the largest listed companies on the Istanbul Stock Exchange during 1992–1998, Guner and Kursat (2002) investigate the effect of ownership structure on firm performance and corporate risk-taking, respectively. Applying ordinary least squares regression for panel data, the authors report significant links between ownership structure and firm performance, and between ownership structure and corporate risk-taking. Ownership structure is tested by two variables, namely, ownership concentration and ownership mix. Ownership mix is tested using dummy variables—foreign ownership, government ownership, family ownership and ownership of conglomerate affiliation. An important finding of this study is that ownership concentration and government ownership are related to firm performance in two opposite directions: a positive impact on market-based measures of firm performance (price/earnings ratios and stock return ratio) and a negative impact on accounting-based performance (return on equity and return on assets). The authors state that the result for ownership concentration is consistent with the findings for other emerging markets such as China and the Czech Republic. In terms of corporate risk-taking (total risk and market risk), firms with highly concentrated ownership and government-owned firms are found to take risks more readily. However, a continual link between ownership structure, corporate risk-taking and firm performance is not investigated in this study.

John et al. (2008) investigate the association between investor protection and corporate risk-taking, and then between corporate risk-taking and country-wide performance (productivity and GDP growth). Using a sample of 39 countries over the period 1992–2002 and another sample for the U.S. market, both cross-country studies and single-country studies were conducted, with ordinary least squares and second-stage least squares regression methods for cross-sectional data. The authors argue that insider or manager ownership is among a number of factors that influence corporate risk-taking, where corporate risk-taking is measured by the standard deviation of EBITDA/assets. In particular, in countries with low investor protection, managers are often the dominant insiders, and they may avoid corporate risk-taking to protect their expected private benefits. Hence, insiders will be less risk-averse if investor protection is enhanced in order to reduce the expected level of private benefits. A positive relationship between corporate risk-taking and growth is also found in this research. An interesting point of this study is that a relationship between insider ownership and corporate risk-taking is also indicated when the link between the latter and investor protection is considered. This is a useful implication for follow-up studies that use data from developing countries because investor protection is poor in most developing markets. Another advantage of this study is that a multiple-country database and analysis are used, which helps in generalising the empirical results. However, the authors do not attempt to examine the intervening role of corporate risk-taking in the association between insider ownership and performance.

In the context of the Korean market, Kim (2011) examines the association between foreign ownership and corporate risk-taking of firms and the relationship between corporate risk-taking and firm growth. While corporate risk-taking is measured as the standard deviation of industry-adjusted annual earnings (EBITDA/assets) over the period 2001–2007, firm growth is based on the growth in total assets and annual sales. Using two-stage least squares regression to control for endogeneity between foreign ownership and corporate risk-taking, and between corporate risk-taking and firm growth, the author reports that foreign ownership is found to be positively related to corporate risk-taking in firms with greater opportunities for investment and that corporate risk-taking, in turn, improves firm growth. On that basis, the author explains that the monitoring incentives of foreign investors encourage corporate risk-taking when firms have growth potential. However, since this study uses cross-sectional data, a limitation is the lack of discussion of the changes in foreign ownership and corporate risk-taking over time, which is important when the time effect is available. Additionally, in the discussion of the association between ownership structure and corporate risk-taking, the author mainly focuses on the analysis of investment decisions of foreign investors and managers. Lastly, the treatment of corporate risk-taking as a connecting point between foreign ownership and firm growth is not within the scope of this study.

## 2.4 Interrelationship between Ownership Structure and Firm Performance

The recent trend of research on the relationship between ownership structure and firm performance is that they are endogenously determined. However, the findings for the interrelationship between ownership structure and firm performance are not consistent across empirical studies.

Specifically, in the Japanese context, Hu and Izumida (2008) examine the causal relationship between ownership concentration and firm performance. The authors propose that four variables, namely ownership concentration, corporate performance, leverage and investment, are interrelated. Using the Granger causality test and two-stage least squares method for a panel data sample, this study finds a U-shaped curve between ownership concentration and firm performance. However, a feedback effect of firm performance on ownership concentration is not found. Although there is no evidence of a reverse effect of corporate performance in the Japanese market, Hu and Izumida enrich the knowledge of transmission mechanisms between ownership structure, capital structure, investment behaviour and firm performance. From a dynamic perspective, however, the authors do not consider the non-contemporaneous interrelationship between ownership concentration and firm value.

In the context of the U.S. market, Bhagat and Bolton (2008) study the relationship between corporate governance and performance by investigating the endogenous relationship between corporate governance, firm performance, capital structure and equity ownership structure. According to the authors, the governance–performance relationship is endogenous in nature, and therefore a simultaneous equation approach is necessary from an econometric viewpoint to examine the relationship between any two of the abovementioned variables. Hence, a system of simultaneous equations with the four endogenous variables is adopted in this study, using panel data and econometric techniques, such as two-stage least squares and three-stage least squares techniques, to control for the potential endogeneity issue. Bhagat and Bolton (2008) find that better corporate governance, including stock ownership of board members, is significantly positively associated with better operating performance (return on assets). This result reveals that ownership structure does matter in terms of its correlation with firm performance. The authors also argue that firm performance is likely to be a determinant of ownership structure. This is due to the exercise of performance-based compensation such as stock options and insider information so that insiders are able to anticipate future performance and then adjust their shareholdings accordingly. However, empirical results are not provided by the authors to support this argument.

In the context of Bangladesh, Farooque et al. (2010) examine the association between dominant ownership and firm performance, investigating the arbitrary policies of the regulatory bodies in relation to ownership concentration. Applying the two-stage least squares approach with a system of two equations, they report that there is a co-deterministic relationship between ownership concentration measured by top-1 shareholder and firm value (return on assets and Tobin's Q). According to the authors, firm performance increases when there is an increase in top-1 shareholder ownership levels and vice versa. However, the generalisation of the results of this study to other markets is a matter that needs more evidence from future research.

In the Taiwanese context, Liang and Lin (2011) also deal with the issue of endogeneity to examine the endogenously determined relationship between ownership and firm performance. By adopting a simultaneous equations approach for panel data, the authors show that institutional ownership, rather than insider ownership, has an impact on the performance (industry-adjusted return on assets) of Taiwanese listed firms. In addition, a new contribution to the literature by Liang and Lin is that firm performance is affected not only by ownership structure but also by life-cycle stages of firms over time. Hence, the authors argue that the impact on performance may vary across firms due to the differences in both ownership structure and a firm's life-cycle stage, such as growth, maturity and stagnation. Notably, Liang and Lin (2011) confirm a significantly negative interrelationship between insider ownership and firm performance in the context of Taiwan, but this finding is relevant to a limited group of emerging Taiwanese listed firms in the maturity stage of development.

Using Australian data, Hassan et al. (2018) attempt to seek a causal relationship between ownership concentration, debt and firm value. Applying the causality test for panel data, the fixed-effect method, and the generalised method of moment estimation, the author finds that there is no causal relation between ownership concentration and firm value; however, firm value negatively causes ownership concentration. Hassan et al. (2018) also argue that there is no direct causality between ownership structure and firm performance, but there may be an indirect link between these two variables. However, such an indirect relationship is not addressed in this study as it was outside the research scope.

In general, it can be argued that the co-deterministic relationship or interrelationship between ownership structure and firm performance is an issue of common concern. While a number of the aforementioned studies report that ownership structure and firm performance are jointly determined, other studies have not confirmed this. These mixed results on the bidirectional relationship may be attributable to the differences in the contexts of study and the approaches to the issue. In particular, prior researchers often consider the contemporaneous interrelationship between ownership structure and firm performance. Hence, there remains a significant gap in the literature that is concerned with the potential bidirectional dynamic relationship between ownership structure and firm performance.

## 2.5 Total Effect of Ownership Structure on Firm Performance

### 2.5.1 Government Ownership and Firm Performance

Government ownership and firm performance are associated with the issue of privatisation. Privatisation is the process through which governments either wholly or partly sell their interests in SOEs to private sector investors in the hope that the inefficient performance of these firms can be improved through application of the discipline associated with private ownership (Megginson et al., 2012). Hence, privatisation theories mostly discuss the efficiency and effects of government ownership on firm performance in comparison with private ownership. When part-government ownership is retained in a privatised company, there is a mixture of ownership structures consisting of both government and private ownership in the firm.

In general, privatisation theories consider that SOEs are less efficient than private corporations and that government ownership is normally associated with inefficiency and bureaucracy; that is, there is a negative relationship between government ownership and firm performance (Djankov and Murrell, 2002, Netter and Megginson, 2001, Thomsen and Pedersen, 2000). However, empirical studies have shown both positive and negative effects of government ownership on firm performance, as discussed below.

Many studies show that government ownership has a negative impact on firm performance. In Europe, Thomsen & Pedersen (2000) argue that the effect of ownership identity on asset returns is significantly negative in the case of government ownership, while it is less strong and not significant for the other identities. Using time-series data for six years (1990–1995) which yields 2610 observations covering 12 countries in Europe, Thomsen & Pedersen (2000) report that government ownership has a negative impact on firm performance in developed European countries where the largest owner is a family, another company or government. A practical implication of this study is that in large European companies where the level of ownership concentration is high, restructuring the ownership structure can improve firm performance by matching ownership structure with corporate strategy.

In developing countries, government ownership has also shown a negative impact on firm performance. Ongore (2011) employs an integrated approach to the issue of ownership structure in relation to corporate performance, by testing simultaneously the effects of ownership concentration and of ownership identity on the performance of 42 listed companies in Kenya. The author highlights a range of conclusions about the relationship between different types of shareowners and identities, including confirmation of a negative impact of government ownership on firm performance. Similarly, a significant negative effect of government ownership on firm performance is also reported by Sabur et al. (2012) for the Botswana market.

However, a large body of existing literature also claims that government ownership can contribute to improving firm performance. Indeed, there is an emerging trend in academic studies that challenges the contemporary viewpoint that government ownership is outperformed by private ownership. It is being shown that the state-owned sector in some developing countries can still be highly profitable and contribute significantly to national economic development. Government ownership can have a positive effect on the efficiency of firms in transition economies where there is a lack of basic capitalist institutions (Anderson, Lee & Murrell; Gupta, Ham & Svejnar, cited in Wei et al., 2005).

Tian and Estrin (2008) use a sample of more than 9000 firm-year observations over a 10-year period (1994–2004) in the Chinese stock markets and find that, if the proportion of government ownership is at least 25%, then it is not negative for firm performance. They argue that government ownership is not detrimental to firm performance but positively related to it when government ownership reaches a certain high level or more than 25%. Accordingly, this relationship is U-shaped, that is, corporate value starts to decrease as government ownership increases, but it begins to increase above a certain threshold of government ownership. Applying two-stage least squares estimation, Tian and Estrin (2008) also find a reverse causality of firm performance, so that current government ownership is affected by past ownership. Hence, this study suggests that government ownership and firm performance are endogenously determined.

Li et al. (2009) report a non-linear and asymmetrical relationship between government ownership and firm performance in China. However, their main finding is different from that of Tian and Estrin (2008), who state that the relationship of corporate performance to government ownership depends on the quantile location of the firm's performance level. Tian and Estrin (2008) argue that there is a strong and significantly negative relation between state shareholding and firm performance 'among, and only among, the more profitable firms' (p. 703), which suggests that it is not significantly negative but positive for the other firms. As a result, a noteworthy implication from Li et al. (2009) is that the equity shareholding by the government in highly profitable firms should be reduced.

Vaaler and Schrage (2009) find that government ownership can also positively contribute to firm performance (cumulative shareholder returns) in the following two contexts: no more than 50% government ownership in a low policy stability country; and no more than 25% government ownership in a low-to-mid policy stability country. These outcomes become negative if the proportion of government ownership is higher than 50%. Even though the dataset of this study is limited to telecommunications companies, these findings suggest that the actual effect of government ownership is subject to certain economic and country-specific conditions.

In short, previous research findings are mixed and can be grouped as having found: positive, negative and non-linear relationships between firm performance and government ownership. This suggests that the effects of government ownership may be determined by certain conditions and circumstances. Therefore, it can be seen that empirical studies are diverse and not entirely consistent with the prevailing privatisation theory that government ownership has a negative effect on firm performance.

### 2.5.2 *Insider Ownership and Firm Performance*

The relationship between insider ownership and firm performance is discussed in numerous studies, particularly in the context of the separation of ownership and control. Insider ownership can be proxied by the fraction of shares owned by directors and/or managers in a firm (Davidson and Singh, 2003, Tan, 2009, Jensen and Meckling, 1976). Thus, the impact of insider ownership can be inferred from discussions of the managerial ownership–firm performance relationship.

There are three main streams of literature regarding the total relationship between managerial ownership and firm performance. The first claims that there is an alignment (or convergence) of interests between the managers (agents) and shareholders (owners) of a firm. Agency theory documents that firm performance changes as a result of a conflict of interest between managers and shareholders, or between majority and minority shareholders (Clacher et al., 2010). If interests are aligned between managers and shareholders, then a higher proportion of managerial ownership can support an improved firm performance level, termed the 'alignment of interest effect' (Jensen and Meckling, 1976).

Berle and Means (1932) are the first researchers who propose that the separation of ownership from control reduces managers' incentive to pursue the goal of corporate profit maximisation. Given the fact that the control of many firms is still handed over to managers, Berle and Mean pose a question as to what is the motivating force, instead of the profit motive, for shareholders to turn over control of their capital to managers. Although an earlier study by Berle and Mean was undertaken for the U.S. market, the issue and questions raised by the authors are still provoking much debate in the literature.

In a similar vein, Jensen and Meckling (1976) initiate the idea of the alignment of interests of the owner and managers. Accordingly, the separation of ownership from control induces managers (agents) to pursue self-benefiting activities at the cost of shareholders (owners). This suggests that the conflict of interest is minimised when managerial ownership is high enough to align the interests of the shareholders and managers. However, the authors do not offer a precise answer as to what level of managerial shareholding is the most effective for this alignment of interests to occur.

The hypothesis of interest alignment is clearly a milestone in research on the impact of managerial ownership and firm performance. This proposition is supported by many researchers, such as Bhagat et al. (2010) and Mehran (1995), who also claim that managerial equity ownership and firm performance are positively associated.

In contrast, the second stream of research develops the managerial entrenchment hypothesis. This argues that there is an 'entrenchment effect' such that, as the proportion of equity ownership by managers increases, they have less incentive to pursue the target of corporate profit maximisation. In other words, managerial ownership and firm performance are negatively related. According to Shleifer and Vishny (2008), managers become involved in non-profit maximising behaviour when they hold up to a certain level of a firm's ownership.

The third stream of literature in this regard argues for a non-linear relationship between managerial ownership and firm performance. The overall effect of managerial ownership on firm performance may depend on the relative strengths of the alignment effect and the entrenchment effect. Accordingly, managerial ownership within a certain range is positive for firm performance if the alignment effect is dominant, and vice versa over some other ranges, if the entrenchment effect dominates (Thomsen and Pedersen, 2000, Morck et al., 1988).

This position is supported by Stulz (1988) when he contends that firm value increases as managerial ownership increases, then this relationship turns negative above a threshold of 50% managerial ownership. Hermalin and Weisbach (1991) show that if insider ownership increases from 0% to 1% of a firm's equity, the impact on firm performance can be positive as a result of the incentive alignment effect, while the entrenchment effect can dominate the range above 1% to 5%, leading to a negative relationship in this regard. Morck et al. (1988) and Holderness et al. (1999) report that the impact on firm performance is positive where insider ownership ranges from 0% to 5%, negative from 5% to 25% and insignificant above 25%. Mcconnell and Servaes (1990) claim that insider ownership is positively related to firm value, not only for the range between 0% to 5%, but also from 5% to 25%. Notably, these authors point out the best range of insider ownership from 30% to 40% of a firm's equity where firm value is maximised.

It can be seen from the above non-linear arguments that insider ownership is examined over different ranges. A shared conclusion from these studies is that the impact of insider ownership on firm performance is positive if insiders hold a relatively small percentage of a firm's equity. However, there is no agreement on a particular range of insider ownership within which firm performance can be significantly enhanced, and the reported results may be relevant for the U.S. market only.

Moreover, none of the above research deals with the mediation effect of agency costs that are associated with a conflict of interest between managers and shareholders, as aforesaid. The interaction between the convergence of interest and the entrenchment effect may also be influenced by the risk preference of inside shareholders. Therefore, there is a need for further research that provides insights into how agency costs and corporate risk-taking attitudes may mediate the impact of managerial ownership on firm performance, particularly in a developing-country context.

### *2.5.3 Foreign Ownership and Firm Performance*

As with other types of ownership structure, studies on the effect of foreign ownership on firm performance have produced mixed empirical findings. However, a greater number of prior studies find a significant positive effect of foreign ownership on firm performance, such as those of Dwivedi and Jain (2005), Sabur et al. (2012) and Sarkar and Sarkar (2000). In contrast, some other studies find that foreign ownership has a significant negative impact on firm performance (Sulong and Nor, 2008, Phung and Le, 2013).

Wei et al. (2005) study the relationship between ownership structure, including foreign ownership, and firm value in Chinese stock markets. This research employs a panel data sample of 5284 firm-year observations of partially privatised former SOEs in China during the period 1991–2001. By adopting two-stage least squares estimation to control for the simultaneous endogeneity, a finding of this study is that foreign ownership has a significantly positive relationship with firm value (proxied by Tobin's Q). However, there is no discussion of why this positive association between foreign ownership and firm value occurs in China's listed firms.

Ferreira and Matos (2008) examine the driving forces and roles of institutional investors in firms around the world. This study uses a large panel dataset of nearly 40% of the world stock market capitalisation, which covers 5300 institutions in 27 countries during the period 2000–2005. Using a three-stage least squares estimation for a system of simultaneous equations, the authors find that firms with higher foreign and independent institutions in their ownership structure have higher firm value, measured by Tobin's Q. Likewise, the relationship between foreign and independent institutions and operating performance (return on assets and net profit margin) is also positive and significant. According to the authors, these results indicate the value-enhancing role of foreign investors for corporations worldwide. Foreign ownership has a positive effect on firm value because foreign institutions act as monitors (the monitoring effect) and also stock prices are pushed up, at least temporarily, by the presence of foreign and independent investors (the overvaluation effect). However, there is no discussion in this paper about the underlying mechanisms that create this positive effect of foreign ownership on firm performance. In addition, Ferreira and Matos (2008) do not attempt to explore this issue from a dynamic perspective.

## 2.6 Literature on Vietnam

There are few empirical studies on the issue of the Vietnamese market. In particular, the mediation approach has not been undertaken in this context of research. As a result, understanding of the equity ownership–firm performance relationship in Vietnam's stock market is limited.

Phung and Le (2013) provide interesting empirical evidence on the association between foreign ownership, debt and firm performance in Vietnam, where debt is treated as a proxy for capital structure. Applying simultaneous equation modelling and panel data techniques for a sample of non-financial listed companies in Vietnam over the period 2008–2011, they report that foreign ownership is negatively related to firm performance. While agreeing that this result is not consistent with most prior studies on the same issue, Phung and Le argue that this negative effect of foreign ownership is because foreign investors lack ownership concentration and information to play a monitoring role in the listed firms in the context of an emerging market. Consequently, foreign investors tend to prefer debt to reduce the agency problem arising from information asymmetry. The application of the simultaneous equation approach in this study is robust in relation to the endogeneity in the ownership–performance relationship, and the findings reflect the fact that foreign shareholding in Vietnamese listed companies is restricted. However, this research is confined to examining only one form of equity ownership, foreign ownership, while other typical types of ownership structure in Vietnam's stock market, such as government ownership and insider ownership, are not tested. In addition, the dataset of this research does not cover those companies listed on the Hanoi Stock Exchange.

Truong (2013) examines the economic performance of SOEs in comparison with that of private and foreign-owned enterprises in Vietnam. By applying the input–output model, for example, using assets as an input variable and profit as an output variable, the author reports that SOEs are less efficient than the private sector, including foreign direct investment enterprises (FDI). Specifically, SOEs are found at the bottom of efficiency rankings in all model settings. This study provides meaningful insights into the issue of firm performance of SOEs in comparison with private enterprises in Vietnam, suggesting that government ownership may not help firms improve performance. However, a noteworthy point is that Truong (2013) addresses the issue from the perspective of the political economy, rather than corporate governance. Additionally, the author does not directly discuss the effect of ownership structure on firm profitability, and the data sample does not cover listed firms in Vietnam.

## 2.7 Summary and Conclusions

This chapter has presented a review of the most relevant literature on the relationship between ownership structure and firm financial performance. The empirical findings on the effect of ownership structure on firm performance are mixed. Likewise, the feedback effect of firm performance on ownership structure is not consistent across different studies. Nevertheless, it is common that the effect of ownership structure on firm performance is investigated from a direct and/or static approach. The mediated relationship between them has not received much attention, leaving a large gap in the knowledge about indirect channels in this relationship, particularly in the context of a developing country like Vietnam. As a result, the mediating roles of both agency costs and corporate risk-taking have not been adequately taken into consideration. However, they are deemed to be inherent in the ownership–performance relationship, as suggested by agency theory. Therefore, undertaking another approach using mediation and dynamic perspectives may serve as a solution in order to fill in these gaps in the literature.

## References

Acock, A. C. 2013. *Discovering structural equation modeling using stata*, College Station, Texas: Stata Press.

Alabdullah, T. T. Y. 2018. The relationship between ownership structure and firm financial performance: Evidence from Jordan. *Benchmarking: An International Journal*, 25, 319–333.

Ang, J. S., Cole, R. A. & Lin, J. W. 2000. Agency costs and ownership structure. *The Journal of Finance*, 55, 81–106.

Baron, R. M. & Kenny, D. A. 1986. The moderator-mediator variable distinction in social psychological research: conceptual, strategic, and statistical considerations. *Journal of Personality and Social Psychology*, 51, 1173–1182.

Berle, A. A. & Means, G. C. 1932. *The modern corporation and private property*. New York: The Macmillan Company.

Bhagat, S. & Bolton, B. 2008. Corporate governance and firm performance. *Journal of Corporate Finance*, 14, 257–273.

Bhagat, S., Bolton, B. & Romano, R. 2010. The effect of corporate governance on performance. *In:* Kent, B. H. & Ronald, A. (eds.) *Corporate governance: A synthesis of theory, research, and practice.* Chichester: Wiley.

Chen, Y. (2011). *Ownership structure, financial structure and R&D investments: Evidence from Korean firms.* Singapore Management University (Singapore). ProQuest Dissertations Publishing database.

Clacher, I., Hillier, D. & Mccolgan, P. 2010. Agency theory: Incomplete contracting and ownership structure. *In:* Kent, B. H. & Ronald, A. (eds.) *Corporate governance: A synthesis of theory, research, and practice.* Chichester: Wiley.

Davidson, W. N. & Singh, M. 2003. Agency costs, ownership structure and corporate governance mechanisms. *Journal of Banking & Finance*, 27, 793–816.

Denis, D. K. 2010. International corporate governance research. *In:* Kent, B. H. & Ronald, A. (eds.) *Corporate governance: A synthesis of theory, research, and practice.* Chichester: Wiley.

Djankov, S. & Murrell, P. 2002. Enterprise restructuring in transition: A quantitative survey. *Journal of Economic Literature*, 40, 739–792.

Dwivedi, N. & Jain, A. K. 2005. Corporate governance and performance of Indian firms: The effect of board size and ownership. *Employee Responsibilities and Rights Journal*, 17, 161–172.

Farooque, O. A., Zijl, T. V., Dunstan, K. & Karim, A. W. 2010. Co-deterministic relationship between ownership concentration and corporate performance: Evidence from an emerging economy. *Accounting Research Journal*, 23, 172–189.

Ferreira, M. A. & Matos, P. 2008. The colors of investors' money: The role of institutional investors around the world. *Journal of Financial Economics*, 88, 499–533.

Guner, G. & Kursat, A. 2002. Equity ownership structure, risk taking, and performance. *Emerging Markets, Finance & Trade*, 38, 6.

Hassan, H., Islam, S. M. N. & Rashid, K. 2018. *Corporate governance, agency theory and firm value: Advanced econometric analysis and empirical evidence.* New York: Nova Science Publishers.

Hermalin, B. E. & Weisbach, M. S. 1991. The effects of board composition and direct incentives on firm performance. *FM: The Journal of the Financial Management Association*, 20, 101–112.

Holderness, C. G., Kroszner, R. S. & Sheehan, D. P. 1999. Were the good old days that good? Changes in managerial stock ownership since the great depression. *Journal of Finance*, 54, 435–469.

Hu, Y. & Izumida, S. 2008. Ownership concentration and corporate performance: A causal analysis with Japanese panel data. *Corporate Governance: An International Review*, 16, 342–358.

Jensen, M. C. & Meckling, W. H. 1976. Theory of the firm: Managerial behavior, agency costs and ownership structure. *Journal of Financial Economics*, 3, 305–360.

John, K., Litov, L. & Yeung, B. 2008. Corporate governance and risk-taking. *The Journal of Finance*, 63, 1679–1728.

Judd, C. M. & Kenny, D. A. 1981. Process analysis: Estimating mediation in treatment evaluations. *Evaluation Review*, 5, 602–619.

Kao, M.-F., Hodgkinson, L. & Jaafar, A. 2019. Ownership structure, board of directors and firm performance: Evidence from Taiwan. *Corporate Governance: The International Journal of Business in Society*, 19, 189–216.

Kim, B. 2011. Do foreign investors encourage value-enhancing corporate risk taking? *Emerging Markets Finance & Trade*, 47, 88–110.

Le, T. V. & Buck, T. 2011. State ownership and listed firm performance: A universally negative governance relationship? *Journal of Management and Governance*, 15, 227–248.

Li, T., Sun, L. & Zou, L. 2009. State ownership and corporate performance: A quantile regression analysis of Chinese listed companies. *China Economic Review*, 20, 703–716.

Liang, C.-J. & Lin, Y.-L. 2011. Does endogenously determined ownership matter on performance? Dynamic evidence from the emerging Taiwan market. *Emerging Markets Finance & Trade*, 47, 120–133.

MacKinnon, D. 2012. *Introduction to statistical mediation analysis*, Hoboken: Taylor and Francis.

Mcconnell, J. J. & Servaes, H. 1990. Additional evidence on equity ownership and corporate value. *Journal of Financial Economics*, 27, 595–612.

Megginson, W. L., Nash, R. C. & Randenborgh, M. 2012. The financial and operating performance of newly privatised firms: An international empirical analysis. *The Journal of Finance*, 49, 403–452.

Mehran, H. 1995. Executive compensation structure, ownership, and firm performance. *Journal of Financial Economics*, 38, 163–184.

Morck, R., Shleifer, A. & Vishny, R. W. 1988. Management ownership and market valuation: An empirical analysis. *Journal of Financial Economics*, 20, 293–315.

Netter, J. & Megginson, W. L. 2001. From state to market: A survey of empirical studies on privatisation. *Journal of Economic Literature*, 39, 321–389.

Ongore, V. O. 2011. The relationship between ownership structure and firm performance: An empirical analysis of listed companies in Kenya. *African Journal of Business Management*, 5, 2120–2128.

Phung, D. N. & Le, T. P. V. 2013. Foreign ownership, capital structure and firm value: Empirical evidence from Vietnamese listed firms. *The IUP Journal of Corporate Governance*, 12, 40–58.

Preacher, K. J. & Hayes, A. F. 2008. Asymptotic and resampling strategies for assessing and comparing indirect effects in multiple mediator models. *Behavior Research Methods*, 40, 879–891.

Sabur, M., Omar Al, F. & Wares, K. 2012. Ownership structure, corporate governance and firm performance. *Studies in Economics and Finance*, 29, 301–319.

Sarkar, J. & Sarkar, S. 2000. Large shareholder activism in corporate governance in developing countries: Evidence from India. *International Review of Finance*, 1, 161–194.

Shleifer, A. & Vishny, R. W. 2008. Large shareholders and corporate control. *In*: Ricketts, M. (ed.) *The Economics of Modern Business Enterprise. Elgar Reference Collection. International Library of Critical Writings in Economics*, vol. 214. Cheltenham, U.K. and Northampton, Mass.: Elgar.

Sobel, M. E. 1982. Asymptotic confidence intervals for indirect effects in structural equation models. *Sociological Methodology*. Washington DC: American Sociology Association: Jossey-Bass Publishers.

Stulz, R. 1988. Managerial control of voting rights. Financing policies and the market for corporate control. *Journal of Financial Economics*, 20, 25–54.

Sulong, Z. & Nor, F. M. 2008. Dividends, ownership structure and board governance on firm value: Empirical evidence from Malaysian listed firms. *Malaysian Accounting Review*, 7, 55–94.

Tan, D. T. 2009. *Corporate governance and firm outcomes: causation or spurious correlations?* PhD, Universtity of New South Wales.

Thomsen, S. & Pedersen, T. 2000. Ownership structure and economic performance in the largest European companies. *Strategic Management Journal*, 21, 689–705.

Tian, L. & Estrin, S. 2008. Retained state shareholding in Chinese PLCs: Does government ownership always reduce corporate value? *Journal of Comparative Economics*, 36, 74–89.

Truong, D. T. 2013. *Public enterprises and economic performance: An examination of Vietnamese state owned enterprises*, 3564645 PhD, The University of Texas at Dallas.

Vaaler, P. M. & Schrage, B. N. 2009. Residual state ownership, policy stability and financial performance following strategic decisions by sprivatising telecoms. *Journal of International Business Studies*, 40, 621–641.

Vanderweele, T. & Vansteelandt, S. 2014. Mediation analysis with multiple mediators. *Epidemiologic Methods*, 2, 95–115.

Wei, Z., Xie, F. & Zhang, S. 2005. Ownership structure and firm value in China's privatised firms: 1991-2001. *Journal of Financial & Quantitative Analysis*, 40, 87–108.

# 3 Equity Ownership Structure and Firm Performance

## Theoretical Framework and Empirical Models

### 3.1 Theoretical Framework

This section begins with a discussion of the relevant aspects of the theoretical perspectives relating to the ownership and performance relationship. Next, the overall conceptual framework is illustrated by a diagram that shows all the possible links among the variables, followed by explanations of how and why these links have been constructed. This section ends with the development of the theoretical models for the relationship between ownership structure and firm performance.

#### *3.1.1 Theoretical Foundation*

##### *3.1.1.1 Agency Theory*

An important concept in agency theory is the agency relationship (Jensen and Meckling, 1976). This is defined as a contract between the principal and the agent under which the latter is delegated with some authority to perform a service on the former's behalf. Agency theory is concerned with two problems in the agency relationship:

1 the conflict between the goals of the principal and of the agent, known as the *agency problem*; and
2 the difference in risk preferences between the principal and the agent, known as the *risk-sharing problem* (Dias and Mroczkowski, 2012, Shankman, 1999).

Since these problems are inherent in the process of managing a firm (Hermalin and Weisbach, 2003), it can be inferred from agency theory that the agency problem and risk-sharing problem are the two core underlying factors for explaining the relationship between equity ownership and firm performance. The theoretical aspects of these two factors are further discussed in this section.

DOI: 10.4324/9781003255741-3

### AGENCY PROBLEM, RISK-SHARING PROBLEM AND LINK BETWEEN OWNERSHIP STRUCTURE AND AGENCY COSTS

According to agency theory, a firm incurs agency costs due to the presence of both agency and risk-sharing problems. While the agency problem implies conflict between the goals of the principal and of the agent, the risk-sharing problem suggests the agent will prefer different courses of actions in comparison with the principal, all other things being equal (Shankman, 1999). Hence, agency theorists argue that there is reason to believe that the agent does not always act in the best interests of the principal (Fama and Jensen, 1983, Jensen and Meckling, 1976, Berle and Means, 1932), and that 'it is impossible for the principal or the agent at zero cost to ensure that the agent will make optimal decisions from the principal's viewpoint' (Jensen and Meckling, 1976).

Jensen and Meckling (1976) summarise that most agency relationships involve some forms of agency costs, which consist of monitoring expenditures by the principal, bonding expenditures by the agent and residual loss. The monitoring expenditures by the principal are the costs designed by the principal to restrict the activities of the agent from diverging from the principal's interests. The bonding expenditures by the agent are the costs paid to the agent to guarantee that they will not take certain actions harmful to the principal, and to demonstrate the commitment of the agent to the principal. The residual loss refers to the reduced welfare in dollars that results from the divergence between the decisions which would maximise the welfare of the principal and the agent's actual decisions.

In a corporation, misalignment of interests between managers and shareholders requires costly actions to be undertaken by managers (Bhagat and Jefferis, 2002). Agency costs are incurred as a consequence of the separation of ownership and control (Copeland et al., 2005). Specifically, when a firm is solely owned by a single owner-manager, no agency costs are generated (zero agency-cost base firm). In contrast, when management does not own the whole amount of a firm's equity (a firm with less than 100 per cent of equity owned by managers), agency costs are present due to management's shirking and perquisite consumption. Intuitively, three forms of agency costs, as mentioned earlier, can be measured together by comparing the difference in the costs associated with a firm with less than 100 per cent of managerial ownership and the costs with a zero agency-cost base firm (Ang et al., 2000).[1]

According to Jensen and Meckling (1976), regardless of the existence of agency costs, shareholders are willing to provide a considerable amount of their capital to corporations run by managers. It is thus common that ownership is widely held. As a result, each type of ownership structure may be related to a certain level of agency costs.

In this regard, ownership structure can affect agency problems in the sense that it can be used as a mechanism to control such problems. For example, if the contract between a firm and managers cannot mitigate agency conflict, an increase in the level of insider shareholding can be an effective corporate governance mechanism for this purpose since it increases managerial monitoring and alignment with shareholders' interests (Bhagat et al., 2010, Agrawal and Knoeber, 1996). In addition, the board of directors can reduce agency problems. Directors have incentives to maintain their independence, to monitor the CEO and to replace the CEO if their performance is poor (Hermalin and Weisbach, 2003).

### RISK-SHARING PROBLEM AND LINK BETWEEN OWNERSHIP STRUCTURE AND CORPORATE RISK-TAKING

The risk-sharing problem in agency theory does not only imply a link between ownership structure and agency costs, but it also suggests a link between ownership structure and corporate risk-taking. Individual shareholders may have different risk preferences, which may be categorised into the following three types: risk averse, risk neutral and risk seeking. Risk-averse shareholders are those who want to avoid or minimise risk. Risk-neutral shareholders focus on expected returns and ignore the dispersion of risk. Risk-seeking shareholders are those who prefer risk (McGuigan et al., 2005, Merna and Al-Thani, 2008). Thus, it is plausible that the risk attitudes of individual shareholders can affect the risk-taking behaviours of the firm or corporate risk-taking.

Nevertheless, most prior literature on corporate risk-taking in the agency context focuses on the behaviour of inside managers and often regards them as risk-averse shareholders (Agrawal & Mandelker; Amihud & Lev; John et al.; Wright et al., cited in Kim 2011). Unlike outside shareholders, who tend to take higher risks to the extent that they can diversify these, it is likely that managers avoid risky projects because the human capital of managers invested in the firm is not diversifiable. The greater the corporate resources the managers expect to divert, the more managers will avoid making risky investments in order to protect their private benefits (Himmelberg et al., 1999).

However, if managers prefer a lower level of risks than do owners, managers may be more involved in risk-taking when they own more shares in firms. This is because the interests of insiders are then more closely aligned with those of owners, according to the 'alignment of interest' hypothesis (Downs and Sommer, 1999). Furthermore, Tirole (2006) implies that both risk-seeking and risk-averse preferences of managers are conditional on their job security. Managers may take risks when their jobs are endangered, but be more conservative when their jobs are secure.

When a company has another type of shareholder, such as foreigners, managers are influenced by foreign investors to take risks that are closer to the optimal level, in the sense that foreign shareholders can effectively reduce managers' incentives to avoid risk (Kim, 2011).

#### OUT-OF-EQUILIBRIUM PHENOMENON AND LINKS BETWEEN OWNERSHIP STRUCTURE, AGENCY COSTS AND FIRM PERFORMANCE

While the conflict-of-interest concept helps depict the link between ownership structure and agency costs, the out-of-equilibrium phenomenon formulated by Hermalin and Weisbach (2003) is useful to explain the links between ownership structure and agency costs, and between agency costs and firm performance. According to the authors, the interpretation of empirical results on the governance–performance relationship is classified into two types: the out-of-equilibrium phenomenon; and the equilibrium phenomenon. As an example of the former, Hermalin and Weisbach (2003) document a negative relationship between the size of boards of directors and firm performance; this is one of the most consistent empirical findings in the economics and finance literature. The underlying mechanism of this link is the out-of-equilibrium phenomenon. The implication of this phenomenon is that any adjustment of the characteristics of a board of directors will result in a change in firm performance because the corporate governance structure is no longer optimal.[2]

This out-of-equilibrium phenomenon is conceptualised as the 'out-of-equilibrium model' by Tan (2009). In this model, any adjustment of corporate governance will result in a direct effect on agency conflict because the corporate governance structure is no longer optimal. In turn, the change in agency conflict will lead to a (negative) change in firm performance. There is an indirect link through agency conflict between corporate governance mechanisms and firm performance. Tan (2009) explains that corporate governance mechanisms are measures or characteristics of a firm that are effective in mitigating agency conflict between managers and shareholders. Agency conflict indicates a misalignment of incentives between them, resulting in managers performing actions that are not in the best interest of shareholders.

It is explicit in the above model that the agency theory can be used to explain the indirect relationship of corporate governance, including ownership structure, to firm performance. In fact, the agency theory and the role of agency costs in the link between ownership structure and firm performance are also indicated in many other studies. As such, agency costs are closely associated with agency conflict (Ang et al., 2000) and so ownership structure can be employed as an instrument to control this agency problem (Agrawal and Knoeber, 1996). Thus, ownership structure may have an effect on agency costs, and consequently on firm performance and investment opportunities (Thomsen and Pedersen, 2000).

Therefore, the out-of-equilibrium model can be adapted to conceptualise the indirect effect of ownership structure via agency costs on firm performance in a mediation model. Nevertheless, it can be argued that the use of a single theory, agency theory, is not sufficient to properly explain how and why ownership structure influences firm performance.

#### *3.1.1.2 Corporate Risk Management Theory*

##### RISK MANAGEMENT AND THE LINK BETWEEN CORPORATE RISK-TAKING AND FIRM PERFORMANCE

As previously discussed, agency theory implies an indirect link between ownership structure and firm performance via agency costs. It also implies a direct link between ownership structure and corporate risk-taking. Besides, corporate risk management theory suggests a direct link between corporate risk-taking and firm performance. According to Léautier (2007), risk management creates firm value through three channels: (1) providing financial flexibility at minimum cost; (2) enhancing capital allocation and performance management; and (3) leveraging operational and strategic flexibility. In the second channel, for example, the logic for value creation of risk management is that: 'by correctly accounting for the risks of assets and businesses (new and existing), firms allocate their capital to the opportunities that offer the highest ex-ante risk-adjusted returns, hence increasing their ex-post observed return' (Léautier, 2007). As a result, the focus of corporate risk management is on the risk–return trade-off (Gordon et al., 2009) and a conventional assumption in finance theories is that 'higher risk' implies 'higher potential return' (Drever et al., 2007).

As a consequence, corporate risk management has become another area of corporate governance. Dealing with corporate risk-taking in entrepreneurism is crucial to ensure that directors are accountable for the firm. Hence, an issue of common concern is how to balance regulation and control on the one hand, and the scope for the corporate risk-taking and innovation necessary for economic growth on the other hand (Farrar, 2008).

Therefore, agency theory and corporate risk management theory together indicate that the impact of ownership structure on firm performance occurs through the intervening roles of agency costs and corporate risk-taking. The theoretical perspectives discussed above have clearly shown that it is possible to conceptualise these associations.

#### *3.1.1.3 Endogeneity Problem in Corporate Governance–Firm Performance Relationship*

Endogeneity is a challenging issue that is almost certain to arise in research on corporate governance and firm performance relationship, as well as financial and accounting decisions.[3] Endogeneity refers to situations in which explanatory variable(s) are correlated with the residuals in a regression model, and hence the variable(s) are endogenous (Brown et al., 2011). The basis of endogeneity is that 'it is generally hard to find exogenous factors or natural experiments with which to identify the relations being examined' (Wintoki et al., 2012). When endogeneity is present, any estimation method that treats corporate governance variables as exogenous, for example, ordinary least squares (OLS) will produce biased and inconsistent estimates if the endogeneity problem is not properly addressed.

Typically, there are two sources of endogeneity in the corporate governance–firm performance relationship. The first is simultaneity, where performance is affected by governance and governance is also affected by performance. Bhagat and Jefferis (2002) indicate that six variables associated with corporate governance are interrelated, including equity ownership structure and firm performance. A possible solution to simultaneity is to use instrumental variables in a system of equations, such as in two-stage least squares (2SLS) estimation (Demsetz and Villalonga, 2001, Bhagat and Bolton, 2008). However, as Wintoki et al. (2012) point out, it is difficult to identify and justify strictly exogenous instruments under such a method. An alternative solution for this simultaneous endogeneity is to use lagged values of endogenous variables as instruments (Mcknight and Weir, 2009).

The second source of endogeneity is unobserved heterogeneity, where both governance and performance variables are affected by some unobservable factor(s). For example, managerial ability, which is generally unobservable, can influence both firm performance and the structure of the board of directors (Wintoki et al., 2012).[4] If panel data is used, it is well known that fixed-effects estimation is a solution to accounting for the unobserved heterogeneity, which contains a fixed or time-invariant component.

In addition, another source of endogeneity in the corporate governance–firm performance relationship is its dynamic nature. It is possible that the current values of governance are determined by past firm performance. This source of endogeneity is often ignored by researchers because they commonly use a static model. For instance, current values of firm performance are a function of current values of board structure. When the relationship between governance and firm performance is considered dynamic, traditional fixed-effects estimation is problematic. This is because it relies on a strong exogeneity assumption that current values of explanatory variables are completely independent of past firm performance, but this is unrealistic (Wintoki et al., 2012).

Furthermore, dynamic endogeneity may also be found in the other direction of the effect of corporate governance on firm performance. According to Hu and Izumida (2008), it is possible that existing firm performance is affected by past ownership structure due to postponed effects. Taken together, there is potential for a non-contemporaneous or lead–lag relationship between ownership structure and firm performance; that is, current values of ownership structure are a function of past firm performance, and current firm performance is a function of past values of ownership structure.

### *3.1.2 Development of Theoretical Framework for This Study*

#### *3.1.2.1 Research Approach*

The overall research approach of this study is positivism, which focuses on the objectivity of quantitative analysis based on facts and observations to describe and explain the external world. Accordingly, theories and models are developed prior to empirical research (Veal, 2005).

This study incorporates all four typical purposes of research, namely: exploratory, descriptive, analytical and predictive (Hussey and Hussey, 1997). First, for the exploratory purpose, previous studies are reviewed to establish the mediated relationship between ownership structure and firm performance. Second, the descriptive purpose of this study is reflected by specific characteristics and relevant information in a developing/transition economy context, including patterns of equity ownership and financial performance of Vietnam's listed companies. Third, as an analytical study, this book separately examines the mediated relationship both with and without the jointly determined relationship between ownership structure and firm performance. Lastly, the predictive purpose is demonstrated by a generalisation of the estimated links among the main variables to similar markets in the future.

In terms of theoretical approaches to the issue, several theories have been used in previous studies to explain the relationship between ownership structure and firm performance. For example, Douma et al. (2006) combine three theories, namely agency theory, resource-based theory and institutional theory, to explain the relationship between ownership structure and performance of firms in India. Tan (2009) utilises agency theory to conceptualise the out-of-equilibrium model, as described earlier, for the relationship between ownership structure, agency costs and firm performance.

Based on the theoretical foundation discussed in Section 3.1.1, this book adopts a combination of the mediation approach and the dynamic approach. The mediation approach is based on agency theory and corporate risk management theory in order to explain the direction of effect from ownership structure to firm performance. This is a mediation approach because it involves mediating variables as the intervening links between ownership structure and firm performance. The two potential mediating variables are agency costs and corporate risk-taking, as

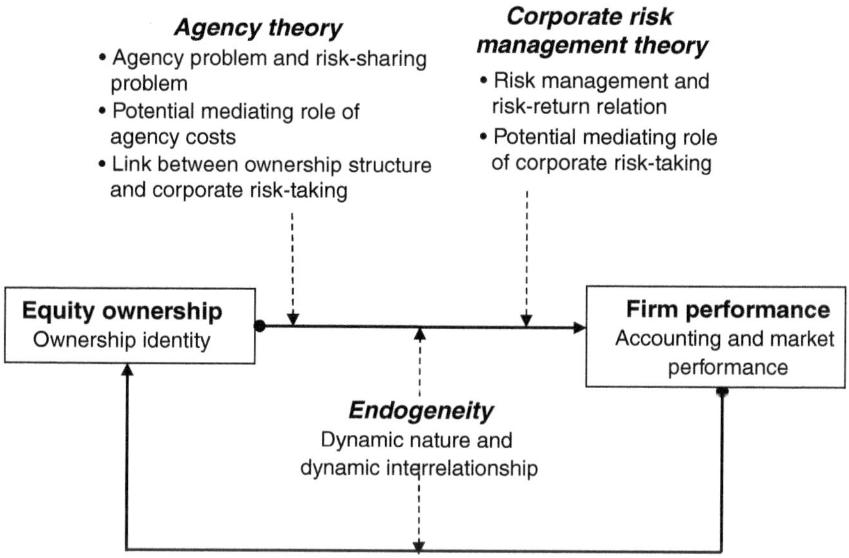


*Figure 3.1* A combination of mediation and dynamic approaches explaining the relationship between ownership structure and firm performance.

suggested by agency theory and corporate risk management theory, respectively. In addition, the dynamic approach is based on the dynamic aspect of endogeneity in the ownership–performance relationship. This approach is used to explain the non-contemporaneous interrelationship between ownership structure and firm performance. Current firm performance is affected by prior ownership structure, while current ownership structure is also affected by prior firm performance. The combination of mediation and dynamic approaches is illustrated in Figure 3.1.

### *3.1.2.2 Conceptual Framework*

As discussed in the above theoretical foundation and research approach, the relationship between ownership structure and firm performance can be established by several pathways, which are summarised as follows:

1 The path between ownership structure and agency costs (agency theory).
2 The path between ownership structure and corporate risk-taking (agency theory).
3 The indirect path via agency costs between ownership structure and firm performance (agency theory).
4 The indirect path via corporate risk-taking between ownership structure and firm performance (agency theory and corporate risk management theory).

5 The bidirectional dynamic paths between ownership structure and firm performance (dynamic endogeneity in the corporate governance–firm performance relationship).

In the mediation context, furthermore, it is suggested in the mediation literature that if variables are measured at the same time, there may not be enough time for the independent variable to affect the mediating variable, or for the mediating variable to affect the outcome variable (Gollob & Reichardt, cited in MacKinnon, 2012). More accurate conclusions about mediation can be obtained by considering the temporal order of change over time (MacKinnon, 2012). It is plausible to hypothesise that it would take at least one period of time for the impact of ownership structure on agency costs, corporate risk-taking and then firm performance to be effective. Hence, it is likely that there are mediated effects of lagged (previous-year) ownership structure through agency costs and corporate risk-taking to firm performance. Similarly, the reverse direction of influence from firm performance to ownership structure can also be hypothesised on a time-lag basis; that is, current changes in ownership structure may be affected by lagged firm performance. As a consequence, it can be said that the mediation approach is suitable for and can be combined with the dynamic endogeneity in explaining the relationship between ownership structure and firm performance.

Based on all of the above propositions, the conceptual framework of this research is developed in the form of the diagram presented in Figure 3.2.

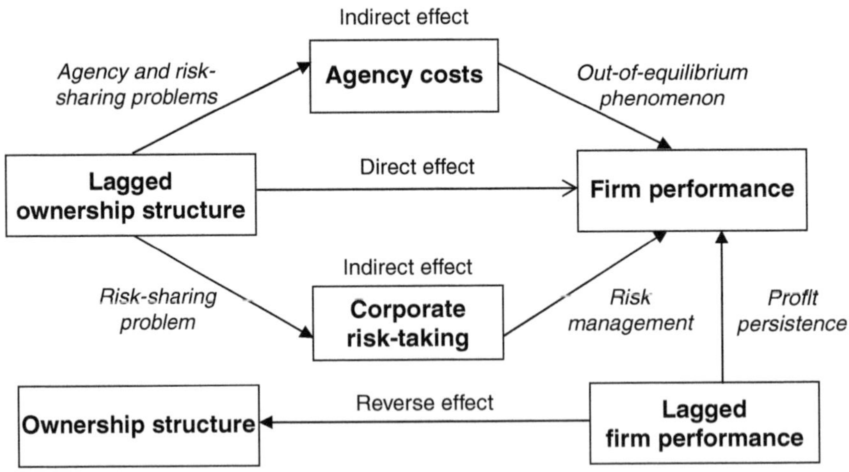


*Figure 3.2* Conceptual framework of the mediated and dynamic relationship between ownership structure and firm performance.

The rationales for the paths between pairs of the main variables are summarised and illustrated next to the arrows in Figure 3.2. In addition to those already discussed, the explanation for the path between lagged firm performance and firm performance is profit persistence; that is, firms may continue to work well if they have performed well previously (Goddard & Wilson, cited in Hu and Izumida 2008).

Overall, Figure 3.2 illustrates a two-mediator mediation model where the mediators are agency costs and corporate risk-taking, whereas most of the literature on mediation analysis relies on a single-mediator model setting (Vanderweele and Vansteelandt, 2014). On the one hand, it is unlikely for the effect of a variable to be mediated by only a single mediating variable in most situations (Preacher and Hayes, 2008). On the other hand, it is suggested in agency theory and risk management theory that agency costs and corporate risk-taking are two potential mediators, as aforementioned. The above conceptual framework is used to develop the theoretical models, and in turn, the empirical models for the relationship between ownership structure and firm performance.

### *3.1.2.3 Theoretical Models of This Study*

The conceptual framework shown in Figure 3.2 can be specified by a single model where all the paths are estimated simultaneously, including the mediated effects of ownership structure and the feedback effect of firm performance. However, the employment of a single model would not provide an in-depth path analysis of the mediated association between ownership structure and firm performance. As the first objective of this book is to test for the flow of mediation from ownership structure to firm performance, as mentioned in Chapter 1, a recursive model which does not take into consideration the feedback effect of firm performance is first used to examine the mediation mechanism from ownership structure to firm performance. The results obtained from this recursive model will then be compared with the full model that covers all paths in order to understand how the mediated relationship is affected by the feedback effect of firm performance.

Based on MacKinnon (2012), the recursive model without the feedback effect of firm performance is developed as follows:

*Theoretical model 1 (recursive model):*

$$\text{Firm performance} = f_1(\text{Ownership structure}(-1),\ C_1,\ \varepsilon_1) \quad (3.1)$$

$$\text{Agency costs} = f_2(\text{Ownership structure}(-1),\ C_2,\ \varepsilon_2) \quad (3.2)$$

$$\text{Corporate risk-taking} = f_3(\text{Ownership structure}(-1),\ C_3,\ \varepsilon_3) \quad (3.3)$$

$$\text{Firm performance} = f_4(\text{Agency costs, Corporate risk-taking, Ownership structure}(-1), C_4, \varepsilon_4) \quad (3.4)$$

Where Equation 3.1 represents the total effect of the one-time lagged value of ownership structure on firm performance; Equations 3.2 and 3.3 represent the effect of the one-time lagged value of ownership structure on agency costs (the first mediator) and on corporate risk-taking (the second mediator), respectively; and Equation 3.4 represents the effect of the one-time lagged value of ownership structure on firm performance, adjusted for agency costs and corporate risk-taking. $C_1$, $C_2$, $C_3$ and $C_4$ are the vectors of the control variables that influence the dependent variables, while $\varepsilon_1$, $\varepsilon_2$, $\varepsilon_3$ and $\varepsilon_4$ are error terms that contain random disturbance and unobserved heterogeneity.

When the feedback effect of firm performance is taken into account, the full model, which is referred to as the non-recursive model, is specified such that: (1) a new equation is added to account for the feedback effect of firm performance on ownership structure; and (2) it allows the simultaneous estimation (system estimation) of all equations to meet the second objective of this study, as stated in Section 1.4. To this end, the non-recursive model is modified from the recursive model. Accordingly, Equation 3.1 in the recursive model is dropped out to avoid having two identical dependent variables in the non-recursive model. This is also reasonable because consideration of the significant total effect of the predictor variable on the outcome variables is not always necessary in order for mediation to occur (Preacher and Hayes, 2008, MacKinnon, 2012). As a result, the non-recursive model takes the following form:

*Theoretical model 2 (non-recursive model):*

$$\text{Agency costs} = f_2(\text{Ownership structure}(-1), C_2, \varepsilon_2) \quad (3.5)$$

$$\text{Corporate risk-taking} = f_3(\text{Ownership structure}(-1), C_3, \varepsilon_3) \quad (3.6)$$

$$\text{Firm performance} = f_4(\text{Agency costs, Corporate risk-taking, Ownership structure}(-1), C_4, \varepsilon_4) \quad (3.7)$$

$$\text{Ownership structure} = f_5(\text{Firm performance}(-1), C_5, \varepsilon_5) \quad (3.8)$$

Where Equation 3.8 represents the feedback effect of firm performance on ownership structure. This is the effect of the one-time lagged value of firm performance on current ownership structure.

The theoretical model 2 is non-recursive because it covers the bidirectional influence between ownership structure and firm performance. Any form of feedback effect of the outcome variable on the independent variable can turn a recursive model into a non-recursive model (Acock, 2013). Moreover, when two endogenous variables have a unidirectional relationship, and their disturbances are allowed to be correlated, a bow-pattern of disturbance correlation is formed, and such a model must be treated as non-recursive (Kline, 2010). This is the case of the non-recursive model in this book because there is a one-way direct effect of the mediating variables on the outcome variables, while the error terms of the mediating variables and the outcome variables, together with those of other equations, are free to be correlated (more details about the correlation of disturbances of the non-recursive model are covered in Section 4.4.2.1).

It should be noted that both theoretical models described above assume that there is no feedback effect of the outcome variable (firm performance) on the two mediating variables (agency costs and corporate risk-taking). If we were to claim that they are contemporaneously correlated, then the above models would require different specifications.

## 3.2 Empirical Models

The purpose of this section is to discuss how the empirical models of this book have been formed on the basis of the theoretical models introduced in previous sections. The first part of this section explains how the variables are defined and measured, including the predictor variable (ownership structure), the mediating variables (agency costs and corporate risk-taking), the outcome variable (firm performance) and the control variables. The second part introduces the two empirical models of this research, of which the first model is used to answer research questions 1 and 2, and the second model is aimed at research questions 3 and 4.

### *3.2.1 Variable Measurement*

This section presents the measurement and/or calculation methods of all variables used in this book. Four groups of variables are described in detail: predictor variables, mediating variables, outcome variables, and control variables.

#### *3.2.1.1 Predictor Variables*

##### LAGGED GOVERNMENT OWNERSHIP (GOV(−1))

This predictor variable is measured as the one-year lagged value of the ratio of common equity owned by government agencies or SOEs over the total common equity of a firm. In fact, the ratios of government ownership can be obtained without any calculation because they are stated in the annual reports of Vietnamese listed firms.

#### LAGGED INSIDER OWNERSHIP (INS(–1))

Following Davidson and Singh (2003) and Tan (2009), INS(–1) in this book is defined as the one-year lagged value of the ratio of common equity owned by the members of the board of directors, including managers, over the total common equity.

Since this proxy consists of shares held by both managers and directors, it is assumed that the interests of both directors and managers are homogeneous, which is appropriate to reflect the problem of little separation of ownership and control in the context of a developing country like Vietnam, as already discussed in Chapter 1. This is also compatible with the traditional focus of economics and finance literature on the agency problems solved or created by the board of directors (Adams et al., 2010). To obtain the accurate amounts of shares owned by insiders, government shares nominally owned by directors are excluded from this ratio.

#### LAGGED FOREIGN OWNERSHIP (FOR(–1))

FOR(–1) is measured as the one-year lagged value of the ratio of common equity held by foreign investors to the total common equity of a firm. It should be noted that the maximum value of foreign ownership is 49% in this research because this was the highest level of foreign ownership in Vietnamese listed firms according to the applicable laws.

### *3.2.1.2 Mediating Variables*

#### AGENCY COSTS (AC)

In the literature, agency costs are often inferred but not directly measured due to the lack of information about sole owner-manager firms; hence, determining the size of agency costs is an empirical issue (Ang et al., 2000). As such, a variety of measurements have been employed to proxy agency costs, such as growth opportunities and the number of acquisitions undertaken per year (Mcknight and Weir, 2009) or the adjusted short-term debt ratio (Chen and Yur-Austin, 2007).

Nevertheless, as already mentioned in Section 3.1.1.1, agency costs can by proxied by the operating expense ratio and asset utilisation ratio. These are the most commonly used proxies for agency costs in the financial and economics literature (Ang et al., 2000). The former ratio is referred to by these authors as 'direct agency costs', calculated as total operating expenses scaled by annual sales. It reflects the difference in dollar expenses between a firm with less than 100 per cent of managerial ownership and a zero agency-cost base firm. The asset utilisation ratio does not directly measure expenses; it is calculated as the ratio of annual sales to total assets and referred as an 'efficiency ratio'. It is a proxy for the dollar revenues lost due to the inefficient use of assets, reflecting the difference in the dollar revenues lost between two types of firms, as mentioned above.

There are variations in valuing the numerator of the expense ratio. It can be total operating expenses (Ang et al., 2000), selling, general and administration expenses (Davidson and Singh, 2003), or all other operating expenses, which do not include general and administration expenses (Fleming et al., 2005). The differences in such calculation methods may reflect the differences in the focus of research, but the implication of this ratio remains the same: a higher value of the operating expense ratio implies a higher level of agency costs.

While the measurement of the operating expense ratio varies, the definition of the asset utilisation ratio is fixed in the literature (annual sales divided by total assets). Following Davidson and Singh (2003) and Mcknight and Weir (2009), therefore, this book employs the asset utilisation ratio as the primary measure of agency costs. A higher value of the asset utilisation ratio implies a lower level of agency costs since it measures the ability of managers to deploy assets efficiently. The operating expense ratio is used for a robustness check only.

#### CORPORATE RISK-TAKING (RT)

In the literature, a typical proxy for corporate risk-taking is the standard deviation of historical stock price volatility/return, which reflects the total risk of a firm (Guner and Kursat, 2002, Niu, 2012). This ratio is often calculated on the basis of the daily or monthly volatility of exchange-traded closing prices of listed stocks.

Therefore, this book adopts a market-based measure of risk-taking that uses historical stock prices. Following Minton et al. (2014), Niu (2012) and Huang and Wang (2015), corporate risk-taking variables are based on daily stock returns during a calendar year and are defined as the standard deviation of the market-adjusted daily stock returns. Specifically, the natural logarithm of variance of daily stock returns is applied to calculate the returns. These values are then adjusted to eliminate the market-driven risk factor by calculating the difference between daily stock returns and daily returns on the stock market index. By subtracting the market-related risk component, this measure better reflects firm-specific risk-taking behaviours. A higher value of the standard deviation indicates a higher corporate risk-taking level and vice versa.

### *3.2.1.3 Outcome Variables*

In the literature, return on assets (ROA), and Tobin's Q (Q) are among the most commonly used measures of firm performance, where the former is an accounting-based performance measure, and the latter is a stock market–based performance measure. ROA is a measure from a backward-looking perspective because it reflects firm performance in the past, while the Q measure can provide a forward-looking perspective on how the firm will perform in the future (Hu and Izumida, 2008, Demsetz and Villalonga, 2001). Recent studies (e.g., among others, Bhagat and Bolton, 2019, Ciftci et al., 2019) also use ROA and Tobin's Q as firm performance measures. Hence, this book employs these two measures to proxy firm performance.

#### ROA

Several measures can be employed individually or collectively for accounting-based performance, such as dividend yield (Ming and Gee, 2008, Ongore, 2011), return on sales, return on assets, return on equity and return on investment (Shah et al., 2011). Thus, the calculation methods for ROA can vary due to differences in the value of the numerator. Accordingly, the return can be earnings before interest and income tax (EBIT) (Hu and Izumida, 2008, Wang and Xiao, 2011, Le and Buck, 2011), net profit plus interest (Shah et al., 2011, Thomsen and Pedersen, 2000), or net profit only (Tian and Estrin, 2008, Li et al., 2009).

In this book, ROA is defined as the ratio of earnings before tax (EBT) to total assets of the firm. It should be noted that net profit is not used because in Vietnam, it was the preferential policy during the initial stage of stock market development that newly listed companies were offered 100% exemption from corporate income tax for the first year of listing, plus 50% exemption over the next two years. As the year of the listing is different among the listed companies in the data sample, EBT is employed to facilitate cross-sectional comparisons.

#### Q

As already noted, Q is one of the most common proxies for the market-based performancc of firms, and it provides an additional dimension of firm performance (a forward-looking perspective). It is arguable that Q suffers from several shortcomings. In China's secondary stock market, for example, government shares in listed firms are not freely traded; thus the valuation of firms may not be accurately reflected by the market prices of the traded shares (Li et al., 2009).

In this book, however, the sample data does not only contain government ownership, and there are significant numbers of listed firms with no government ownership. As in many other studies, therefore, Q is employed as a proxy of market firm performance in this book.

Q is here defined as the simplified Tobin's Q (Tian and Estrin, 2008, Hu and Izumida, 2008, Wei et al., 2005), where book value is used to measure the market value of debt. Q is thus calculated as the ratio of the market value of common stock plus the book value of preferred stock and liabilities to the book value of total assets. The numerator of Q can be regarded as the value of the firm and the denominator represents the replacement value of assets (Himmelberg et al., 1999). As preferred stocks were rarely issued in Vietnam during the period of study, the value of preferred stocks in the numerator is not included in the calculation of Q.

### *3.2.1.4 Control Variables*

Based on both the literature on the issue and the country-specific context of research, the following control variables are employed in this study (see Section 3.2.2 and Section 3.2.3 for justifications for the use of these control variables):

1 *Financial leverage (LEV)*: This ratio is calculated as total liabilities divided by total assets of a firm, where the numerator encompasses all liabilities, including interest-bearing debt. As an important firm-specific characteristic, LEV is used to capture the influence of financial leverage on agency costs, corporate risk-taking, firm performance, government ownership and foreign ownership.
2 *Firm size (SIZE)*: This variable is defined as the natural logarithm of total assets. There may be significant differences between large firms and small ones. SIZE is used to capture the influence of firm size on agency costs equations, firm performance equations and ownership structure equations.
3 *Firm age (AGE)*: This variable is defined as the difference between the observed year and the initial year of listing on national stock exchanges. Hence, it shows how long a firm has been trading on stock exchanges. AGE is employed to account for the influence it may have on agency costs.
4 *Firm growth (GRO)*: This proxy is calculated as the percentage of change in annual sales divided by one-year lagged sales (Hu and Izumida, 2008). GRO is employed to account for the influence of firm growth on corporate risk-taking, insider ownership and foreign ownership.

5 *Financial investment (FIN)*: This variable is defined as the sum of short-term and long-term financial investments scaled by total assets. Short-term financial investments include marketable securities (e.g. short-term stocks and bonds) and other financial assets which are available for sale within one fiscal year. Long-term financial investments consist of capital investments in long-term projects, such as equity holdings in unconsolidated companies. FIN is used to control for corporate risk-taking.
6 *Prior firm performance (FP(–1))*: This variable is defined as the one-year lagged value of firm performance (both ROA and Q). FP(–1) is used as the control variable in firm performance equations and ownership structure equations.
7 *Big-4 audit company (BIG4)*: This is a dummy variable to control for the influence of the audit quality offered by international Big-4 audit companies on corporate risk-taking and firm performance. BIG4 takes a value of 1 if the firm's financial statements are audited by one of the Big-4 international audit companies and zero otherwise.
8 *Formerly state-owned enterprise (SOE)*: This is a dummy variable to capture the distinction between privatised SOEs and private-owned firms, which may influence the level of government ownership in Vietnamese listed firms. Hence, it is used in government ownership equations. SOE would take a value of 1 if the firm was wholly owned by the government before listing on the stock market and zero otherwise.
9 *Industry classification (IND):* This is a dummy variable to control for the influence of industry differences on government ownership. It is assigned a value of 1 if a listed firm belongs to a relevant industry and zero otherwise. This variable is built on the first level of ICB-based industry classification developed by a securities data provider in Vietnam (FiinGroup).
10 *Listing market (MARKET)*: Since the main board of stock exchanges in Vietnam is at the Ho Chi Minh Stock Exchange (HSX), this dummy variable is used to capture the influence of the listing market on foreign ownership. MARKET is assigned the value of 1 if a firm is listed on the HSX and zero if a firm is listed on the Hanoi Stock Exchange (HNX).

Table 3.1 summarises the definitions of all four groups of variables employed in this study.

*Table 3.1* Summary of variables

| *Denotation* | *Definition* |
|---|---|
| *Predictor variables* | |
| GOV(−1) | Lagged government ownership. It is the one-year lagged value of the ratio of shares owned by government over total common shares. |
| INS(−1) | Lagged insider ownership. It is the one-year lagged value of the ratio of shares owned by the board of directors over total common shares. |
| FOR(−1) | Lagged foreign ownership. It is the one-year lagged value of the ratio of shares owned by foreign investors over total common shares. |
| *Mediating variables* | |
| AC | Asset utilisation ratio. It is calculated as annual sales divided by total assets. |
| RT | Corporate risk-taking. It is calculated as the standard deviation of market-adjusted stock returns, where stock returns are the natural logarithms of variance of daily closing prices of stocks. |
| *Outcome variables* | |
| ROA | Return on assets. It is a proxy of accounting-based firm performance and calculated as earnings before tax (EBT) over total assets. |
| Q | Tobin's Q. It is a proxy of market-based firm performance and calculated as the ratio of market value of equity plus book value of liabilities over book value of assets. |
| *Control variables* | |
| LEV | Financial leverage. It is calculated as ratio of total liabilities over total assets. |
| SIZE | Firm size. It is calculated as the natural logarithm of the book value of total assets. |
| AGE | Firm age. It is calculated as the difference between the observed year and listed year of a firm. |
| GRO | Firm growth. It is calculated as the percentage change in annual sales to one-year lagged sales. |
| FIN | Financial investment. It is calculated as the ratio of total financial investment over total assets. |
| FP(−1) | Prior firm performance. It is the one-year lagged value of the ROA or Q. |
| BIG4 | Big-4 audit company. This is a dummy variable which is equal to 1 if a firm's financial statements are audited by one of international Big-4 audit companies and zero otherwise. |
| SOE | Formerly state-owned enterprise. This is a dummy variable which is equal to 1 if a firm was wholly owned by government before listing on the stock market and zero otherwise. |
| IND | Industry classification. This is a dummy variable which is equal to 1 if a listed firm belongs to a relevant industry and zero otherwise. |
| MARKET | Listing market. This is a dummy variable which is equal to 1 if a firm is listed on the Ho Chi Minh Stock Exchange (HSX) and zero if listed on the Hanoi Stock Exchange (HNX). |

### *3.2.2 Recursive Model*

Based on the theoretical model 1 described in Section 3.1.2.3, the empirical form of the recursive model is as follows, aimed at answering research questions 1 and 2.

*Recursive model:*

$$FP_{it} = \alpha_1 + \beta_{11}GOV(-1)_{it} + \beta_{12}INS(-1)_{it} + \beta_{13}FOR(-1)_{it} + \beta_{14}LEV_{it} + \beta_{15}SIZE_{it} + \beta_{16}BIG4_{it} + \beta_{17}FP(-1)_{it} + \varepsilon_{1it} \quad (3.9)$$

$$AC_{it} = \alpha_2 + \beta_{21}GOV(-1)_{it} + \beta_{22}INS(-1)_{it} + \beta_{23}FOR(-1)_{it} + \beta_{24}LEV_{it} + \beta_{25}SIZE_{it} + \beta_{26}AGE_{it} + \varepsilon_{2it} \quad (3.10)$$

$$RT_{it} = \alpha_3 + \beta_{31}GOV(-1)_{it} + \beta_{32}INS(-1)_{it} + \beta_{33}FOR(-1)_{it} + \beta_{34}LEV_{it} + \beta_{35}BIG4_{it} + \beta_{36}GRO_{it} + \beta_{37}FIN_{it} + \varepsilon_{3it} \quad (3.11)$$

$$FP_{it} = \alpha_4 + \beta_{41}AC_{it} + \beta_{42}RT_{it} + \beta_{43}GOV(-1)_{it} + \beta_{44}INS(-1)_{it} + \beta_{45}FOR(-1)_{it} + \beta_{46}LEV_{it} + \beta_{47}SIZE_{it} + \beta_{48}BIG4_{it} + \beta_{49}FP(-1)_{it} + \varepsilon_{4it} \quad (3.12)$$

Where the *i* and *t* subscripts stand for firm and year, AC and RT denote agency costs and corporate risk-taking, respectively, and FP denotes firm performance, consisting of two alternative measures: ROA and Q. GOV (–1), INS(–1) and FOR(–1) denote lagged government ownership, lagged ownership and lagged foreign ownership, respectively. Control variables consist of LEV for financial leverage, SIZE for firm size, AGE for firm age, GRO for firm growth and FIN for financial investment. BIG4 is a dummy variable for Big-4 audit company. FP(–1) is prior firm performance. $\varepsilon_1$, $\varepsilon_2$, $\varepsilon_3$, and $\varepsilon_4$ are the error terms containing random disturbance and unobserved heterogeneity.

*Equation 3.9* is the regression of the determinant of firm performance, which is aimed at estimating the total effect of ownership structure on firm performance. As already reviewed in Chapter 2, Tian and Estrin (2008), Li et al. (2009), and Vaaler and Schrage (2009) point out that under certain conditions in a developing country, it is possible that government ownership has a positive impact on firm performance. Hence, the total effect of past government ownership on current firm performance in Equation 3.9 is expected to be positive. Likewise, it is assumed that the 'alignment of interests' effect also holds in the context of Vietnamese listed firms; thus, past insider ownership might have a positive total effect on current firm performance. On the other hand, it is reported that foreign ownership in Vietnam's listed firms has a negative impact on firm performance due to the lack of a monitoring role as a consequence of non-concentrated ownership (Phung and Le, 2013).

Therefore, it is expected that past foreign ownership has a negative effect on current firm performance in this book.

With regard to the control variables, financial leverage (LEV) is an indicator of capital structure that is correlated with both accounting and market firm performance (Tian and Estrin, 2008). A higher value of LEV means that the firm has to cover more interest expenses. Hence, LEV is likely to be negatively related to firm performance (Morck et al., 1988). In the period of study from 2008 to 2012, this negative relationship could be significant due to high inflation rates in the Vietnamese economy, which can incur large interest expenses for listed firms. Firm size (SIZE) may also have a negative relationship with firm performance. Large companies may produce worse or better outcomes than small ones (Chhibber and Majumdar, 1998). In a developing country like Vietnam, it is likely that smaller firms are more efficient than larger ones. Following Al Farooque et al. (2007), Big-4 audit company dummy (BIG4) is introduced in Equation 3.9 to reflect the difference in firm performance rendered by the service of international Big-4 audit affiliates for Vietnamese listed firms. Lastly, prior firm performance, FP(–1), is expected to be positively correlated with current firm performance due to the persistence of profits (Hu and Izumida, 2008).

*Equation 3.10* is the regression of agency costs on ownership structure and other control variables. Ownership structure is represented by three main variables, namely, lagged government ownership, lagged insider ownership and lagged foreign ownership. It is worth reiterating that the indirect proxy of agency costs (the asset utilisation ratio) is used in this equation. Therefore, when a positive association with the utilisation ratio is mentioned, a negative association with agency costs is implied.

In terms of the impact of government ownership on agency costs, Le and Buck (2011) find that the effect of government ownership on firm performance is positively mediated by agency costs in the Chinese context. That is, a higher percentage of government ownership is correlated with a lower level of agency costs, while lower agency costs are correlated with improved firm performance. Since Vietnam shares similar characteristics with China in terms of the dominant role of government ownership in the economy, it is likely that agency costs also have a positive mediating role in the relationship between past government ownership and current firm performance. Hence, lagged government ownership (GOV(–1)) is expected to have a positive relationship with the asset utilisation measure of agency costs, which reflects a negative association between lagged government ownership and agency costs.

With respect to insider ownership, the 'alignment of interest' hypothesis (Jensen and Meckling, 1976) suggests that the higher the level of insider ownership, the less conflict of interest, and hence the lower the level of agency costs. Thus, it is expected that lagged insider ownership (INS(–1)) is positively related to the asset utilisation measure of agency costs.

Foreign ownership is a typical form of ownership in developing countries. Prior studies generally show that agency costs are mitigated by the involvement of foreign investors. The higher ratio of foreign ownership, the lower the level of agency costs, and vice versa. Hence, lagged foreign ownership (FOR(–1)) is expected to have a positive effect on the asset utilisation measure of agency costs.

Financial leverage (LEV) is an important influencing factor that is used to control for agency costs by previous researchers such as Davidson and Singh (2003) and Mcknight and Weir (2009). LEV is expected to be positively related to the asset utilisation ratio (and so negatively related to agency costs) because a higher level of debt can also reduce agency problems (Jensen and Meckling, 1976).

Firm size (SIZE) is expected to be negatively correlated with the asset utilisation ratio measure of agency costs, which implies that larger firms have greater agency costs (Himmelberg et al., 1999). In contrast, firm age (AGE) is assumed to be negatively associated with agency costs, or positively associated with the asset utilisation ratio. In Vietnam's stock market, a firm with greater years of listing may be associated with a lower level of agency costs, because the firm may come under greater pressure from outside shareholders and investors in terms of controlling for operating costs in order to increase shareholder value, as compared to unlisted or newly listed firms.

*Equation 3.11* is the regression of the determinants of corporate risk-taking to help detect the second channel of mediation via corporate risk-taking. For political and power reasons, government shareholders may have strong incentives for preserving and increasing the value of the state capital in listed firms. As a result, they might tend to seek potential returns by supporting risky investment projects. Hence, it is expected that lagged government ownership (GOV(–1)) is positively related to corporate risk-taking.

As for the effect of insider ownership on corporate risk-taking, it is suggested in previous literature that insiders are risk-averse owners because their human capital is not diversified (Himmelberg et al., 1999). Thus, lagged insider ownership is assumed to be negatively associated with corporate risk-taking; that is, a higher proportion of lagged insider ownership is associated with a lower level of corporate risk-taking in firms.

Since foreign ownership does not control shareholding and was restricted to 49% in the Vietnamese stock market at the time of this study, it is plausible that foreign investors in this market do not have long-term commitments to local listed firms. Hence, they might choose to avoid risky investment projects. Lagged foreign ownership is thus expected to have a negative relationship with corporate risk-taking.

Financial leverage (LEV) might have a negative relationship with corporate risk-taking, because it is likely that firms with abundant debt are not willing to take risks (Kim, 2011). Regarding the dummy variable BIG4, it is expected that there is a significant difference in corporate risk-taking level between the companies audited by Big-4 audit firms and the others. In contrast, firm growth (GRO) may have a positive influence on corporate risk-taking, because firms with more growth opportunities are expected to be positively associated with higher corporate risk-taking levels (Panaretou et al., 2013, Nguyen, 2011).

Financial investment (FIN) is introduced into Equation 3.11 to reflect the specific context of Vietnam's stock market. As such, financial investment might have a positive impact on corporate risk-taking. A higher involvement of listed firms in financial investment may be associated with greater corporate risk-taking in two aspects:

1 there is greater exposure of a firm to market risk due to a possible change in the market value of such financial assets, which is 'the possibility that prices of traded assets will differ from what is desired, expected, or planned... it also includes risk for untraded or thinly traded securities when prices can be modelled or inferred' (Coleman, 2012); and
2 there is a higher level of liquidity risk when a firm finds it difficult to sell such investments at favourable prices under typical market conditions (McGuigan et al., 2005).

*Equation 3.12* is the final equation in the recursive model. It contains firm performance as the dependent variable, and the addition of agency costs and corporate risk-taking as the explanatory variables. The purpose of this equation is to estimate the direct effect of ownership structure on firm performance after adjusting for the effects of the mediating variables. As for the first mediator, since a firm with lower agency costs is more efficient, the asset utilisation ratio measure of agency costs (AC) is expected to have a positive relationship with both measures of firm performance (ROA and Q). Regarding the second mediator, based on the assumption of 'high risk – high return', corporate risk-taking (RT) is expected to have a positive relationship with accounting firm performance. Nevertheless, corporate risk-taking might have a negative association with market firm performance. As mentioned in Chapter 1, the risk-seeking preference was common among Vietnam's listed firms in the period of study, and resulted in large losses in terms of the market value of these firms. This might be due to a lack of efficient risk management by the firms and, hence, a negative correlation between corporate risk-taking and market firm performance is assumed in this book.

When agency costs and corporate risk-taking are controlled in this equation, the coefficients of ownership variables indicate the direct effect of ownership structure on firm performance. For the mediation mechanism to occur, it is expected that the signs of the direct effects of ownership structure will remain the same, as mentioned above for Equation 3.9, but that the magnitudes of the effects will be smaller or no longer significant. In addition, it is likely that the influence of the control variables is similar in Equation 3.12 as in Equation 3.9.

### *3.2.3 Non-Recursive Model*

With regard to research questions 3 and 4, the recursive model described in previous sections is modified to take into account the feedback effect of firm performance. Based on the theoretical model 2 described in Section 3.1.2.3, the empirical form of the non-recursive model is as follows:

*Non-recursive model:*

$$\begin{aligned} AC_{it} = \pi_1 + \lambda_{11}GOV(-1)_{it} + \lambda_{12}INS(-1)_{it} + \lambda_{13}FOR(-1)_{it} \\ + \lambda_{14}LEV_{it} + \lambda_{15}SIZE_{it} + \lambda_{16}AGE_{it} + u_{1it} \end{aligned} \quad (3.13)$$

$$\begin{aligned} RT_{it} = \pi_2 + \lambda_{21}GOV(-1)_{it} + \lambda_{22}INS(-1)_{it} + \lambda_{23}FOR(-1)_{it} \\ + \lambda_{24}LEV_{it} + \lambda_{25}BIG4_{it} + \lambda_{26}GRO_{it} + \lambda_{27}FIN_{it} + u_{2it} \end{aligned} \quad (3.14)$$

$$\begin{aligned} ROA_{it} = \pi_3 + \lambda_{31}AC_{it} + \lambda_{32}RT_{it} + \lambda_{33}GOV(-1)_{it} + \lambda_{34}INS(-1)_{it} \\ + \lambda_{35}FOR(-1)_{it} + \lambda_{36}LEV_{it} + \lambda_{37}SIZE_{it} + \lambda_{38}BIG4_{it} \\ + \lambda_{39}ROA(-1)_{it} + u_{3it} \end{aligned} \quad (3.15)$$

$$\begin{aligned} Q_{it} = \pi_4 + \lambda_{41}AC_{it} + \lambda_{42}RT_{it} + \lambda_{43}GOV(-1)_{it} + \lambda_{44}INS(-1)_{it} \\ + \lambda_{45}FOR(-1)_{it} + \lambda_{46}LEV_{it} + \lambda_{47}SIZE_{it} + \lambda_{48}BIG4_{it} \\ + \lambda_{49}Q(-1)_{it} + u_{4it} \end{aligned} \quad (3.16)$$

$$\begin{aligned} GOV_{it} = \pi_5 + \lambda_{51}ROA(-1)_{it} + \lambda_{52}Q(-1)_{it} + \lambda_{53}LEV_{it} \\ + \lambda_{54}SIZE_{it} + \lambda_{55}SOE_{it} + \sum_{k=1}^{14} \omega_k IND_{kit} + u_{5it} \end{aligned} \quad (3.17)$$

$$\begin{aligned} INS_{it} = \pi_6 + \lambda_{61}ROA(-1)_{it} + \lambda_{62}Q(-1)_{it} + \lambda_{63}SIZE_{it} \\ + \lambda_{64}AGE_{it} + \lambda_{65}GRO_{it} + u_{6it} \end{aligned} \quad (3.18)$$

$$\begin{aligned} FOR_{it} = \pi_7 + \lambda_{71}ROA(-1)_{it} + \lambda_{72}Q(-1)_{it} + \lambda_{73}LEV_{it} \\ + \lambda_{74}SIZE_{it} + \lambda_{75}GRO_{it} + \lambda_{76}MARKET_{it} + u_{7it} \end{aligned} \quad (3.19)$$

Where the *i* and *t* subscripts stand for firm and year, AC and RT denote agency costs and corporate risk-taking, respectively, and ROA and Q are accounting and market firm performance, respectively. GOV(–1), INS (–1) and FOR(–1) denote lagged government ownership, lagged insider ownership and lagged foreign ownership, respectively. Control variables include LEV for financial leverage, SIZE for firm size, AGE for firm age, GRO for firm growth, FIN for financial investment, ROA(–1) for prior ROA and Q(–1) for prior Q. Other control variables are dummies, including BIG4 for Big-4 audit companies, MARKET for listing market and IND for industry classification. $u_1, u_2, u_3, \ldots, u_7$ are the error terms containing random disturbance and unobserved heterogeneity.

Unlike in the recursive model, it should be noted that both measures of firm performance (ROA and Q) are used simultaneously in the non-recursive model. It can be argued that ROA and Q are two different proxies of firm performance: the former is based on profit value, while the latter is based on market value; thus, each of them reflects a different aspect of firm performance. Consequently, it is natural that the feedback effects of both measures of firm performance are considered at the same time in ownership structure equations (Equations 3.17–3.19). Specifically, it is assumed that a change in the current ownership structure is affected by both past ROA and past Q. In the literature, ROA and Q are also employed collectively as determinants of ownership structure in corporate governance studies such as those of Ng et al. (2009); and Wei and Varela (2003).

All three types of ownership structures are employed simultaneously in the non-recursive model. It can be argued that the feedback effect of firm performance can occur simultaneously for all three types of ownership structures used in this book (Equations 3.17–3.19).

The signs of all coefficients in the first four equations of the above system (Equations 3.13–3.16) are expected to remain the same as argued for the recursive model. But it is likely that their magnitude of effect and significance levels are changed since all the paths of the non-recursive model are estimated simultaneously. In addition, it is expected that the specific indirect effect of at least one type of ownership variable is significant in the non-recursive model for the mediation mechanism to be confirmed.

In Equations 3.17–3.19, it is expected that past firm performance has a positive feedback effect on all forms of current ownership structure employed in this book. The current level of government ownership might be influenced by the prior performance level (Tian and Estrin, 2008). Likewise, it might be that insider ownership is also determined by past firm performance. Foreign investors may tend to invest in profitable firms due to their short-term investment horizon in Vietnam's stock market, as argued earlier.

With respect to the control variables in the ownership structure equations, following Tian and Estrin (2008), financial leverage (LEV) and firm size (SIZE) are used as control variables in the government ownership equation (Equation 3.17). According to Tian and Estrin (2008), government shareholders tend to hold shares in strategic industries. Thus, industry dummies (IND) are also employed as control variables in Equation 3.17. Another dummy variable that is also introduced in this equation is the former SOE. In the Vietnamese context, government shareholdings tend to be retained or invested more significantly in listed firms that were privatised from former SOEs, while the level of government ownership in other firms may be relatively small.

Among the control variables in Equation 3.18, firm size (SIZE) is expected to have a positive relationship with insider ownership (Himmelberg et al., 1999). The proportion of insider ownership might also be positively influenced by firm growth (GRO), because a higher growth rate may encourage board members to increase their shareholdings as a long-term commitment to such a high growth rate of the firm. Likewise, it is assumed that firm age (AGE) has a negative relationship with insider ownership. It is likely that the proportion of insider ownership is relatively small over the years of listing because the number of outside investors will increase over time when the firm issues more shares to raise funds on stock markets.

In Equation 3.19, foreign investors are less attracted by firms with higher financial leverage and also tend to invest in larger firms (Mishra, 2013). Hence, financial leverage (LEV) and firm size (SIZE) are respectively expected to have negative and positive effects on foreign ownership. Firm growth (GRO) is expected to have a positive relationship with firm performance because firms with higher growth bring about higher expected returns, hence attracting foreign investors to buy the shares of these firms. Lastly, it is likely that foreign investors prefer to own more shares of the firms listed on the main board (the Ho Chi Minh Stock Exchange in the case of Vietnam's stock market). Hence, the sign of the listing market (MARKET) might be positive.

## 3.3 Summary and Conclusions

The theoretical and empirical models employed in this book have been developed on the basis of agency theory, corporate risk management theory and the dynamic endogeneity in the ownership–performance relationship. The former two theories suggest continuing paths from last-year ownership structure through current-year agency costs and current-year corporate risk-taking to current-year firm performance. The latter helps specify the dynamic bidirectional relationship between ownership structure and firm performance.

On that basis, a two-mediator theoretical model has been developed in this chapter where the predictor variables consist of three types of ownership structure, namely, lagged government ownership, lagged insider ownership and lagged foreign ownership; the mediating variables are agency costs and corporate risk-taking; and the outcome variables are return on assets and Q. This theoretical model is specified into two empirical models: (1) the recursive model aimed at research questions 1 and 2; and (2) the non-recursive model aimed at the remaining research questions. All in all, it is argued in this book that the model specifications of the non-recursive model are helpful for obtaining a more accurate and comprehensive understanding of the relationship between ownership structure and firm performance.

## Notes

1 For example, Ang et al. (2000) employ the operating expense ratio and the asset utilisation ratio to proxy agency costs; the former ratio is assumed to be the difference in dollar expenses between two types of the abovementioned firms (see Section 3.2.1.2 for more details of why these two proxies are often selected in empirical studies).
2 According to Hermalin and Weisbach (2003), the other common finding in the literature, the 'equilibrium phenomenon', implies that there are certain factors causing both board size and firm performance and, hence, the relationship between board size and firm performance is spurious.
3 Corporate governance in this context also includes ownership structure, because the latter is often considered an internal mechanism of the former in the literature.
4 Board structure reflects board size, independence of board members and/or duality, i.e. whether the CEO is also the chair of the board (Wintoki et al., 2012).

## References

Acock, A. C. 2013. *Discovering structural equation modeling using stata*, College Station, Texas: Stata Press.

Adams, R. B., Hermalin, B. E. & Weisbach, M. S. 2010. The role of boards of directors in corporate governance: A conceptual framework and survey. *Journal of Economic Literature*, 48, 58–107.

Agrawal, A. & Knoeber, C. R. 1996. Firm performance and mechanisms to control agency problems between managers and shareholders. *Journal of Financial & Quantitative Analysis*, 31, 377–397.

Al Farooque, O., Van Zijl, T., Dunstan, K. & Karim, A. K. M. W. 2007. Corporate governance in Bangladesh: Link between ownership and financial performance. *Corporate Governance: An International Review*, 15, 1453–1468.

Ang, J. S., Cole, R. A. & Lin, J. W. 2000. Agency costs and ownership structure. *The Journal of Finance*, 55, 81–106.

Berle, A. A. & Means, G. C. 1932. *The modern corporation and private property*.

Bhagat, S. & Bolton, B. 2008. Corporate governance and firm performance. *Journal of Corporate Finance*, 14, 257–273.

Bhagat, S. & Bolton, B. 2019. Corporate governance and firm performance: The sequel. *Journal of Corporate Finance*, 58, 142–168.

Bhagat, S., Bolton, B. & Romano, R. 2010. The effect of corporate governance on performance. *In:* Kent, B. H. & Ronald, A. (eds.) *Corporate governance: A synthesis of theory, research, and practice*. Chichester: Wiley.

Bhagat, S. & Jefferis, R. H. 2002. *The econometrics of corporate governance studies*, Cambridge, Mass: MIT.

Brown, P., Beekes, W. & Verhoeven, P. 2011. Corporate governance, accounting and finance: A review. *Accounting and Finance*, 51, 96–172.

Chen, X. & Yur-Austin, J. 2007. Re-measuring agency costs: The effectiveness of blockholders. *Quarterly Review of Economics and Finance*, 47, 588–601.

Chhibber, P. & Majumdar, S. K. 1998. State as investor and state as owner: Consequences for firm performance in India. *Economic Development and Cultural Change*, 46, 561–580.

Ciftci, I., Tatoglu, E., Wood, G., Demirbag, M. & Zaim, S. 2019. Corporate governance and firm performance in emerging markets: Evidence from Turkey. *International Business Review*, 28, 90–103.

Coleman, T. S. 2012. *Quantitative risk management: A practical guide to financial risk*, New York: Wiley.

Copeland, T. E., Weston, J. F. & Shastri, K. 2005. *Financial theory and corporate policy*, Boston, MA: Addison-Wesley, 4th ed.

Davidson, W. N. & Singh, M. 2003. Agency costs, ownership structure and corporate governance mechanisms. *Journal of Banking & Finance*, 27, 793–816.

Demsetz, H. & Villalonga, B. 2001. Ownership structure and corporate performance. *Journal of Corporate Finance*, 7, 209–233.

Dias, R. & Mroczkowski, N. A. 2012. Do banks use credit default swaps to hedge or speculate? An agency theoretic perspective. *International Journal of Critical Accounting*, 4, 283.

Douma, S., George, R. & Kabir, R. 2006. Foreign and domestic ownership, business groups, and firm performance: Evidence from a large emerging market. *Strategic Management Journal*, 27, 637–657.

Downs, D. H. & Sommer, D. W. 1999. Monitoring, ownership, and risk-taking: The impact of guaranty funds. *The Journal of Risk and Insurance*, 66, 477–479.

Drever, M., Stanton, P. A. & Mcgowan, S. 2007. *Contemporary issues in accounting*, Milton, Qld: John Wiley & Sons Australia.

Fama, E. F. & Jensen, M. C. 1983. Separation of ownership and control. *Journal of law and economics*, 301–325.

Farrar, J. H. 2008. *Corporate governance: Theories, principles and practice*, South Melbourne, Vic: Oxford University Press.

Fleming, G., Heaney, R. & Mccosker, R. 2005. Agency costs and ownership structure in Australia. *Pacific-Basin Finance Journal*, 13, 29–52.

Gordon, L. A., Loeb, M. P. & Tseng, C.-Y. 2009. Enterprise risk management and firm performance: A contingency perspective. *Journal of Accounting and Public Policy*, 28, 301–327.

Guner, G. & Kursat, A. 2002. Equity ownership structure, risk taking, and performance. *Emerging Markets, Finance & Trade*, 38, 6.

Hermalin, B. E. & Weisbach, M. S. 2003. Boards of directors as an endogenously determined institution: A survey of the economic literature. *Economic Policy Review*, 9, 7–26.

Himmelberg, C. P., Hubbard, R. G. & Palia, D. 1999. Understanding the determinants of managerial ownership and the link between ownership and performance. *Journal of Financial Economics*, 53, 353–384.

Hu, Y. & Izumida, S. 2008. Ownership concentration and corporate performance: A causal analysis with Japanese panel data. *Corporate Governance: An International Review*, 16, 342–358.

Huang, Y. S. & Wang, C.-J. 2015. Corporate governance and risk-taking of Chinese firms: The role of board size. *International Review of Economics & Finance*, 37, 96–113.

Hussey, J. & Hussey, R. 1997. *Business research: A practical guide for undergraduate and postgraduate students*, London: Macmillan.

Jensen, M. C. & Meckling, W. H. 1976. Theory of the firm: Managerial behavior, agency costs and ownership structure. *Journal of Financial Economics*, 3, 305–360.

Kim, B. 2011. Do foreign investors encourage value-enhancing corporate risk taking? *Emerging markets finance & trade*, 47, 88–110.

Kline, R. B. 2010. *Principles and practice of structural equation modeling*, New York: Guilford Press.

Le, T. V. & Buck, T. 2011. State ownership and listed firm performance: A universally negative governance relationship? *Journal of Management and Governance*, 15, 227–248.

Léautier, T.-O. 2007. *Corporate risk management for value creation: A guide to real-life applications*, London: Risk.

Li, T., Sun, L. & Zou, L. 2009. State ownership and corporate performance: A quantile regression analysis of Chinese listed companies. *China Economic Review*, 20, 703–716.

MacKinnon, D. 2012. *Introduction to Statistical Mediation Analysis*, Hoboken: Taylor and Francis.

Mcguigan, J. R., Moyer, R. C. & Harris, F. H. D. 2005. *Managerial economics: Applications, strategy, and tactics*, Mason, Ohio: Thomson / South-Western, 10th ed.

Mcknight, P. J. & Weir, C. 2009. Agency costs, corporate governance mechanisms and ownership structure in large UK publicly quoted companies: A panel data analysis. *Quarterly Review of Economics and Finance*, 49, 139–158.

Merna, T. & Al-Thani, F. F. 2008. *Corporate risk management*, Chichester, England: Wiley.

Ming, T. C. & Gee, C. S. 2008. The influence of ownership structure on the corporate performance of Malaysian public listed companies. *ASEAN Economic Bulletin*, 25, 195.

Minton, B. A., Taillard, J. P. & Williamson, R. 2014. Financial expertise of the board, risk taking, and performance: Evidence from bank holding companies. *Journal of Financial & Quantitative Analysis*, 49, 351–380.

Mishra, A. V. 2013. Foreign ownership in Australian firms. *Research in International Business and Finance*, 28, 1–18.

Morck, R., Shleifer, A. & Vishny, R. W. 1988. Management ownership and market valuation: An empirical analysis. *Journal of Financial Economics*, 20, 293–315.

Ng, A., Chen, E. & Yuce, A. 2009. Determinants of state equity ownership, and its effect on value/performance: China's privatised firms. *Pacific Basin Finance Journal*, 17, 413–443.

Nguyen, P. 2011. Corporate governance and risk-taking: Evidence from Japanese firms. *Pacific-Basin Finance Journal*, 19, 278–297.

Niu, J. 2012. An empirical analysis of the relation between bank charter value and risk taking. *The Quarterly Review of Economics and Finance*, 52, 298–304.

Ongore, V. O. 2011. The relationship between ownership structure and firm performance: An empirical analysis of listed companies in Kenya. *African Journal of Business Management*, 5, 2120–2128.

Panaretou, A., Shackleton, M. B. & Taylor, P. A. 2013. Corporate risk management and hedge accounting. *Contemporary Accounting Research*, 30, 116–139.

Phung, D. N. & Le, T. P. V. 2013. Foreign ownership, capital structure and firm value: empirical evidence from Vietnamese listed firms. *The IUP Journal of Corporate Governance*, 12, 40–58.

Preacher, K. J. & Hayes, A. F. 2008. Asymptotic and resampling strategies for assessing and comparing indirect effects in multiple mediator models. *Behavior Research Methods*, 40, 879–891.

Shah, S. Z. A., Butt, S. A. & Saeed, M. M. 2011. Ownership structure and performance of firms: Empirical evidence from an emerging market. *African Journal of Business Management*, 5, 515–523.

Shankman, N. A. 1999. Reframing the debate between agency and stakeholder theories of the firm. *Journal of Business Ethics*, 19, 319–334.

Tan, D. T. 2009. *Corporate governance and firm outcomes: causation or spurious correlations?* PhD, Universtity of New South Wales.

Thomsen, S. & Pedersen, T. 2000. Ownership structure and economic performance in the largest European companies. *Strategic Management Journal*, 21, 689–705.

Tian, L. & Estrin, S. 2008. Retained state shareholding in Chinese PLCs: Does government ownership always reduce corporate value? *Journal of Comparative Economics*, 36, 74–89.

Tirole, J. 2006. *The theory of corporate finance*, Princeton, NJ: Princeton University Press.

Vaaler, P. M. & Schrage, B. N. 2009. Residual state ownership, policy stability and financial performance following strategic decisions by sprivatising telecoms. *Journal of International Business Studies*, 40, 621–641.

Vanderweele, T. & Vansteelandt, S. 2014. Mediation analysis with multiple mediators. *Epidemiologic Methods*, 2, 95–115.

Veal, A. J. 2005. *Business research methods: A managerial approach*, South Melbourne.: Pearson Addison Wesley.

Wang, K. & Xiao, X. 2011. Controlling shareholders' tunneling and executive compensation: Evidence from China. *Journal of Accounting and Public Policy*, 30, 89–100.

Wei, Z. & Varela, O. 2003. State equity ownership and firm market performance: Evidence from China's newly privatised firms. *Global Finance Journal*, 14, 65.

Wei, Z., Xie, F. & Zhang, S. 2005. Ownership structure and firm value in China's privatised Firms: 1991–2001. *Journal of Financial & Quantitative Analysis*, 40, 87–108.

Wintoki, M. B., Linck, J. S. & Netter, J. M. 2012. Endogeneity and the dynamics of internal corporate governance. *Journal of Financial Economics*, 105, 581–606.

# 4 Corporate Governance, Ownership Structure and Firm Performance

## Data and Estimation Methods

### 4.1 Panel Data Selection

This study employs a panel dataset. Panel data analysis has become popular in social science, and it offers a range of estimation methods (Asteriou and Hall, 2011). In comparison with either cross-sectional or time-series data, the advantage of panel data is that it produces an increase in the number of observations and it allows the examination of changes within both individuals and cross-sections (MacKinnon, 2012). Hence, the use of panel data is better for research on complex issues of dynamic behaviour (Baltagi, 2011).

Panel data is also believed to enable researchers to address the biased estimates caused by unobserved heterogeneity among individuals (Coles et al., 2012, Wintoki et al., 2012, Hu and Izumida, 2008, Baltagi, 2011). The use of panel data with cross-sectional fixed effects is also a solution to the endogeneity problem (Coles et al., 2012), which is often encountered by researchers of corporate governance.

In mediation analysis, as a result, more information regarding the temporal dependence of the independent variable, mediating variable and dependent variable is provided by panel data (MacKinnon, 2012). Furthermore, panel data is a preferred method of mediation testing thanks to its ability to improve statistical inference and investigate intra-firm variation, whereas the traditional application of cross-sectional data has a number of fundamental problems (Selig and Preacher, 2009).

### 4.2 Sample

#### *4.2.1 Data Sources*

In this book, the financial data of listed firms have been obtained from audited annual financial statements, which were sourced from DataStream. Stock price data has been retrieved from the databases of stock exchanges, which were available on the websites of the Hanoi Stock Exchange and Ho Chi Minh Stock Exchange.[1] Ownership data has been hand-collected

DOI: 10.4324/9781003255741-4

from company annual reports, which were also downloadable from the websites mentioned above. Since all this data is publicly disclosed as required by securities law, an advantage of this data collection is that every single item in the data sample can be cross-checked for accuracy from different sources on the markets, including the databases of securities companies and listed companies themselves.

### *4.2.2 Sample Collection and Data Cleansing Procedures*

The data in this book started with a population of 288 firms, which is the number of all listed companies on Vietnam's stock market in 2008, including both the Hanoi Stock Exchange and the Ho Chi Minh Stock Exchange. The period from 2008 to 2012 has been selected for the following three reasons:

1 the year 2008 was one year after the Securities Law of 2007 in Vietnam came into effect, which is believed to enhance the quality of mandatory information disclosure due to stricter legal enforcement;
2 the data from 2008 on Vietnam's listed companies and stock market was provided in international data terminals such as DataStream; and
3 almost all financial reporting standards applicable in Vietnam's stock market, which are based on the International Financial Reporting Standards (IFRS), were completed and adopted after 2008.

The listed companies must have had a full five years of continuous listing in the period from 2008 to 2012, to enable the efficient use of lagged values of variables. Following previous studies, financial companies were excluded due to the incompatibility or differences in their financial statements as compared to those of non-financial companies. To maintain the quality of the data, companies with incomplete data, that is, lacking annual reports or financial statements of one or more fiscal years, were also removed. Finally, a balanced panel data sample has been obtained with 475 observations in total (95 firms over five years).

In order to mitigate the effect of potential outliers, the most common procedure is to winsorise variables (Leone et al., 2014). In comparison with other procedures of data accommodation, such as trimming (deleting) or piecewise linear regression, winsorising is unaffected by sample size, and it helps a regression model to fit the data well while having a low level of prediction error (Kennedy et al., 1992). Unfortunately, there is no generally accepted guideline for an appropriate fraction of observations to be winsorised. The percentage of gross errors can be few in average-quality data and realistically 10% in fairly low-quality data (Hampel, 1986).

In this book, potential outliers have been detected by constructing ranges of quartile values in Excel. Observations at the distance of

1.5 interquartile ranges adjacent to the lower and upper quartiles were identified as outliers. These outliers were then double-checked by using box plots in Stata. Next, each variable was winsorised at the percentage and tail of outliers found from the above steps, where the percentage of outliers is the fraction of the number of outliers over the total observations for the variable. It should be noted that all dependent and independent variables, except the dummy ones, were winsorised. This is because winsorising predictor variables, but not dependent variables, can lead to biased coefficients (Leone et al., 2014).

Specifically, in constructing the ranges of quartile values in Excel, the QUARTILE function was employed to calculate the upper boundary and lower boundary. The upper boundary is equal to the 3rd quartile of data plus 1.5*IQR, and the lower boundary is equal to the 1st quartile of data minus 1.5*IQR, where IQR denotes interquartile range, which is the difference between the 3rd and the 1st quartile. Any observation that was greater than the upper boundary or smaller than the lower boundary was considered an outlier. Table 4.1 presents the results of the identification of outliers, which includes the percentage and tail of the outliers for all variables except the dummies.

For winsorisation to mitigate the effect of outliers, the identified outliers are not removed as in the trimming technique but are replaced by the next value counting inwards from the extreme values. In Stata, the *winsor* command is used for this purpose.[2]

*Table 4.1* Identification of outliers for winsorisation

| *Variable* | *Percentage of outliers* | *Tail of outliers* |
|---|---|---|
| Government ownership | 0 | N/A |
| Insider ownership | 6.7 | High only |
| Foreign ownership | 7.1 | High only |
| Agency costs | 3.8 | High only |
| Corporate risk-taking | 1.2 | High only |
| ROA | 4.6 | Two tails |
| Q | 9.8 | Two tails |
| Firm size | 2.5 | Two tails |
| Firm age | 0 | N/A |
| Firm growth | 5.8 | Two tails |
| Financial leverage | 0 | N/A |
| Financial investment | 6.7 | High only |

Notes: Percentages of outliers were calculated as the number of outliers divided by the total number of observations. Tails of outliers were N/A (not applicable) if no outlier was found, 'high only' if there were no outliers below the lower boundary and 'two tails' if some outliers were found greater than the upper boundary and some others smaller than the lower boundary. Other variables that were used to test for robustness also followed the same procedures for detecting outliers, but the results are not included in this table for brevity.

## 4.3 Description of Data

### *4.3.1 Summary Statistics*

Table 4.2 presents the summary statistics of the full dataset (except the dummy variables), which is referred to as the raw data. All variables in the raw data have not been processed with cleansing procedures. As already described, this is a balanced panel dataset that covers 95 listed firms in Vietnam's stock market over the five-year period from 2008 to 2012. Hence, there are in total 475 firm-year observations. All one-year lagged ownership and performance variables contain 380 observations (a loss of 95 observations due to the lag operation).

Next, Table 4.3 shows the summary of statistics of all the main variables, which were winsorised at the percentage and tail identified in the cleansing steps mentioned above to mitigate the influence of outliers. As can be seen from this table, government ownership (GOV) ranges from zero to 75%, with a standard deviation of 22.3% around the mean of 29.18%. The standard deviation and average value of government ownership are the largest in comparison with those of insider ownership and

*Table 4.2* Raw data

| *Variable* | *Observations* | *Mean* | *Standard Deviation* | *Minimum* | *Maximum* |
|---|---|---|---|---|---|
| GOV | 475 | 29.18 | 22.30 | 0 | 75 |
| GOV(−1) | 380 | 29.38 | 22.29 | 0 | 75 |
| INS | 475 | 12.25 | 15.43 | 0.002 | 83.02 |
| INS(−1) | 380 | 12.34 | 15.58 | 0.003 | 83.02 |
| FOR | 475 | 9.37 | 12.13 | 0 | 49 |
| FOR(−1) | 380 | 9.35 | 12.14 | 0 | 49 |
| AC | 475 | 1.26 | 1.16 | 0.02 | 10.55 |
| RT | 475 | 3.00 | 0.87 | 1.18 | 7.48 |
| ROA | 475 | 8.75 | 9.47 | −34.48 | 50.26 |
| ROA(−1) | 380 | 9.31 | 9.25 | −34.48 | 50.26 |
| Q | 475 | 1.06 | 0.49 | 0.06 | 4.26 |
| Q(−1) | 380 | 1.10 | 0.49 | 0.43 | 4.26 |
| LEV | 475 | 49.77 | 22.45 | 3.90 | 92.44 |
| AGE | 475 | 3.41 | 1.92 | 0 | 10 |
| SIZE | 475 | 20.05 | 1.38 | 16.67 | 24.75 |
| GRO | 475 | 20.89 | 58.45 | −86.30 | 725.5 |
| FIN | 475 | 11.84 | 15.25 | 0 | 91.87 |

Notes: This table reports the summary of statistics of the raw data (i.e. the variables before winsorisation). Variables are denoted as follows: GOV is government ownership. GOV(−1) is lagged government ownership. INS is insider ownership. INS(−1) is lagged insider ownership. FOR is foreign ownership. FOR(−1) is lagged foreign ownership. AC is agency costs. RT is corporate risk-taking. ROA is return on assets. ROA(−1) is prior return on assets. Q is Tobin's Q. Q(−1) is prior Tobin's Q. LEV is financial leverage. AGE is firm age. SIZE is firm size. GRO is firm growth. FIN is financial investment.

*Table 4.3* Winsorised data

| *Variable* | *Observations* | *Mean* | *Standard Deviation* | *Minimum* | *Maximum* |
|---|---|---|---|---|---|
| GOV | 475 | 29.18 | 22.30 | 0 | 75 |
| GOV(−1) | 380 | 29.38 | 22.29 | 0 | 75 |
| INS | 475 | 11.37 | 12.78 | 0.002 | 42.70 |
| INS(−1) | 380 | 11.41 | 12.83 | 0.003 | 42.70 |
| FOR | 475 | 8.82 | 10.64 | 0 | 33.74 |
| FOR(−1) | 380 | 8.79 | 10.66 | 0 | 33.74 |
| AC | 475 | 1.17 | 0.79 | 0.02 | 3.21 |
| RT | 475 | 2.99 | 0.84 | 1.18 | 5.41 |
| ROA | 475 | 8.56 | 7.65 | −3.57 | 26.49 |
| ROA(−1) | 380 | 9.09 | 7.44 | −3.57 | 26.49 |
| Q | 475 | 1.00 | 0.26 | 0.68 | 1.54 |
| Q(−1) | 380 | 1.03 | 0.26 | 0.68 | 1.54 |
| LEV | 475 | 49.77 | 22.45 | 3.90 | 92.44 |
| AGE | 475 | 3.41 | 1.92 | 0 | 10 |
| SIZE | 475 | 20.05 | 1.31 | 17.38 | 23.19 |
| GRO | 475 | 15.95 | 29.78 | −30.13 | 78.85 |
| FIN | 475 | 10.86 | 12.30 | 0 | 40.42 |

Notes: This table reports the summary of statistics of the winsorised variables. Variables are denoted as follows: GOV is government ownership. GOV(−1) is lagged government ownership. INS is insider ownership. INS(−1) is lagged insider ownership. FOR is foreign ownership. FOR(−1) is lagged foreign ownership. AC is agency costs. RT is corporate risk-taking. ROA is return on assets. ROA(−1) is prior return on assets. Q is Tobin's Q. Q(−1) is prior Tobin's Q. LEV is financial leverage. AGE is firm age. SIZE is firm size. GRO is firm growth. FIN is financial investment.

foreign ownership. Such high values of government ownership suggest that the distribution of the government variable is quite dispersed and that the government is the major shareholder in many of Vietnam's listed firms.

Similarly, there is a large difference between the minimum and maximum levels of insider ownership (INS) at nearly zero and 42.7%, respectively. The very small proportion of insider ownership at the lower end is applicable to some listed SOEs where some members of the board are nominal government owners. Since only their own shareholdings are calculated as insider ownership, as defined in Section 3.2.1.1, the abovementioned low ratio in these firms is reasonable.

The range of foreign ownership (FOR) is from zero to 33.74%. This is because foreign investors do not own any shares in a number of Vietnam's listed companies, while they are restricted to 49% of common equity in the others. The mean and standard deviation of foreign ownership are the smallest in comparison with the two other types of ownership, which are 8.8% and 10.64%, respectively.

The summary statistics of lagged ownership variables, including GOV (−1), INS(−1) and FOR(−1), are almost similar to the original ones. The only exception is that the number of observations is reduced by 95 due to the lagging process of these variables.

There is a large difference in the extreme values of agency costs (AC), which vary between 0.023 and 3.21. The standard deviation of AC is 0.79, around a mean of 1.17. The values of corporate risk-taking (RT) are also largely dispersed, from 1.18 to 5.41. The mean value and the standard deviation of corporate risk-taking are higher than those of agency costs.

In terms of firm performance variables, the minimum value, maximum value and standard deviation of ROA are –.57%, 26.49% and 7.65%, respectively. The negative value of minimum ROA shows that some listed companies suffered from loss during the period of study. However, ROA is averaged at 8.56%, indicating that most of the listed companies in this sample are profitable. As for Q, the lowest value of Q (0.68) shows that the market value of some firms is smaller than the value of their assets. On average, however, the mean value of Q is about 1 and the standard deviation of Q is 0.26. The statistics for lagged ROA and lagged Q are not much different from those of ROA and Q.

With respect to the control variables, the standard deviation of financial leverage (LEV) is quite high at 22.45%, around a mean of 49.77%; while the extreme points of LEV are 3.90% at the lowest and 92.44 at the highest. In particular, the average value of LEV, nearly half of total assets, reveals that financial leverage is excessively employed by Vietnam's listed firms.

The year of listing or firm age (AGE) ranges between 0 and 10, with a standard deviation of nearly 2 years around a mean of 3.41 years. The lowest, mean and largest observations of firm size (SIZE) are 17.38, 20.05 and 23.19, respectively. There is not much difference in the size of firms, as indicated by the standard deviation of SIZE at 1.38.

In contrast, a quite large standard deviation of 29.78% around a mean of 15.95% is shown for firm growth (GRO), which corresponds to a wide range between the minimum and maximum levels of –30.13 % and –78.85%, respectively. The negative value of GRO reflects the fact, as aforesaid, that some listed companies were making losses during the period of study.

The last control variable, financial investment (FIN), has an average value of 10.86% and a standard deviation of 12.30%. The two extreme values of FIN are zero at the minimum and 40.42% at the maximum, suggesting that not all listed companies engage in portfolio investment.

### *4.3.2 Pairwise Correlations*

The correlation matrix in Table 4.4 shows that almost all the coefficients are small. The exceptions are high-correlation coefficients between the ownership or firm performance variables and their one-year lagged values due to their correlated nature; for example, government ownership and lagged government ownership, ROA and lagged ROA.

*Table 4.4* Pairwise correlation matrix

| | *GOV* | *GOV(–1)* | *INS* | *INS(–1)* | *FOR* | *FOR(–1)* | *AC* | *RT* | *ROA* |
|---|---|---|---|---|---|---|---|---|---|
| GOV | 1 | | | | | | | | |
| GOV(–1) | 0.9792* | 1 | | | | | | | |
| INS | –0.6530* | –0.6568* | 1 | | | | | | |
| INS(–1) | –0.6553* | –0.6581* | 0.8957* | 1 | | | | | |
| FOR | –0.1424* | –0.1051* | 0.0952* | 0.0932* | 1 | | | | |
| FOR(–1) | –0.1568* | –0.1400* | 0.0888* | 0.0940* | 0.8972* | 1 | | | |
| AC | 0.1018* | 0.1151* | –0.0238 | –0.0473 | –0.0391 | –0.0447 | 1 | | |
| RT | –0.0846* | –0.0529 | 0.0062 | 0.0431 | –0.2768* | –0.2459* | 0.0166 | 1 | |
| ROA | 0.1559* | 0.1507* | –0.1374* | –0.1280* | 0.3500* | 0.3243* | 0.0721 | –0.1077* | 1 |
| ROA(–1) | 0.1250* | 0.1296* | –0.1407* | –0.1323* | 0.4280* | 0.3487* | 0.0384 | –0.1375* | 0.7707* |
| Q | 0.0571 | 0.0491 | 0.0005 | 0.0203 | 0.2914* | 0.2703* | –0.0881* | –0.0168 | 0.5857* |
| Q(–1) | 0.0573 | 0.0470 | –0.0080 | 0.0096 | 0.3343* | 0.2760* | –0.1091* | –0.0343 | 0.4787* |
| LEV | –0.0340 | –0.0391 | 0.1004* | 0.1149* | –0.2494* | –0.2517* | 0.0608 | 0.2130* | –0.5867* |
| AGE | 0.0207 | 0.0226 | –0.1146* | –0.1359* | 0.1091* | 0.1377* | –0.0373 | –0.2315* | –0.0249 |
| SIZE | –0.0409 | –0.0507 | 0.1837* | 0.1964* | 0.4538* | 0.4626* | –0.2112* | –0.4296* | –0.0368 |
| GRO | –0.0200 | –0.0289 | 0.0345 | 0.0577 | 0.0204 | 0.00440 | 0.1035* | 0.0515 | 0.1341* |
| FIN | –0.0872* | –0.0872* | 0.0490 | 0.0308 | 0.1293* | 0.1224* | –0.3196* | –0.0795* | 0.2330* |
| | ROA(–1) | Q | Q(–1) | LEV | AGE | SIZE | GRO | FIN | |
| ROA(–1) | 1 | | | | | | | | |
| Q | 0.5177* | 1 | | | | | | | |
| Q(–1) | 0.5756* | 0.6247* | 1 | | | | | | |
| LEV | –0.5336* | –0.1439* | –0.1632* | 1 | | | | | |
| AGE | 0.0372 | –0.2248* | –0.1693* | –0.1004* | 1 | | | | |
| SIZE | 0.0077 | 0.1846* | 0.2057* | 0.1347* | 0.1536* | 1 | | | |
| GRO | 0.0228 | 0.1553* | 0.2028* | 0.1116* | –0.2083* | 0.0987* | 1 | | |
| FIN | 0.2090* | 0.1679* | 0.1707* | –0.3759* | 0.0196 | 0.0939* | –0.0282 | 1 | |

Notes: This table reports the correlation coefficients of all variables except the dummy ones. Variables are denoted as follows. GOV is government ownership. GOV(–1) is lagged government ownership. INS is insider ownership. INS(–1) is lagged insider ownership. FOR is foreign ownership. FOR(–1) is lagged foreign ownership. AC is agency costs. RT is corporate risk-taking. ROA is return on assets. ROA(–1) is prior return on assets. Q is Tobin's Q. Q(–1) is prior Tobin's Q. LEV is financial leverage. AGE is firm age. SIZE is firm size. GRO is firm growth. FIN is financial investment. * denotes $p<0.1$.

The significantly positive coefficient between agency costs and government ownership suggests that higher lagged government ownership may be associated with higher asset efficiency or lower agency costs. In contrast, the correlations between agency costs and lagged insider ownership, and between agency costs and lagged foreign ownership are not significant.

The correlation between corporate risk-taking and lagged foreign ownership is significantly negative, indicating that foreign investors may be risk-averse shareholders in Vietnamese listed firms. Meanwhile, the coefficients for corporate risk-taking lagged government ownership and corporate risk-taking lagged insider ownership correlation are not significant.

All three forms of ownership are reported to have significant correlations with ROA, where lagged government ownership and lagged foreign ownership are positively correlated with ROA, and lagged insider ownership is negatively correlated with ROA.

The sign of the correlation coefficient between agency costs on ROA is positive but not significant at the 10% level. On the other hand, the sign of the coefficient between agency costs and Q is significantly negative. This suggests that higher levels of the asset utilisation ratio may not be associated with higher firm performance. Corporate risk-taking is significantly negatively correlated with both measures of firm performance, but only the correlation with ROA is significant.

As an important control variable, Table 4.3 shows that financial leverage is not significantly correlated with government ownership, but financial leverage is positively (negatively) correlated with higher insider ownership (and foreign ownership). However, the magnitude of such correlations is not great. Financial leverage is significantly positively correlated with corporate risk-taking, and it is significantly negatively correlated with both measures of firm performance.

## 4.4 Estimation Methods

This section justifies the choice of estimation methods and regression techniques, including explanations of how they are applied to address the two empirical models developed in Chapter 3. Accordingly, causal-steps regressions with the generalised method of moments and the fixed-effects regression with Driscoll-Kraay standard errors are used for the recursive model, which depicts the direction of effects from past ownership structure to current firm performance. The product-of-coefficients approach is used to estimate for the recursive model, with endogenous mediating variables and the non-recursive model with the feedback effects from past firm performance to the current ownership structure.

### 4.4.1 Causal-Steps Approach

As already mentioned in Section 1.4, the causal-steps approach of Baron and Kenny (1986) is applied to the recursive model to find answers to research questions 1 and 2. Under this approach, each path, and hence each equation, in this model is tested separately (step by step).[3] This is possible because Equations 3.10 and 3.11 (agency costs and corporate risk-taking) are independent of Equations 3.9 and 3.12 (firm performance). The disturbances of the agency costs and corporate risk-taking equations are not allowed to co-vary under this approach. According to Preacher and Hayes (2008) and MacKinnon (2012), the causal-steps approach can be used in a multiple-mediator context, and the main concern under such an approach is the significance of the paths defining the specific indirect effects. As summarised by Preacher and Hayes (2008) and MacKinnon (2012), the causal-steps approach can be applied to the recursive model to confirm the mediating effects if the following conditions are met:

1 The relationship between the predictor variables (here ownership structure) and the outcome variables (here firm performance) is significant (Equation 3.9).
2 The relationship between the predictor variables (here ownership structure) and the mediating variables (here agency costs and corporate risk-taking) is significant (Equations 3.10 and 3.11).
3 The effect of the mediating variables (here agency costs and corporate risk-taking) on the outcome variables (here firm performance) while controlling for the predictor variables (here ownership structure) is significant (Equation 3.12).
4 The effect of the predictor variables (here ownership structure) on the outcome variable (here firm performance) decreases substantially when both predictor variables and mediating variables are simultaneously regressed.

Following the above conditions, each equation in the recursive model is regressed individually, starting from Equation 3.9. Hence there are in total four steps of regression. Under the fourth condition, a *partial* mediating effect is established if the effect of the predictor variables is low but still significant, and there is a *full* mediating effect when this effect is no longer significant.

#### 4.4.1.1 Generalised Method of Moments (GMM) Estimation for Dynamic Panel Data

It is common knowledge in econometrics that the GMM method can be applied to estimate a dynamic panel data model which is characterised by the presence of a lagged dependent variable among the explanatory variables together with an unobserved effect (Wooldridge, 2001). According to Baltagi (2011), the specification of a dynamic panel model is as follows:

$$y_{it} = \delta y_{i,t-1} + x'_{it}\beta + \mu_i + \nu_{it} \tag{4.1}$$

Where *i* and *t* denote cross-sections and t denotes time periods, with $i = 1, 2, \ldots, N$ and $t = 1, 2, \ldots, T$. $y_{it}$ is the *it*-th observation on the dependent variable. $x'_{it}$ is the *it*-th observation on the *K* explanatory variables. $\delta$ is scalar. $\beta$ is $K \times 1$. $\mu_i$ and $\nu_{it}$ are two components of the error term, where $\mu_i$'s are the cross-section-specific components (time-invariant heterogeneity) and $\nu_{it}$ are the remainder effects (random disturbances).

In this model, $y_{i,t-1}$ is also a function of $\mu_i$ because $y_{it}$ is a function of $\mu_i$. Hence, $y_{i,t-1}$ is correlated with the error term and so the endogeneity problem is present in this model. In this case, the ordinary least squares (OLS) estimation is biased and inconsistent even if the $\nu_{it}$ values are not serially correlated.

Alternatively, as summarised in Hu and Izumida (2008) and Tan (2009), the dynamic GMM panel specifications developed by Arellano and Bond (1991) can overcome the problems of the dynamic effects and endogeneity in the explanatory variables by employing a valid set of internal instruments, hence producing unbiased and consistent estimates.

Specifically, the idea behind dynamic GMM estimation is to use the first-differenced form of Equation 4.1 to remove unobserved heterogeneity, and then use instruments to deal with the other sources of endogeneity. There are two types of GMM estimators for dynamic panel data, namely, difference GMM and system GMM. While the former uses the first-differenced equation, the latter employs both the first-differenced and level equation (e.g. Equation 4.1). In the difference GMM estimator, the instruments include suitable lagged levels of the endogenous variables and any other variables that may be specified. In the latter estimator, the instruments include both lagged levels and lagged differences of the variables (Baum, 2006).[4]

In this book, both Equations 3.9 and 3.12 have a lagged dependent variable (past firm performance) employed as the explanatory variable. As mentioned earlier, unobserved firm fixed effects are possible in these equations because firms are not homogenous. In addition, endogeneity exists in these equations since past firm performance is correlated with the error terms of current firm performance. Therefore, the dynamic GMM method is employed to estimate Equations 3.9 and 3.12 to obtain unbiased and consistent results. In selecting an appropriate dynamic GMM technique (difference GMM or system GMM, a one-step or two-step procedure), this book employs a two-step dynamic system GMM estimator to address Equations 3.9 and 3.12. The two-step procedure is considered more efficient than the one-step procedure (Roodman, 2009)[5]. Additionally, system GMM regressors are more efficient than difference GMM regressors because of the increased number of instruments as a result of the addition of the level equation.

#### 4.4.1.2 *Fixed-Effects (FE) Regression with Driscoll-Kraay Standard Errors*

The fixed-effects method is commonly used in corporate governance literature (Brown et al., 2011). As presented in Baltagi (2011), a fixed-effects model can take the following form:

$$y_{it} = \alpha + X'_{it}\beta + \sum_{i=1}^{N} \mu_i D_i + v_{it} \tag{4.2}$$

Where $i$ and $t$ denote cross-sections and t denotes time periods, with $i = 1, 2, \ldots, N$ and $t = 1, 2, \ldots, T$. $y_{it}$ is the *it*-th observation on the dependent variable. $X'_{it}$ is the *it*-th observation on the $K$ explanatory variables. α is scalar. $\beta$ is $K \times 1$. $\mu_i$ and $v_{it}$ are two components of the error term, where $\mu_i$ is the cross-section-specific component (time-invariant heterogeneity). $D_i$ is a dummy variable for the i-*th* individual (e.g. household or firm). $\sum_{i=1}^{N}\mu_i D_i$ is considered a fixed parameter. $v_{it}$ are the remainder effects (random disturbances). $\sum_{i=1}^{N}\mu_i D_i$ and $v_{it}$ are the two components of the error term.

The time-invariant component in the fixed-effects model captures the unobserved heterogeneity of firms and allows a limited form of endogeneity since it is correlated with the explanatory variables (Cameron and Trivedi, 2010). Hence, the advantage of the fixed-effects method is that it accounts for the endogeneity caused by unobserved heterogeneity across firms and over time, capturing all time-invariant variables which affect firm performance.

The fixed-effects estimation is performed by first removing the panel-level averages from each side of Equation 4.2. The purpose is to remove the fixed effects from the model. To illustrate, assuming that Equation 4.2 has only one independent variable, then this model becomes:

$$y_{it} = \alpha + \beta x_{it} + \mu_i + v_{it} \tag{4.3}$$

Removing the panel-level averages from each side of Equation 4.3 means that:

$$y_{it} - \bar{y}_i = \beta(x_{it} - \bar{x}_i) + (v_{it} - \bar{v}_i) \tag{4.4}$$

Where $\bar{y}_i$, $\bar{x}_i$, $\bar{v}_i$ are the average values over time of the dependent variables, independent variable and disturbance term, respectively and $\bar{y}_i = \alpha + \beta\bar{x}_i + \mu_i + \bar{v}_i$

Equation 4.4 implies that

$$\tilde{y}_{it} = \beta\tilde{x}_{it} + \tilde{v}_{it} \tag{4.5}$$

Where $\tilde{y}_{it}$ is defined as $(y_{it} - \bar{y}_i)$ while $\tilde{x}_{it}$ and $\tilde{v}_{it}$ are defined as $(x_{it} - \bar{x}_i)$ and $(v_{it} - \bar{v}_i)$, respectively.

The fixed-effects estimation now requires running an ordinary least squares estimation (OLS) on Equation 4.5. OLS regression on the within-transformed data will produce consistent coefficient estimates (Baum, 2006).

This book also adopts fixed-effects estimation for Equations 3.10 and 3.11, under the assumption that firms are heterogeneous due to the unobserved effect across firms, which is constant over time. Diagnostic tests are also performed to determine whether fixed-effects estimation is appropriate.

In addition to the unobserved firm fixed effect, the unobserved time effect (cross-sectional dependence) is another common form of dependence found in finance applications. While the former refers to the residuals of a given firm correlated across years for a given firm, the latter is for the residuals of a given year correlated across different firms (Petersen, 2009). If such two types of dependence are present, several approaches such as the White/Huber, Rogers or Newey-West estimators are not suitable for obtaining the standard errors, which are robust in relation to such violations of regression assumption, because they do not account for the cross-sectional dependence dimension (Hoechle, 2007).

Since this book uses panel data, it is highly likely that the two dimensions of dependence mentioned above are present in Equations 3.10 and 3.11. Diagnostic tests for cross-sectional dependence are conducted (details reported in Section 5.1).

If both the firm effect and the time effect exist in the dataset, several estimation methods can be applied. First, the feasible generalised least squares estimation (FGLS) for panel data is an option. However, this method tends to produce optimistic standard errors. Additionally, the time dimension $T$ is required to be larger than the cross-sectional dimension $N$ to make this method feasible (Hoechle, 2007). This is not the case for the dataset of this research. Second, a more possible option for Equations 3.10 and 3.11 is the Prais-Winsten regression with panel corrected standard errors (PCSE). The standard errors produced by the PCSE method are also more reliable than those produced by the FGLS method (Beck and Katz, 2006). However, since the PCSE estimators are based on a large-T asymptotic assumption, this method may not be an appropriate method because the time dimension in the dataset of this book is short ($t = 5$).

Consequently, fixed-effects regression with Driscoll-Kraay standard errors has been selected in case both firm and time fixed effects are present.[6] According to Hoechle (2007), the estimates obtained from this method are known to be efficient and robust to heteroscedasticity, cross-sectional dependence and autocorrelation up to some lags. Generally, fixed-effects regression with Driscoll-Kraay standard errors is also performed through the two steps as described earlier (i.e. within-transformation to remove fixed effects and then OLS regression). However, 'Driscoll-Kraay standard errors for the coefficient estimates are obtained as the square roots of the diagonal elements of the asymptotic covariance matrix' (Hoechle, 2007). Also relying on a large-T asymptotic assumption, these standard errors are obtained independently of the cross-sectional dimension *N* and thus, this approach overcomes the abovementioned drawbacks of the FGLS and PCSE approaches.

### 4.4.2 Product-of-Coefficients Approach

The product-of-coefficient approach is used to find the answers to research questions 3 and 4 in this book. This approach is also termed the Sobel test (Sobel, 1982, 1986), which focuses on the product of two individual paths defining specific indirect effects (Preacher and Hayes, 2008). This is in sharp contrast with the causal-steps approach of Baron and Kenny (1986), which focuses on testing individual paths in a mediation model.

The advantage of the product-of-coefficient approach is that the disturbances of the endogenous variables can be imposed to be correlated. This is because all hypothesised paths in the mediation model can be estimated simultaneously rather than separately. Therefore, this approach is used to address research questions 3 and 4 in this book, as already noted. To this end, two estimation methods are applied collectively: (1) full-information maximum likelihood estimation; and (2) the Sobel test. While the former method is employed to obtain the coefficients on all paths of the model, the latter method utilises all such coefficients to decompose the effects of ownership structure on firm performance into different types of effects (direct effect, indirect effect and total effect). Further justifications for the use of the two methods are presented in the following parts of this section.

#### 4.4.2.1 Full-Information Maximum Likelihood (ML) Estimation

As already mentioned in Section 1.4, ML estimation is employed for the non-recursive model to find answers to research questions 3 and 4. It is also used for the recursive model in aiming at Research question 2. The answers to research questions 2 and 3 can be obtained directly from the results of ML estimation. However, the answers to Research question 4 rely on the results of the Sobel test, which is conducted after ML estimation is finalised.

The basic objective of ML estimation is to choose the values of $\mu$ (mean) and $\sigma^2$ (standard deviation) of a random sample such that the probability of obtaining this sample is maximised (Baltagi, 2011). According to the author, the marginal probability density function for a random sample of $n$ observations of $X$ variable, assuming X is normally distributed $X_i \sim N(\mu, \sigma^2)$, is as follows:

$$f_i(X_i; \mu, \sigma^2) = \left(\frac{1}{\sigma\sqrt{2\pi}}\right)\exp\left\{-\frac{(X_i-\mu)^2}{2\sigma^2}\right\} \quad -\infty < X_i < +\infty \qquad (4.6)$$

Given that $X_1,\ldots, X_n$ are independent and identically distributed, the joint probability density function is the product of the marginal probability density functions, which is expressed as follows:

$$f(X_1,\ldots,X_n; \mu, \sigma^2) = \prod_{i=1}^{n} f_i(X_i; \mu, \sigma^2) = \left(\frac{1}{2\pi\sigma^2}\right)^{n/2} \exp\left\{-\frac{(X_i-\mu)^2}{2\sigma^2}\right\} \qquad (4.7)$$

This joint probability density function is treated as the likelihood function $L(\mu, \sigma^2)$. Thus, ML estimation seeks to maximise $L(\mu, \sigma^2)$ with respect to $\mu$ and $\sigma^2$.

ML estimation is applicable to a large variety of regression models. It can be employed to estimate a fixed-effect model such as Equation 4.2 described in Section 4.4.1.2. In addition, according to Mátyás and Sevestre (2008), the ML method is an alternative to GMM estimation for dynamic equations in short panels (such as Equation 4.1 represented in Section 4.4.1.1), but this requires the assumption that both the individual effect and idiosyncratic errors are normally distributed. When the assumption of independent and homoscedastic errors is no longer valid and the variance–covariance structure of the residuals is used instead, ML estimation still helps in obtaining unbiased and efficient estimates. While other techniques can also produce unbiased estimates, they are not the best linear unbiased estimators (Mátyás and Sevestre, 2008).

The ML estimation in this book is performed by Stata's *cmp* command (Roodman, 2011). This is a new technique in Stata that can be applied to mediation models using panel data[7] as well as to various other models. According to the author, *cmp* can be used to fit models that were previously much harder to estimate and it is appropriate for both types of maximum likelihood estimations: (1) full-information maximum likelihood estimation, where all estimated parameters are structural; and (2) limited-information maximum likelihood estimation, where only the final stages' parameters are structural. Similar to the *sem* command, the *cmp* command helps the clustering of panel or time variables, which is necessary when the normal assumption of error terms is not met. Additionally, the *cmp* command permits the simultaneous estimation of all equations in a system and particularly the correlation of cross-equation disturbances. This is necessary because the error terms of potentially endogenous regressors are recommended to be correlated in mediation models (Antonakis et al., 2010).

In this regard, as firm fixed effects and cross-sectional dependence (time effects) are possible in the panel data context, an important task in using ML regression is to control for such problems. In general, a common approach in empirical finance research is to use dummy variables for one dimension and then estimate standard errors clustered on the other dimension; for example, including time dummies to absorb time effects and then clustering standard errors by firm (Petersen, 2009). Alternatively, we can add full sets of individual dummies and full sets of time dummies (Mátyás and Sevestre, 2008). According to Petersen (2009), if the time effect is not fixed, the cross-sectional dependence is not removed completely by time dummies and so the firm clustering can produce biased standard errors. A solution for this is to cluster on both time and firm dimensions (two-way clustering).

In this book, it is assumed that the time effect is not constant across years. There were different shocks in macroeconomic policy and stock market regulations during the period of study from 2008 to 2012. For example, in 2009, the Vietnamese Government implemented an expansionary monetary policy characterised by a decrease in benchmark interest rates and adoption of an economic stimulus package. In 2010, however, the monetary policy entered a tightening phase with a significant increase in interest rates. The amendment of the Securities Law was also adopted in the same year. In 2012, the government enacted a regulation that government capital invested by SOEs in non-core business areas should be withdrawn.

Thus, year clustering is used together with firm dummies to control for varied time effects and unobserved firm fixed effects in ML estimation. Since all equations in both recursive and non-recursive models are structural (i.e. without equations of reduced form), the ML method using *cmp* is full-information maximum likelihood estimation.

In practice, a limited-information maximum likelihood method such as two-stage least squares (2SLS) estimation can also be used to estimate a system of equations. 2SLS estimation can serve as a solution to control for both the unobserved heterogeneity and simultaneous causality of the corporate governance variables (Mcknight and Weir, 2009, Brown et al., 2011). However, the 2SLS method relies on the use of internal instruments that are generated within the system of simultaneous equations. Thus the validity of these instruments is a matter of concern. As pointed out by Baltagi (2011), in instrument variable estimation such as 2SLS, different choices of instrument variables may yield different estimates in finite samples.

Practically, when the 2SLS method is performed on an equation-by-equation basis, that is, equations are estimated separately (such as by *xtivreg2* or *ivreg2* command in Stata), it does not account for the cross-equation correlation of disturbances. Another option is the *reg3* command in Stata, which can be used to estimate the entire system under the 2SLS method, that is, all equations are estimated simultaneously. System estimators account for the variance–covariance matrix of the disturbances of the whole system (Baltagi, 2011). However, a problem with this command is that it appears not to be suitable for panel data with dynamic equations, that is, when there are dynamic equations such as Equations 3.15 and 3.16. Therefore, the ML method using Stata's *cmp* command is selected to estimate for the non-recursive model in this book due to its advantages over the 2SLS method, as discussed above.

#### *4.4.2.2 The Sobel Test*

As already mentioned, the calculation of the direct effects, indirect effects and total effects using the Sobel test (Sobel, 1982, 1986) can be done after the ML estimation under the product-of-coefficient approach in order to provide the answers to Research question 4 of this book. Importantly, this test can calculate the standard errors of the above effects and hence the significance levels of these effects.

The Sobel test is based on the multivariate delta method (Preacher and Hayes, 2008, MacKinnon, 2012). It is primarily used for testing the specific indirect effects by multiplying the coefficients on the paths defining the indirect effects in order to derive the magnitudes and the standard errors of these specific indirect effects. To illustrate, assume that the Sobel test (Sobel, 1982, 1986) is applied to a single-mediator mediation model. The Sobel test calculates the indirect effect (or mediated effect) of predictor variable X on outcome variable Y via mediating variable M by multiplying $\hat{a}$ and $\hat{b}$, where $\hat{a}$ is the estimated coefficient for the path from X to M and $\hat{b}$ is the estimated coefficient for the path from M to Y. Next, as summarised in Li (2011), the standard errors of this indirect effect can be estimated in the Sobel test by using the following formula:

$$s_{\hat{a}\hat{b}} = \sqrt{s_{\hat{a}}^2\hat{b}^2 + s_{\hat{b}}^2\hat{a}^2} \tag{4.8}$$

Where $s_{\hat{a}}^2$ is the variance of $\hat{a}$ coefficient and $s_{\hat{b}}^2$ is the variance of $\hat{b}$ coefficient.

It is also suggested in the literature that the Sobel test is not limited to testing specific indirect effects only, but can be applied to testing the other types of effects, such as the total indirect effect, which is the sum of the specific indirect effects (Preacher and Hayes, 2008). In this book, the Sobel test is used to decompose the effect of ownership structure on firm performance, consisting of the direct effect of ownership structure, the specific indirect effect via agency costs, the specific indirect effect via risk-taking, and the total effect of ownership structure on firm performance. These estimates are obtained by using the *nlcom* command in Stata.

## 4.5 Summary and Conclusions

This chapter has discussed all relevant aspects of the data used in this book, including the advantages of using panel data, data sources, data cleansing procedures and a description of the data sample. Another focus of this chapter has been to justify how each model is estimated. Accordingly, the main estimation method for the recursive model is causal-steps regression, where each equation is estimated separately using either Generalised Method of Moments or Fixed-Effects estimation. The non-recursive model is estimated simultaneously using Maximum Likelihood estimation techniques, where the cross-equation correlation of disturbances is allowed. It is worth noting that the system estimation for the non-recursive model is comprehensive, because all hypothesised paths are assessed in a single estimation.

## Notes

1 www.hsx.vn; www.hnx.vn
2 For example, the following syntax was used to winsorise insider ownership: *winsor ins, gen(Nins) p(0.067) highonly.*
3 The term 'causal' in 'causal-steps approach' does not necessarily indicate a causal relationship among the variables in a mediation model. As stated in MacKinnon (2012), 'true causal relations cannot be known exactly' and 'the only true way to identify causality is with randomized experiments because only with this design is it possible to rule out alternative explanations of results'.
4 The results of GMM estimation reported in Sections 5.2.1 and 5.2.4 are examples of the instruments for the first-differenced equation and level equation in the system GMM estimator.
5 *xtabond2* command in Stata.
6 *xtscc* command in Stata.
7 In Stata, *sem* and *sureg* commands can also be used to estimate mediation models (Acock, 2013).

## References

Acock, A. C. 2013. *Discovering structural equation modeling using stata*, College Station, Texas: Stata Press.

Antonakis, J., Bendahan, S., Jacquart, P. & Lalive, R. 2010. On making causal claims: A review and recommendations. *The Leadership Quarterly*, 21, 1086–1120.

Arellano, M. & Bond, S. 1991. Some tests of specification for panel data: Monte Carlo evidence and an application to employment equations. *The Review of Economic Studies*, 58, 277–297.

Asteriou, D. & Hall, S. G. 2011. *Applied econometrics*, Basingstoke [England], New York: Palgrave Macmillan.

Baltagi, B. H. 2011. *Econometrics*, Berlin, Heidelberg, New York: Springer.

Baron, R. M. & Kenny, D. A. 1986. The moderator-mediator variable distinction in social psychological research: Conceptual, strategic, and statistical considerations. *Journal of Personality and Social Psychology*, 51, 1173–1182.

Baum, C. F. 2006. *An introduction to modern econometrics using Stata*, College Station, Tex.: Stata Press.

Beck, N. & Katz, J. N. 2006. What to do (and not to do) with time-series cross-section data. *American Political Science Review*, 100, 676–677.

Brown, P., Beekes, W. & Verhoeven, P. 2011. Corporate governance, accounting and finance: A review. *Accounting and Finance*, 51, 96–172.

Cameron, A. C. & Trivedi, P. K. 2010. *Microeconometrics using Stata*, College Station, Tex.: Stata Press.

Coles, J. L., Lemmon, M. L. & Felix Meschke, J. 2012. Structural models and endogeneity in corporate finance: The link between managerial ownership and corporate performance. *Journal of Financial Economics*, 103, 149–168.

Hampel, F. R. 1986. *Robust statistics the approach based on influence functions*, New York: Wiley.

Hoechle, D. 2007. Robust standard errors for panel regressions with cross-sectional dependence. *Stata Journal*, 7, 281–312.

Hu, Y. & Izumida, S. 2008. Ownership concentration and corporate performance: A causal analysis with Japanese panel data. *Corporate Governance: An International Review*, 16, 342–358.

Kennedy, D., Lakonishok, J. & Shaw, W. H. 1992. Accommodating outliers and nonlinearity in decision models. *Journal of Accounting, Auditing & Finance*, 7, 161–190.

Leone, A. J., Minutti-Meza, M. & Wasley, C. E. 2014. Influential observations and inference in accounting research. *SSRN Working Paper*. Available at: http://ssrn.com/abstract=2407967.

Li, S. D. 2011. Testing mediation using multiple regression and structural equation modeling analyses in secondary data. *Evaluation Review*, 35, 240–268.

MacKinnon, D. 2012. *Introduction to statistical mediation analysis*, Hoboken: Taylor and Francis.

Mátyás, L. & Sevestre, P. 2008. *The econometrics of panel data. Fundamentals and recent developments in theory and practice*, New York: Springer.

Mcknight, P. J. & Weir, C. 2009. Agency costs, corporate governance mechanisms and ownership structure in large UK publicly quoted companies: A panel data analysis. *Quarterly Review of Economics and Finance*, 49, 139–158.

Petersen, M. A. 2009. Estimating standard errors in finance panel data sets: Comparing approaches. *Review of Financial Studies*, 22, 435–480.

Preacher, K. J. & Hayes, A. F. 2008. Asymptotic and resampling strategies for assessing and comparing indirect effects in multiple mediator models. *Behavior Research Methods*, 40, 879–891.

Roodman, D. 2009. How to do xtabond2: An introduction to difference and system GMM in Stata. *Stata Journal*, 9, 86–136.

Roodman, D. 2011. Fitting fully observed recursive mixed-process models with cmp. *Stata Journal*, 11, 159–206.

Selig, J. P. & Preacher, K. J. 2009. Mediation models for longitudinal data in developmental research. *Research In Human Development*, 6, 144–164.

Sobel, M. E. 1982. Asymptotic confidence intervals for indirect effects in structural equation models. *Sociological Methodology*. Washington DC: American Sociology Association, Jossey-Bass Publishers.

Sobel, M. E. 1986. Some new results on indirect effects and their standard errors in covariance structure models. *Sociological Methodology*, 159–186.

Tan, D. T. 2009. *Corporate governance and firm outcomes: causation or spurious correlations?* PhD, Universtity of New South Wales.

Wintoki, M. B., Linck, J. S. & Netter, J. M. 2012. Endogeneity and the dynamics of internal corporate governance. *Journal of Financial Economics*, 105, 581–606.

Wooldridge, J. M. 2001. Applications of generalised method of moments estimation. *Journal of Economic Perspectives*, 15, 87–100.

# 5 The Recursive Model and the Non-Recursive Model

## Empirical Estimations and Analysis

### 5.1 Results for Recursive Model

This section presents the empirical results for the recursive model, consisting of Equations 3.9–3.12. Each of these equations is regressed individually under the causal-steps approach. Hence, there are four groups of results for four estimated paths. The results of additional tests for robustness are included in the final part of this section.

#### *5.1.1 Total Effect of Ownership Structure on Firm Performance*

As mentioned in Section 4.4.1, the first regression of the causal-steps approach for the recursive model in this study is to estimate the total effects of ownership structure on firm performance in Equation 3.9:

$$FP_{it} = \alpha_1 + \beta_{11}GOV(-1)_{it} + \beta_{12}INS(-1)_{it} + \beta_{13}FOR(-1)_{it} + \beta_{14}LEV_{it} + \beta_{15}SIZE_{it} + \beta_{16}BIG4_{it} + \beta_{17}FP(-1)_{it} + \varepsilon_{1it} \quad (3.9)$$

Where *i* and *t* subscripts stand for firm and year, and FP is firm performance, consisting of ROA or Q. GOV(–1), INS(–1), and FOR(–1) denote lagged government ownership, lagged insider ownership and lagged foreign ownership, respectively. The control variables consist of LEV for financial leverage, SIZE for firm size, BIG4, a dummy variable, for Big-4 audit company and FP(–1) for prior firm performance. $\varepsilon_{1it}$ is the error term containing random disturbance and unobserved heterogeneity.

##### *5.1.1.1 Treatment of Variables in GMM Estimation*

Since GMM estimation is applied to this equation as mentioned earlier, a primary task is to classify the endogenous, predetermined and exogenous variables. All explanatory variables of interest, consisting of lagged government ownership, lagged insider ownership and lagged foreign

DOI: 10.4324/9781003255741-5

ownership, are treated as endogenous. The Durbin–Wu–Hausman test of endogeneity of these variables confirms this treatment, but this result is not consistent when excluded instruments are replaced. Following Hassan et al. (2018) and Mcknight and Weir (2009), only the variables of interest (i.e. the ownership variables) are treated as endogenous, assuming that they are correlated with the unobserved fixed effects of the firm.

Among the control variables, it is plausible to argue that financial leverage, firm size and lagged firm performance are not strictly exogenous, since they can be affected by prior shocks or changes in firm-specific characteristics. For instance, firm performance is potentially predetermined because the firm value has persistence (Hu and Izumida, 2008). Hence, financial leverage, firm size and lagged firm performance are treated as predetermined variables in the dynamic GMM regression of Equation 3.9.

According to Roodman (2009), one assumption for the use of system GMM regression is that there is no correlation across individuals (firms) in the idiosyncratic disturbances, and the inclusion of time dummies can make this assumption more likely to hold. Therefore, year dummy variables are added to Equation 3.9 to control for the common effects of the same year, such as changes in policy or macroeconomic situations. In addition, industry dummies are added to account for the industry fixed effects. As dummy variables, the Big-4 audit, time dummies and industries dummies are treated as exogenous in Equation 3.9.

#### *5.1.1.2 Empirical Results*

The GMM regression of Equation 3.9 for the determinants of accounting firm performance (ROA) and market firm performance (Q) are presented in Table 5.1. When ROA is employed as the dependent variable, in the transformed equation, the lags 2 of the endogenous variables and lags 1 of the predetermined variables are used as the instruments. In the level equation, the first lags of the differenced endogenous variables and the contemporaneous differenced predetermined variables are used as the instruments.

When Q is the dependent variable, in the transformed equation, the lags 1 to lags 2 of the endogenous variables and the contemporaneous lags to lags 1 of the predetermined variables are used as the instruments. In the level equation, the lags 2 of the differenced endogenous variables and the first lags of the differenced predetermined variables are used as the instruments.

In the regression with ROA, the total effects of both lagged government ownership and lagged insider ownership on current ROA are found to be significantly positive at the 5% level. These are the expected results. However, the coefficient on lagged foreign ownership is also positive and significant at the 10% level, which does not meet the expectation of a negative sign for foreign ownership as argued in Section 3.2.2.

*Table 5.1* Total effects of ownership structure on firm performance

| *Dependent variable*<br>*Equation* | *ROA*<br>*(3.9)* | *Q*<br>*(3.9)* |
|---|---|---|
| GOV(–1) | 0.150 | 0.001 |
| | (0.060)** | (0.002) |
| INS(–1) | 0.333 | 0.008 |
| | (0.156)** | (0.004)* |
| FOR(–1) | 0.197 | 0.003 |
| | (0.115)* | (0.003) |
| LEV | –0.242 | 0.002 |
| | (0.074)*** | (0.001)** |
| SIZE | 2.498 | 0.007 |
| | (1.748) | (0.037) |
| BIG4 | –4.770 | –0.001 |
| | (2.509)* | (0.068) |
| ROA(–1) | 0.340 | |
| | (0.129)*** | |
| Q(–1) | | 0.509 |
| | | (0.110)*** |
| _cons | –13.563 | 0.681 |
| | (40.339) | (1.174) |
| Observations | 380 | 380 |
| Number of instruments | 50 | 50 |
| Number of groups | 95 | 95 |
| AR(1) | –2.05 | –3.59 |
| [P-value] | (0.040) | (0.000) |
| AR(2) | –1.69 | 0.03 |
| [P-value] | (0.091) | (0.977) |
| Hansen test | 30.83 | 28.21 |
| [P-value] | (0.235) | (0.348) |
| Difference-in-Hansen test | 26.75 | 16.08 |
| [P-value] | (0.062) | (0.518) |
| F–statistics | 3.01 | 24.27 |
| [P-value] | (0.000) | (0.000) |
| Time effects | Included | Included |
| Industry effects | Included | Included |

Notes: This table reports the results of dynamic system GMM regression of both measures of firm performance in Equation 3.9. It examines how firm performance is affected by ownership structure and other control variables. Variables are denoted as follows. ROA is return on assets. Q is Tobin's Q. GOV(–1) is lagged government ownership. INS(–1) is lagged insider ownership. FOR(–1) is lagged foreign ownership. LEV is financial leverage. SIZE is firm size. BIG4 is Big-4 audit company. ROA(–1) is prior return on assets. Q(–1) is prior Tobin's Q. Endogenous variables are GOV(–1), INS(–1) and FOR(–1). Predetermined variables are LEV, SIZE, ROA(–1) and Q(–1). Exogenous variables are BIG4, time dummies and industry dummies. The parameters are estimated using two-step procedures for dynamic system GMM. Robust standard errors using the Windmeijer correction for small samples are given in parentheses under the coefficients. Estimates of year and industry dummies are excluded from the table for brevity. The individual coefficient is statistically significant at the *10%, **5% or ***1% significance levels.

Among the control variables of ROA, as expected, higher financial leverage is significantly associated with ROA at the 1% level. Firm size does not have any influence on ROA in this equation, as expected. Firms audited by Big-4 audit affiliates have lower ROA levels than the other firms. Lastly, the effect of lagged ROA on current ROA is positive and significant at the 1% level.

In Q regression, it is found that lagged insider ownership has a significantly positive total effect on current Q at the 10% level. The coefficient on financial leverage is positive and significant at the 5% level. Lagged Q has a significantly positive effect on current Q at the 1% level. The effects of all other variables on Q are weak and insignificant.

Therefore, it is estimated that all three forms of ownership employed in this study have significant total effects on ROA, while only lagged insider ownership has a significant total effect on Q. Referring to the list of four conditions of mediation described in Section 4.4.1, the *first condition* for the mediating effect of agency costs and corporate risk-taking is met for lagged government ownership, lagged insider ownership and lagged foreign ownership in relationship with ROA, and for lagged insider ownership in relationship with Q.

### *5.1.2 Direct Effect of Ownership Structure on Agency Costs*

The second step for testing mediation effects in the recursive model is to regress agency costs on ownership structure and other controlling variables, to investigate whether the direct effects of ownership structure on agency costs are significant. Equation 3.10 is employed for this purpose:

$$AC_{it} = \alpha_2 + \beta_{21}GOV(-1)_{it} + \beta_{22}INS(-1)_{it} + \beta_{23}FOR(-1)_{it} + \beta_{24}LEV_{it} + \beta_{25}SIZE_{it} + \beta_{26}AGE_{it} + \varepsilon_{2it} \tag{3.10}$$

Where *i* and *t* subscripts stand for firm and year and AC denotes agency costs. GOV(–1), INS(–1) and FOR(–1) denote lagged government ownership, lagged insider ownership and lagged foreign ownership, respectively. The control variables consist of LEV for financial leverage, SIZE for firm size and AGE for firm age. $\varepsilon_{2it}$ is the error term containing random disturbance and unobserved heterogeneity.

#### *5.1.2.1 Diagnostic Tests*

Relevant diagnostic tests for panel data are performed for Equation 3.10. The first is the multicollinearity test. The result shows that the problem of collinearity among the explanatory variables in this equation is not present since all the variance inflation factors (VIF) are less than 10 and the mean VIF value is 5.47.

Equation 3.10 is then tested for firm fixed effect. The result of the F-test rejects the null hypothesis that there is a common intercept for all firms, meaning that there is an unobserved firm fixed effect ($F = 43.21$, $p < 0.01$). The Hausman test also indicates that a fixed-effects model is appropriate (chi-square statistic=17.96, $p<0.01$). The Wooldridge test for serial correlation indicates that the first-order autocorrelation is present in this equation, since the null hypothesis is rejected ($F = 30.545$, $p < 0.01$).

Since Equation 3.10 is involved with fixed effects, the result of Pesaran's test of the cross-sectional dependence problem in fixed-effects model is conducted. This test is suitable for large-N and small-T data samples (De Hoyos and Sarafidis, 2006). The test result indicates that the cross-sectional dependence problem is present in Equation 3.10. The average absolute value of correlation among the residuals is quite high at 0.57, corresponding to a strong rejection of the null hypothesis of no cross-sectional dependence. This result is confirmed by Frees's test.

The modified Wald test for groupwise heteroscedasticity in fixed-effect regression models rejects the null hypothesis of no heteroscedasticity. In addition, the likelihood-ratio test for panel data shows that the heteroscedasticity problem is present (the LR chi-square value is 482.99, $p < 0.01$).

To sum up, the following problems are detected for the error terms of Equation 3.10: the unobserved firm fixed effect; heteroscedasticity; first-order autocorrelation; and cross-sectional dependence. As discussed in Section 4.4.1.2, fixed-effects estimation with Driscoll-Kraay standard errors is employed to control for the above problems found in Equation 3.10.

#### *5.1.2.2 Empirical Results*

Empirical results for the direct effects of lagged ownership structure and other control variables on agency costs are shown in Table 5.2.

In terms of the effect of ownership variables, the direct link between lagged government ownership and the utilisation measure of agency costs is as expected, which is positive and significant at the 1% level. The signs of the coefficients of lagged insider ownership and lagged foreign ownership are also as expected, but their effects are not significant at all.

All control variables are found to have significant relationships with agency costs at the 1% level. However, the sign of the coefficients of financial leverage does not support the expectation that financial leverage is a mechanism to reduce agency costs, as mentioned in Section 3.2.2. In contrast, the influence of firm size and firm age on the

*Table 5.2* Direct effects of ownership structure on agency costs (asset utilisation ratio)

| *Dependent variable*<br>*Equation* | *AC*<br>*(3.10)* |
|---|---|
| GOV(–1) | 0.005<br>(0.001)*** |
| INS(–1) | 0.001<br>(0.002) |
| FOR(–1) | 0.001<br>(0.002) |
| LEV | –0.003<br>(0.001)*** |
| SIZE | –0.373<br>(0.035)*** |
| AGE | 0.052<br>(0.009)*** |
| _cons | 8.441<br>(0.705)*** |
| Observations | 380 |
| Number of groups | 95 |
| F–statistic | 142.36 |
| Within R–squared | 0.1409 |

Notes: This table reports the results of Equation 3.10 for agency costs (asset utilisation ratio) using fixed-effects regression with Driscoll-Kraay standard error. It examines how agency costs are affected by ownership structure and other control variables. Variables are denoted as follows. AC is agency costs. GOV(–1) is lagged government ownership. INS(–1) is lagged insider ownership. FOR(–1) is lagged foreign ownership. LEV is financial leverage. SIZE is firm size. AGE is firm age. Robust standard errors are reported in parentheses under the coefficients. The individual coefficient is statistically significant at the *10%, **5% or ***1% significance levels.

asset utilisation ratio is as expected, suggesting that larger firms have greater agency costs than smaller firms, and firms that are listed on stock markets for a longer time are associated with a lower level of agency costs.

At this step of the regression, it is found that the direct path between lagged government ownership and agency costs is significant, whereas the paths between the other forms of ownership structure and agency costs are not significant. An increase in the proportion of government ownership in one year is followed by a higher asset utilisation ratio or lower agency costs in the next year. Hence, the *second condition* of mediation is satisfied for lagged government ownership, but this is only valid for the mediation channel via agency costs.

### *5.1.3 Direct Effect of Ownership Structure on Corporate Risk-Taking*

The third step of testing the mediation mechanism in the recursive model in this study is the regression of corporate risk-taking on ownership structure and other control variables in Equation 3.11:

$$RT_{it} = \alpha_3 + \beta_{31}GOV(-1)_{it} + \beta_{32}INS(-1)_{it} + \beta_{33}FOR(-1)_{it} + \beta_{34}LEV_{it} + \beta_{35}BIG4_{it} + \beta_{36}GRO_{it} + \beta_{37}FIN_{it} + \varepsilon_{3it} \quad (3.11)$$

Where *i* and *t* subscripts stand for firm and year and RT denotes corporate risk-taking. GOV(–1), INS(–1) and FOR(–1) denote lagged government ownership, lagged insider ownership and lagged foreign ownership, respectively. The control variables consist of LEV for financial leverage, GRO for firm growth and FIN for financial investment. BIG4 is a dummy for Big-4 audit company. $\varepsilon_{3it}$ is the error terms containing random disturbance and unobserved heterogeneity.

#### *5.1.3.1 Diagnostic Tests*

The test for multicollinearity is conducted first. The result shows that the problem of collinearity among the explanatory variables is not present in Equation 3.11, since all the variance inflation factors (VIF) are less than 10 and the mean VIF value is 5.13.

The likelihood-ratio test for heteroscedasticity rejects the null hypothesis that the error terms are homoscedastic (LR chi-square value is 158.91, $p < 0.01$).

The F-test for fixed effects shows that there is an unobserved firm fixed effect in Equation 3.11 (F-statistic = 3.03, $p < 0.01$). The Hausman test also confirms that a fixed-effects model is suitable (chi-square statistic = 24.36, $p < 0.01$). Next, the serial correlation test is conducted. The result indicates that first-order autocorrelation is not present in Equation 3.11 (F statistic = 0.005, $p > 0.05$).

The Pesaran's (2004) CD test for cross-sectional dependence in fixed-effect models is performed for Equation 3.11. The result shows a problem of cross-sectional dependence. The null hypothesis of no cross-sectional dependence is strongly rejected at the 1% significance level, and the average absolute value of correlation among residuals is 0.501. The Frees' test does not confirm this result since the Frees' statistic is smaller than the critical value at $\alpha = 0.10$. However, a decision can be made based on the result of Pesaran's test, which is preferred in dynamic panels (De Hoyos and Sarafidis, 2006). Additionally, the average absolute correlation of the residuals is a very high value (0.501). Therefore, there is reason to conclude that cross-sectional dependence is also present in Equation 3.11, similar to Equation 3.10.

As a result, it can be said that Equation 3.11 is involved with the unobserved firm fixed effect, heteroscedasticity and cross-sectional dependence. Similar to Equation 3.10, the fixed-effects estimation with Driscoll-Kraay standard errors is also applied for Equation 3.11.

#### *5.1.3.2 Empirical Results*

Empirical results for Equation 3.11 for the direct effect of lagged ownership structure and other control variables on corporate risk-taking are presented in Table 5.3.

An interesting result is that all three forms of ownership variables employed in this study are estimated to have significantly positive relationships with corporate risk-taking at the 1% level. The magnitude of the direct effects of past government and past insider shareholders on

*Table 5.3* Direct effect of ownership structure on corporate risk-taking

| *Dependent variable*<br>*Equation* | *RT*<br>*(3.11)* |
|---|---|
| GOV(–1) | 0.011<br>(0.001)*** |
| INS(–1) | 0.013<br>(0.005)*** |
| FOR(–1) | 0.004<br>(0.002)*** |
| LEV | –0.002<br>(0.003) |
| BIG4 | 0.046<br>(0.063) |
| GRO | –0.000<br>(0.000) |
| FIN | 0.010<br>(0.006) |
| _cons | 2.458<br>(0.177)*** |
| Observations | 380 |
| Number of groups | 95 |
| F-statistic | 131.89 |
| Within R-squared | 0.0267 |

Notes: This table reports the results of Equation 3.11 for corporate risk-taking using fixed-effects regression with Driscoll-Kraay standard error. It examines how corporate risk-taking is affected by ownership structure and other control variables. Variables are denoted as follows. RT is corporate risk-taking. GOV (–1) is lagged government ownership. INS(–1) is lagged insider ownership. FOR (–1) is lagged foreign ownership. LEV is financial leverage. BIG4 is Big-4 audit company. GRO is firm growth. FIN is financial leverage. Robust standard errors are reported in parentheses under the coefficients. The individual coefficient is statistically significant at the *10%, **5% or ***1% significance levels.

current corporate risk-taking is larger than that of past foreign shareholders. While the positive effect of lagged government ownership on corporate risk-taking is as expected, the positive effects of lagged insider ownership and lagged foreign ownership are not in conformity with the assumptions set out in Section 3.2.2.

In terms of the control variables, the sign of the effect of financial leverage on corporate risk-taking is negative as expected. However, the influence of this variable on corporate risk-taking is not meaningful. On the other hand, no significant influence of the Big-4 audit service on corporate risk-taking is estimated, which indicates that the difference between Big-4 audited firms and the other listed firms is small. Lastly, financial investment is found to have a positive effect on corporate risk-taking as expected, but the impact of financial investment is not significant.

With the abovementioned results, the *second condition* is met for corporate risk-taking to be a mediator in the links between all forms of ownership structure used in this research and firm performance because there are significant direct relationships between them and corporate risk-taking.

### *5.1.4 Direct Effects of Ownership Structure, Agency Costs and Corporate Risk-Taking on Firm Performance*

The final step of the causal-steps regression for the recursive model is the estimation of Equation 3.12, which is revised from Equation 3.9 to include the effects of agency costs and corporate risk-taking. This equation is needed to estimate the direct effects of ownership structure on firm performance when the mediating variables are controlled, as well as the direct effects of the mediating variables on firm performance.

$$\begin{aligned} FP_{it} = \alpha_4 &+ \beta_{41}AC_{it} + \beta_{42}RT_{it} + \beta_{43}GOV(-1)_{it} + \beta_{44}INS(-1)_{it} \\ &+ \beta_{45}FOR(-1)_{it} + \beta_{46}LEV_{it} + \beta_{47}SIZE_{it} + \beta_{48}BIG4_{it} \\ &+ \beta_{49}FP(-1)_{it} + \varepsilon_{4it} \qquad (3.12) \end{aligned}$$

Where *i* and *t* subscripts stand for firm and year and AC and RT denote agency costs and corporate risk-taking, respectively. FP is firm performance, consisting of ROA or Q. GOV(–1), INS(–1) and FOR(–1) denote lagged government ownership, lagged insider ownership and lagged foreign ownership, respectively. The control variables consist of LEV for financial leverage, SIZE for firm size, BIG4, a dummy variable, for Big-4 audit company and FP(–1) for prior firm performance. $\varepsilon_{4it}$ is the error term containing random disturbance and unobserved heterogeneity.

#### *5.1.4.1 Treatment of Variables in GMM Estimation*

In Equation 3.12, the explanatory variables of interest are ownership structure, agency costs and corporate risk-taking. As already discussed in Section 5.1.1, the ownership structure variables are treated as endogenous, and financial leverage, firm size and lagged firm performance are considered predetermined variables. Additionally, agency costs and corporate risk-taking are treated as predetermined variables in GMM estimation of Equation 3.12 because in this book, a change in previous-year ownership structure is assumed to influence the current-year levels of agency costs and corporate risk-taking.

Other treatments that are similar to Equation 3.9 include: time dummies added to Equation 3.12 to strengthen the assumption of no cross-sectional dependence; industry dummies added to control for industry fixed effects; and Big4-audit dummy, time and industry dummies treated as exogenous variables.

#### *5.1.4.2 Empirical Results*

The empirical results obtained from GMM regression for the direct effects of ownership structure adjusted for agency costs and corporate risk-taking on ROA and Q in Equation 3.12 are presented in columns 1 and 2 of Table 5.4. To facilitate convenient comparison with Equation 3.9, the results of Equation 3.9 are added to column 1 of Table 5.4.

*Table 5.4* Direct effects of ownership structure on firm performance before and after adjusting for agency costs and corporate risk-taking

| *Dependent variable* | *ROA* | | *Q* | |
|---|---|---|---|---|
| *Equation* | *(3.9)*<br>*(1)* | *(3.12)*<br>*(2)* | *(3.9)*<br>*(1)* | *(3.12)*<br>*(2)* |
| AC | | 5.619<br>(1.909)*** | | 0.086<br>(0.046)* |
| RT | | 0.271<br>(0.513) | | 0.020<br>(0.025) |
| GOV(−1) | 0.150<br>(0.060)** | 0.055<br>(0.061) | 0.001<br>(0.002) | 0.000<br>(0.002) |
| INS(−1) | 0.333<br>(0.156)** | 0.227<br>(0.117)* | 0.008<br>(0.004)* | 0.003<br>(0.004) |
| FOR(−1) | 0.197<br>(0.115)* | 0.022<br>(0.119) | 0.003<br>(0.003) | −0.001<br>(0.003) |
| LEV | −0.242<br>(0.074)*** | −0.228<br>(0.039)*** | 0.002<br>(0.001)** | 0.000<br>(0.001) |

*(Continued)*

*Table 5.4* (Continued)

| *Dependent variable* | *ROA* | | *Q* | |
|---|---|---|---|---|
| *Equation* | *(3.9)* *(1)* | *(3.12)* *(2)* | *(3.9)* *(1)* | *(3.12)* *(2)* |
| **SIZE** | 2.498 | 1.335 | 0.007 | 0.049 |
| | (1.748) | (1.043) | (0.037) | (0.024)** |
| **BIG4** | –4.770 | –1.108 | –0.001 | –0.002 |
| | (2.509)* | (1.767) | (0.068) | (0.052) |
| **ROA(–1)** | 0.340 | 0.369 | | |
| | (0.129)*** | (0.099)*** | | |
| **Q(–1)** | | | 0.509 | 0.481 |
| | | | (0.110)*** | (0.083)*** |
| **_cons** | –13.563 | –14.029 | 0.681 | 0.178 |
| | (40.339) | (16.377) | (1.174) | (0.891) |
| **Observations** | 380 | 380 | 380 | 380 |
| **Number of instruments** | 50 | 64 | 50 | 81 |
| **Number of groups** | 95 | 95 | 95 | 95 |
| **AR(1)** | –2.05 | –2.95 | –3.59 | –3.55 |
| **[P-value]** | [0.040] | [0.003] | [0.000] | [0.000] |
| **AR(2)** | –1.69 | –1.91 | 0.03 | 0.30 |
| **[P-value]** | [0.091] | [0.056] | [0.977] | [0.762] |
| **Hansen test** | 30.83 | 31.08 | 28.21 | 61.29 |
| **[P-value]** | [0.235] | [0.779] | [0.348] | [0.261] |
| **Difference-in-Hansen test [P-value]** | 26.75 [0.062] | 22.89 [0.584] | 16.08 [0.518] | 20.14 [0.740] |
| **F-statistics** | 3.01 | 55.23 | 24.27 | 41.04 |
| **[P-value]** | [0.000] | [0.000] | [0.000] | [0.000] |
| **Time effects** | Included | Included | Included | Included |
| **Industry effects** | Included | Included | Included | Included |

Notes: This table reports the results of dynamic system GMM regression of Equation 3.12 in column (2). It examines how firm performance is directly affected by ownership structure, agency costs, corporate risk-taking and the other control variables. The results of Equation 3.9 are also repeated in column (1) to facilitate convenient comparison with Equation 3.12. Variables are denoted as follows. ROA is return on assets. Q is Tobin's Q. AC is agency costs. RT is corporate risk-taking. GOV(–1) is lagged government ownership. INS(–1) is lagged insider ownership. FOR(–1) is lagged foreign ownership. LEV is financial leverage. SIZE is firm size. BIG4 is Big-4 audit company. ROA(–1) is prior return on assets. Q(–1) is prior Tobin's Q. Endogenous variables are GOV(–1), INS(–1) and FOR(–1). Predetermined variables are AC, RT, LEV, SIZE, ROA(–1) and Q(–1). Exogenous variables are BIG4 dummy, time dummies and industry dummies. The parameters are estimated using two-step procedures for dynamic system GMM. The robust standard errors using the Windmeijer correction for small samples are included in parentheses under the coefficients. Estimates of year and industry dummies are excluded from the table for brevity. The individual coefficient is statistically significant at the *10%, **5% or ***1% significance levels.

When ROA is regressed, in the transformed equation, the lags 2 of the endogenous variables and lags 1 of the predetermined variables are used as the instruments. In the level equation, the first lags of the differenced endogenous variables and the contemporaneous differenced predetermined variables are used as the instruments.

When Q is regressed, in the transformed equation, the lags 2 to lags 3 of the endogenous variables and the lags 1 to lags 2 of the predetermined variables are used as the instruments. In the level equation, the first lags of the differenced endogenous variables and the contemporaneous lags of the differenced predetermined variables are used as the instruments.

In regression with ROA (column 2), agency costs are found to have a significantly positive relation with ROA at the 1% level. An increase of 1 in the asset utilisation ratio is associated with about a 5.6% increase in ROA of the same year, holding all other variables constant. Hence, *the third condition* for the mediating effect of agency costs is satisfied. However, the third condition for corporate risk-taking is not met because a direct link between corporate risk-taking and ROA is not found (insignificant).

As already stated, the *fourth condition* for the mediating effect is that the direct effects of the predictor variables on the outcome variables are reduced or no longer significant when the mediating variables are controlled for. To compare, the results in column 2 of ROA regression show that when agency costs and corporate risk-taking are added to Equation 3.12, the direct positive effects of lagged government ownership and lagged foreign ownership become insignificant, while that of lagged insider ownership is still significant although smaller in magnitude. Taken together with the results of previous equations, the conclusion can be drawn that *agency costs fully mediate the positive effect of lagged government ownership on ROA*. Agency costs do not play such a mediating role in the relationship between lagged insider ownership and ROA, nor between lagged foreign ownership and ROA, because the links between agency costs and lagged insider ownership/lagged foreign ownership are not established, as reported in Section 5.1.2.

In regression with Q (column 2), it is found that agency costs are significantly positively associated with Q. Precisely, an increase of 1 in the asset utilisation ratio corresponds with an increase of nearly 0.09 in Q. The direct effect of lagged insider ownership on Q found in Equation 3.9 becomes weak and insignificant when agency costs and corporate risk-taking are added. However, the mediating role of agency costs is not found in the relationship between lagged insider ownership and Q, because the effect of lagged insider ownership on agency costs is not meaningful, as mentioned above. As in ROA regression, there is no significant relationship between corporate risk-taking and Q. As a result, there is no mediating role of corporate risk-taking in the relationship between ownership structure and Q.

In terms of the control variables, the signs and significance levels of financial leverage and lagged ROA in ROA regression are unchanged in both columns, but the influence of Big4 audit company on ROA is no longer significant when agency costs and corporate risk-taking are added into Equation 3.12. The effect of financial leverage on Q disappears in column 2, whereas the positive effect of firm size on Q becomes significant at the 5% level. The explanatory power of all other variables on Q remains insignificant regardless of adjusting for agency costs and corporate risk-taking. In general, the influence of all control variables is reduced in explanatory power as expected when the mediating variables are added into the firm performance equation.

Overall, it can be concluded that a full mediating role of agency costs is found for the relationship between lagged government ownership and ROA. As for the second mediator, although the direct links between all three types of ownership structure used in this research and corporate risk-taking are highly significant, it turns out that a mediating role of corporate risk-taking is not confirmed due to the lack of a significant link between corporate risk-taking and firm performance. Nevertheless, it should be reiterated that these results have been found in the recursive model using causal-steps regression.

### *5.1.5 Robustness Tests of Recursive Model*

Several additional regressions are conducted to check for robustness of the estimated coefficients of all variables of interest, including ownership structure, firm performance, agency costs and corporate risk-taking variables.

#### *5.1.5.1 Replacing and Removing Insignificant Control Variables in Equations 3.9 and 3.12*

It is worth reiterating that both Equations 3.9 and 3.12 are firm performance equations in the recursive model. The purpose of robustness checks in this section is to replace or remove a control variable that does not have significant explanatory power in relation to firm performance.

When ROA was used to proxy firm performance in Equations 3.9 and 3.12, it was already reported that firm size (SIZE) does not have significant impact on ROA in both equations. To check whether or not the effects of the variables of interests on ROA are sensitive to a change in firm size, therefore, another measure of firm size (SIZE2) is employed. Specifically, SIZE2 is calculated as the natural logarithm of the market capitalisation of the firm. This variable is also treated with similar procedures as for other variables (i.e. detecting for outliers and winsorising at the detected percentage and tails of outliers). Then, Equations 3.9 and 3.12 with ROA as the dependent variable are re-estimated using the GMM estimation method, but with SIZE replaced by SIZE2.

The results indicate that there are no significant changes in the estimated coefficients of the variables of interest in both equations (see Appendix A5.2a for detailed results). In Equation 3.9, the total effects of lagged government ownership and lagged insider ownership on ROA are still significantly positive. The sign of the coefficient on lagged foreign ownership remains positive, but the standard error of this estimate is slightly varied; hence the total effect of lagged foreign ownership on ROA is not significant at the 10% level, as reported in the initial estimation of Equation 3.9 with SIZE.

In Equation 3.12, when SIZE2 is used instead of SIZE, the effect of agency costs and corporate risk-taking on ROA do not change: agency costs have a significantly positive impact on ROA, while corporate risk-taking does not explain ROA. The direct effects of ownership structure variables on ROA are similar to those found in the initial regression; but the effect of lagged insider ownership is no longer significant at the 10% level. However, the inference for mediation analysis remains the same: the effect of lagged insider ownership on ROA is reduced or insignificant when agency costs and corporate risk-taking are controlled for in Equation 3.12.

When Q is employed to measure firm performance in Equations 3.9 and 3.12, Big-4 audit company (BIG4) is found to be an insignificant control variable in both equations, as reported in Section 5.1.4. To check for the robustness of the effects of the variables of interest on Q, BIG4 is removed from these two equations when they are re-estimated with the same GMM estimation method. The results show that all the estimates of ownership structure variables and mediating variables are similar to those obtained in the estimations with BIG4.[1]

Taken together, it can be said that the empirical results of Equations 3.9 and 3.12 in the recursive model are robust to a change in control variables. Applying the same GMM estimation techniques for the robustness checks, no significant changes are found for the estimates of all variables of interest in these equations.

#### *5.1.5.2 Using an Alternative Measure of Agency Costs in Equation3.10*

Operating expense ratio (AC2), another measure of agency costs, is used for the robustness test of the validity of agency costs. As mentioned in Section 3.2.1.2, there are various methods to measure operating expenses, and it appears that there is no perfect measure that fully captures all sources of agency costs. Even with the total operating expense measure, Ang et al. (2000) note that it may underestimate total agency costs because indirect agency costs at the firm level are not fully measured.

Following Davidson and Singh (2003), AC2 in this book is calculated as selling, general and administration expenses (SG&A) scaled by total assets. This is a direct measure of agency costs in the sense that a higher value of AC2 implies a higher level of agency costs, and vice versa. Hence, it is expected that the coefficients of the explanatory variables of AC2 have opposite signs to those obtained with the asset utilisation ratio measure of agency costs (AC).

When Equation 3.10 is retested with AC2, the result shows that lagged government ownership has a significantly negative relationship with AC2, which confirms the result found previously for AC, that a higher proportion of government ownership is associated with a lower level of agency costs. However, it can be observed that the estimates of lagged insider ownership and lagged foreign ownership are not as expected. While the effects of these two ownership variables are not significant with the asset utilisation measure of agency costs (AC), they become significant with the operating expense measure of agency costs (AC2). This reveals that there are some gaps between AC and AC2 in terms of reflecting agency costs. At least, it can be said that the result for the main variable of interest in Equation 3.10 (i.e. lagged government ownership) is robust to the employment of a different measure of agency costs (see Appendix A5.2b for detailed results).

#### *5.1.5.3 Replacing and Removing Financial Leverage in Equation 3.11*

Two tests for the robustness of the corporate risk-taking equation (Equation 3.11) are performed:

1. replacing LEV with another proxy of financial leverage; and
2. removing LEV from Equation 3.11.

For the first test, it is commonly argued in finance literature that financial leverage is associated with the default risk or credit risk of firms. Thus, financial risk might account for a significant part of the variation in corporate risk-taking. However, such a potential effect of financial leverage on corporate risk-taking has not been found in the FE estimation performed earlier (in Equation 3.11), because the coefficient on LEV is not significant. The use of another proxy of financial leverage may confirm a significant role of financial leverage and alter the impact of the ownership variable on corporate risk-taking.

Therefore, this book employs LEV2 to proxy financial leverage for the robustness test of the corporate risk-taking equation. LEV2 is calculated as the ratio of total liabilities over the book value of common equity. This ratio is also checked for potential outliers, like other variables employed in this study, and then winsorised at the percentage and tail of outliers found in the above step. The results for the corporate risk-taking equation are not considered to be robust if there are substantial changes in the estimated parameters due to the replacement of financial leverage (LEV) with the second proxy (LEV2).

When Equation 3.11 is re-estimated with LEV2 using the same fixed-effects estimation with Driscoll-Kraay standard errors, the results show that the coefficients of all ownership structure variables on corporate risk-taking are almost the same as found previously. Consistently, the effects of LEV2, Big-4 auditing and firm growth remain insignificant. The only significant change in this test is that the coefficient on financial investment in corporate risk-taking equation is confirmed to be significantly positive at the 10% level.

For the second test, financial leverage may also correlate with the ownership structure variables, because both financial leverage and ownership structure are components of the capital structure of a firm. In this case, the estimated effects of ownership structure on corporate risk-taking may be biased due to multicollinearity. It should be noted that the test for multicollinearity among the independent variables of Equation 3.11 has already been performed and showed that this problem is not present. Thus, retesting Equation 3.11 without financial leverage is also to double-check this multicollinearity test. More importantly, there should not be any significant variation in the estimates of the variables of interest, that is, the ownership structure variables, when LEV is dropped out.

The fixed-effects estimation with Driscoll-Kraay standard errors for Equation 3.11 without LEV shows that all the estimated coefficients are consistent with the results found with LEV. The effects of all ownership structure variables on corporate risk-taking remain positive and significant at the 1% level.

Taken together, it can be argued that the estimates for the effects of the ownership variables on corporate risk-taking are robust and not sensitive to a change in the explanatory variables.

### *5.1.6 What if Agency Costs and Corporate Risk-Taking are Endogenous Covariates?*

#### *5.1.6.1 ML Estimation as Solution*

As mentioned in Section 4.4.2.1, maximum likelihood estimation (ML) is applied to test the recursive model when the two mediators are treated as endogenous covariates. The purpose of this estimation is to answer Research question 2. To reiterate, the ML estimation technique is advantageous in terms of allowing the cross-equation correlation structure of error terms. In this way, the endogeneity of the two mediators is accounted for, which otherwise cannot be resolved in causal-steps regression.

Since ML estimation is a completely different method of regression, it is possible that the results obtained from ML estimation are different from those of FE and GMM estimation under causal-steps regression. To compare with causal-steps regression, therefore, it is important to make sure that the variation in the mediating role of agency costs and corporate risk-taking found in ML estimation, if any, is not simply due to the application of different estimation techniques but is instead because of the endogenous nature of agency costs and corporate risk-taking.

To this end, it is required that ML estimation produces estimates consistent with those of FE and GMM estimation under the same condition, that each equation in the recursive model is regressed separately. If this is the case, ML estimation allowing covariance in the error terms of agency costs and corporate risk-taking can be safely applied to the recursive model.

Therefore, the covariance structure of errors in ML estimation of the recursive model is firstly imposed to be independent, so that individual equations are treated independently. For consistency, it should be noted that Equation 3.9 of the recursive model is not included in any ML estimations, because the next steps of ML estimation (in the non-recursive model) would be system estimation rather than equation-by-equation estimation (see Section 3.1.2.3 for specific reasons for the dropping of Equation 3.9 in the non-recursive model).

When ROA is used to measure firm performance in the recursive model, the results show that there is no significant difference between the causal-steps approach and the ML approach, where the latter uses firm dummies, year clustering and independent covariance structure of error terms. The signs and significance levels of all variables, including the main variables, are almost consistent. This consistency is not obtained if standard errors are clustered by firms. Specific results are presented in Table 5.5.

*Table 5.5* Comparison of causal-steps regression and ML regression of recursive model with *independent disturbances* (firm performance proxied by ROA)

| *Dependent variable* | *Regressor* | *Causal–steps regression* | *ML regression* |
|---|---|---|---|
| **AC** | **GOV (–1)** | 0.005 | 0.005 |
| (Equation 3.10) | | (0.001)*** | (0.001)*** |
| | **INS(–1)** | 0.001 | 0.001 |
| | | (0.002) | (0.003) |
| | **FOR (–1)** | 0.001 | 0.001 |
| | | (0.002) | (0.002) |
| | **LEV** | –0.003 | –0.003 |
| | | (0.001)*** | (0.001)*** |
| | **SIZE** | –0.373 | –0.373 |
| | | (0.035)*** | (0.052)*** |
| | **AGE** | 0.052 | 0.052 |
| | | (0.009)*** | (0.011)*** |
| | **_cons** | 8.441 | 8.397 |
| | | (0.705)*** | (1.152)*** |

(*Continued*)

*Table 5.5* (Continued)

| *Dependent variable* | *Regressor* | *Causal–steps regression* | *ML regression* |
|---|---|---|---|
| **RT** | **GOV (–1)** | 0.011 | 0.011 |
| (Equation 3.11) | | (0.001)*** | (0.002)*** |
| | **INS(–1)** | 0.013 | 0.013 |
| | | (0.005)*** | (0.005)** |
| | **FOR (–1)** | 0.004 | 0.004 |
| | | (0.002)*** | (0.002)* |
| | **LEV** | –0.002 | –0.002 |
| | | (0.003) | (0.004) |
| | **BIG4** | 0.046 | 0.046 |
| | | (0.063) | (0.064) |
| | **GRO** | –0.000 | –0.000 |
| | | (0.000) | (0.001) |
| | **FIN** | 0.010 | 0.010 |
| | | (0.006) | (0.008) |
| | **_cons** | 2.458 | 1.499 |
| | | (0.177)*** | (0.173)*** |
| **ROA** | **AC** | 5.619 | 3.883 |
| (Equation 3.12) | | (1.909)*** | (0.133)*** |
| | **RT** | 0.271 | 0.750 |
| | | (0.513) | (0.485) |
| | **GOV (–1)** | 0.055 | 0.009 |
| | | (0.061) | (0.054) |
| | **INS(–1)** | 0.227 | 0.098 |
| | | (0.117)* | (0.033)*** |
| | **FOR (–1)** | 0.022 | –0.028 |
| | | (0.119) | (0.035) |
| | **LEV** | –0.228 | –0.125 |
| | | (0.039)*** | (0.014)*** |
| | **SIZE** | 1.335 | –2.975 |
| | | (1.043) | (0.851)*** |
| | **BIG4** | –1.108 | –2.687 |
| | | (1.767) | (0.785)*** |
| | **ROA(–1)** | 0.369 | 0.101 |
| | | (0.099)*** | (0.113) |
| | **_cons** | –14.029 | 74.138 |
| | | (16.377) | (17.820)*** |
| *N* | | 380 | 380 |

Notes: This table compares the results of causal-steps regression and those of ML estimation for the recursive model where firm performance is measured by ROA. The purpose of this comparison is to determine whether the two estimation methods produce consistent estimates. The results for causal-steps regression are restated from FE and GMM estimations as reported in Section 5.1. In ML regression, covariance structures of disturbances are specified as independent (i.e. equations are separately estimated) and standard errors are clustered by year. Variables are denoted as follows. AC is agency costs. RT is corporate risk-taking. ROA is return on assets. GOV(–1) is lagged government ownership. INS(–1) is lagged insider ownership. FOR(–1) is lagged foreign ownership. LEV is financial leverage. SIZE is firm size. AGE is firm age. BIG4 is Big-4 audit company. GRO is firm growth. FIN is financial investment. ROA(–1) is prior return on assets. Robust standard errors are presented in parentheses under the coefficients. All firm dummy estimates are excluded from the table for brevity. The individual coefficient is statistically significant at the *10%, **5% or ***1% significance levels.

As can be observed in Table 5.5, the ML method yields nearly identical estimates and significance levels in comparison with FE estimations for Equations 3.10 and 3.11. In Equation 3.12, there are several slight differences between ML and dynamic system GMM estimation, but the variation is not significant. The coefficients of the main variables under ML estimation tend to be smaller in magnitude, while the sign of the coefficient on a control variable (firm size) is found to be opposite to that obtained in GMM estimation. The reason for such variations may be that industry dummies in GMM estimation do not fully capture the unobserved firm fixed effects, which is possible in ML with the inclusion of firm dummies. Using firm dummies in a two-step system GMM estimation for this equation is not feasible because of the instrument proliferation problem, which cannot be tackled by the *collapse* technique as suggested in Stata's *xtabond2* command.[2] Hence, it can be said that ML estimation works better in comparison with GMM estimation, as shown in the results of Equation 3.12.

Next, when market firm performance (Q) is employed, similar techniques of ML estimation, i.e. firm dummies, time clustering and independent cross-equation error terms, are also applied. The results show that there are large differences between ML estimation and GMM estimation in terms of the estimates for Equations 3.9 and 3.12. Consequently, this ML estimation and causal-steps regression should not be compared for consistency when firm performance is measured by Q. Therefore, it is not plausible to apply ML estimation as such for the recursive model using Q as firm performance to answer Research question 2 of this book.

Consequently, an interesting outcome that has emerged is that ML estimation with firm dummies, year clustering and independent cross-equation error terms is nearly of exact equivalence to causal-steps regression using FE and GMM estimations. This is seen when ROA is used to proxy firm performance in the recursive model. Hence, it can be concluded that ML estimation with firm dummies and year clustering of error terms can be safely employed to estimate for the recursive model when the mediators are treated as endogenous variables, but this method is applicable when firm performance is ROA only. The task of finding answers to Research question 2 is thus confined to the recursive model with firm performance proxied by ROA.

#### *5.1.6.2 Recursive Model with Correlated Disturbances*

As indicated in Research question 2, a concern in this research is whether the mediating roles of agency costs and corporate risk-taking found in the causal-steps approach are varied if the two mediating variables are permitted to co-vary (i.e. they are endogenous). To find the answer to this question, ML techniques as described in the above section (i.e. for firm dummies and year clustering) are used to test the recursive model, but this time the error terms of agency costs and corporate risk-taking equations are free to be correlated. In addition, it should be restated that the ML method is applicable only when ROA is used to proxy firm performance in the recursive model.

To make an easy comparison with the causal-steps regression, the results for ML estimation of the recursive model with correlated disturbances are presented in parallel with those obtained from the causal-steps approach in Table 5.6.

*Table 5.6* Comparison of causal-steps regression and ML regression of recursive model with *correlated disturbances* (firm performance proxied by ROA)

| *Dependent variable* | *Regressor* | *Causal-steps regression* | *ML regression* |
|---|---|---|---|
| AC | GOV (–1) | 0.005 | 0.005 |
| (Equation 3.10) | | (0.001)*** | (0.001)*** |
| | INS(–1) | 0.001 | 0.001 |
| | | (0.002) | (0.003) |
| | FOR (–1) | 0.001 | 0.001 |
| | | (0.002) | (0.002) |
| | LEV | –0.003 | –0.003 |
| | | (0.001)*** | (0.001)*** |
| | SIZE | –0.373 | –0.390 |
| | | (0.035)*** | (0.044)*** |
| | AGE | 0.052 | –0.706 |
| | | (0.009)*** | (0.129)*** |
| | _cons | 8.441 | 12.516 |
| | | (0.705)*** | (1.490)*** |
| RT | GOV (–1) | 0.011 | 0.007 |
| (Equation 3.11) | | (0.001)*** | (0.004)* |
| | INS(–1) | 0.013 | 0.012 |
| | | (0.005)*** | (0.004)*** |
| | FOR (–1) | 0.004 | 0.002 |
| | | (0.002)*** | (0.003) |
| | LEV | –0.002 | –0.001 |
| | | (0.003) | (0.005) |
| | BIG4 | 0.046 | 0.079 |
| | | (0.063) | (0.068) |
| | GRO | –0.000 | –0.001 |
| | | (0.000) | (0.001)* |
| | FIN | 0.010 | 0.000 |
| | | (0.006) | (0.001) |
| | _cons | 2.458 | 1.501 |
| | | (0.177)*** | (0.255)*** |
| ROA | AC | 5.619 | 6.570 |
| (Equation 3.12) | | (1.909)*** | (1.488)*** |
| | RT | 0.271 | –13.609 |
| | | (0.513) | (4.094)*** |

(*Continued*)

*Table 5.6* (Continued)

| *Dependent variable* | *Regressor* | *Causal-steps regression* | *ML regression* |
|---|---|---|---|
| | GOV (−1) | 0.055 | 0.052 |
| | | (0.061) | (0.105) |
| | INS(−1) | 0.227 | 0.265 |
| | | (0.117)* | (0.046)*** |
| | FOR (−1) | 0.022 | −0.011 |
| | | (0.119) | (0.055) |
| | LEV | −0.228 | −0.116 |
| | | (0.039)*** | (0.078) |
| | SIZE | 1.335 | 1.274 |
| | | (1.043) | (0.262)*** |
| | BIG4 | −1.108 | −1.049 |
| | | (1.767) | (1.805) |
| | ROA(−1) | 0.369 | 0.057 |
| | | (0.099)*** | (0.087) |
| | _cons | −14.029 | 0.886 |
| | | (16.377) | (0.000) |
| *N* | | 380 | 380 |

Notes: This table compares the results of ML estimation and those of causal-steps regression for the recursive model where firm performance is measured by ROA. The purpose is to determine whether the mediating role of agency costs and corporate risk-taking are varied when they are treated as endogenous. In ML regression, the covariance structures of disturbances are unstructured (i.e. free to be correlated) and standard errors are clustered by year. The results for causal-steps regression are restated from FE and GMM estimations as reported from Section 5.1. Variables are denoted as follows. AC is agency costs. RT is corporate risk-taking. ROA is return on assets. GOV(−1) is lagged government ownership. INS(−1) is lagged insider ownership. FOR(−1) is lagged foreign ownership. LEV is financial leverage. SIZE is firm size. AGE is firm age. BIG4 is Big-4 audit company. GRO is firm growth. FIN is financial investment. ROA(−1) is prior return on assets. Robust standard errors are presented in parentheses under the coefficients. All firm dummy estimates are excluded from the table for brevity. The individual coefficient is statistically significant at the *10%, **5% or ***1% significance levels.

With respect to the agency costs equation (Equation 3.10) and to compare with the causal-steps regression (FE estimation), all estimates remain almost the same in both magnitude and significance level. In particular, the coefficient on the variable of interest in this equation (lagged government ownership) does not vary at all. In ML estimation, however, there is a change in the influence of firm age on agency costs, which turns negative at the same significance level of 1%.

In terms of the corporate risk-taking equation (Equation 3.11), the estimated values in both columns are fairly similar, but there is a significant change in ML estimation in comparison with causal-steps regression (FE estimation): lagged foreign ownership loses its explanatory power in relation to corporate risk-taking. However, the effects of lagged government ownership and past insider ownership on current corporate risk-taking remain significantly positive, with a slight reduction in the magnitude of effect.

The most significant variation when agency costs and corporate risk-taking are treated as endogenous is found in the firm performance equation (Equation 3.12). In causal-steps regression (GMM estimation), the effect of corporate risk-taking on accounting firm performance (ROA) is not significant at all when agency costs and corporate risk-taking are independent. In contrast, this effect becomes strong and significantly negative at the 1% level in ML estimation with correlated disturbances. The coefficient on the other mediating variable (agency costs) remains positive and significant at the 1% level, but the magnitude of effect is stronger in ML estimation.

Since there are large variations in the effects of corporate risk-taking in ML estimation of the recursive model when the two mediating variables are treated as endogenous covariates, it is reasonable to argue that agency costs and corporate risk-taking are not exogenous in reality but are affected by unobserved common causes that have not been accounted for in causal-steps regression. Thus, Baron and Kenny (1986) causal-steps approach, which treats the two mediators as exogenous, is likely to produce spurious results. This calls for a system estimator of all paths, such as ML estimation, which permits the disturbances of mediators to be correlated to avoid biased estimates, as suggested by Antonakis et al. (2010). This result also endorses the recommendation by other authors such as Preacher and Hayes (2008) and Acock (2013) that the covariance of two mediators should be allowed in mediation analysis with two-mediator mediation models. Therefore, the results obtained previously in the causal-steps approach by FE and GMM estimation are not regarded as the final findings on the issue but as a robustness exercise for ML estimation in this book.

In this regard, several paths among the variables of interests are found to be robust throughout all three estimation methods applied above (causal-steps regression, ML with independent cross-equation disturbances and ML with correlated cross-equation disturbances), including four pairs of relationships as follows:

1. lagged government ownership–agency costs;
2. agency costs–ROA;
3. lagged government ownership–corporate risk-taking; and
4. lagged insider ownership–corporate risk-taking.

Specifically, an increase in lagged government ownership is associated with an increase in the asset utilisation ratio, which reflects a reduction in agency costs. In turn, lower agency costs are associated with higher ROA. In addition, changes in the percentages of last-year government ownership and insider ownership are positively followed by a change in current-year corporate risk-taking.

It can be said that there is strong evidence of the positive mediating role of agency costs in the relationship between lagged government ownership and current ROA. The mediation channel via agency costs is not changed when agency costs and corporate risk-taking are allowed to co-vary. However, the mediating role of corporate risk-taking is changed completely. The results of ML estimation indicate that corporate risk-taking has a significantly negative impact on ROA and, hence, negatively mediates the effect of lagged government ownership and lagged insider ownership, but not lagged foreign ownership, on ROA.

## 5.2 Results for Non-Recursive Model

This section reports the empirical results of the non-recursive model, which is estimated simultaneously for all paths in the model using the ML method. The results of all equations are reported first, followed by the results of the robustness tests. The final part of this section presents the results of Sobel tests for the decomposition of effects from ownership structure to firm performance and the bootstrapping results for the significance of the total effect of ownership structure on firm performance.

As already presented in Chapter 3, the non-recursive model is aimed at answering Research questions 3 and 4. The specification of this model is restated as follows:

$$\begin{aligned} AC_{it} = {} & \pi_1 + \lambda_{11}GOV(-1)_{it} + \lambda_{12}INS(-1)_{it} + \lambda_{13}FOR(-1)_{it} \\ & + \lambda_{14}LEV_{it} + \lambda_{15}SIZE_{it} + \lambda_{16}AGE_{it} + u_{1it} \end{aligned} \quad (3.13)$$

$$\begin{aligned} RT_{it} = {} & \pi_2 + \lambda_{21}GOV(-1)_{it} + \lambda_{22}INS(-1)_{it} + \lambda_{23}FOR(-1)_{it} \\ & + \lambda_{24}LEV_{it} + \lambda_{25}BIG4_{it} + \lambda_{26}GRO_{it} + \lambda_{27}FIN_{it} + u_{2it} \end{aligned} \quad (3.14)$$

$$\begin{aligned} ROA_{it} = {} & \pi_3 + \lambda_{31}AC_{it} + \lambda_{32}RT_{it} + \lambda_{33}GOV(-1)_{it} + \lambda_{34}INS(-1)_{it} \\ & + \lambda_{35}FOR(-1)_{it} + \lambda_{36}LEV_{it} + \lambda_{37}SIZE_{it} + \lambda_{38}BIG4_{it} \\ & + \lambda_{39}ROA(-1)_{it} + u_{3it} \end{aligned} \quad (3.15)$$

$$\begin{aligned} Q_{it} = {} & \pi_4 + \lambda_{41}AC_{it} + \lambda_{42}RT_{it} + \lambda_{43}GOV(-1)_{it} + \lambda_{44}INS(-1)_{it} \\ & + \lambda_{45}FOR(-1)_{it} + \lambda_{46}LEV_{it} + \lambda_{47}SIZE_{it} + \lambda_{48}BIG4_{it} \\ & + \lambda_{49}Q(-1)_{it} + u_{4it} \end{aligned} \quad (3.16)$$

$$\begin{aligned} GOV_{it} = {} & \pi_5 + \lambda_{51}ROA(-1)_{it} + \lambda_{52}Q(-1)_{it} + \lambda_{53}LEV_{it} \\ & + \lambda_{54}SIZE_{it} + \lambda_{55}SOE_{it} + \sum_{k=1}^{14} \omega_k IND_{kit} + u_{5it} \end{aligned} \quad (3.17)$$

$$\text{INS}_{\text{it}} = \pi_6 + \lambda_{61}\text{ROA}(-1)_{\text{it}} + \lambda_{62}\text{Q}(-1)_{\text{it}} + \lambda_{63}\text{SIZE}_{\text{it}} + \lambda_{64}\text{AGE}_{\text{it}} + \lambda_{65}\text{GRO}_{\text{it}} + u_{6\text{it}} \quad (3.18)$$

$$\text{FOR}_{\text{it}} = \pi_7 + \lambda_{71}\text{ROA}(-1)_{\text{it}} + \lambda_{72}\text{Q}(-1)_{\text{it}} + \lambda_{73}\text{LEV}_{\text{it}} + \lambda_{74}\text{SIZE}_{\text{it}} + \lambda_{75}\text{GRO}_{\text{it}} + \lambda_{76}\text{MARKET}_{\text{it}} + u_{7\text{it}} \quad (3.19)$$

Where $i$ and $t$ subscripts stand for firm and year and AC and RT denote agency costs and corporate risk-taking, respectively. ROA and Q are accounting and market firm performance respectively. GOV(–1), INS(–1) and FOR(–1) denote lagged government ownership, lagged insider ownership and lagged foreign ownership, respectively. The control variables include LEV for financial leverage, SIZE for firm size, AGE for firm age, GRO for firm growth, FIN for financial investment, ROA(–1) for prior return on assets and Q(–1) for prior Tobin's Q. The other control variables are dummies, including BIG4 for Big-4 audit company, MARKET for listing market and IND for industry classification. $u_1, u_2, u_3, ..., u_7$ are the error terms containing random disturbance and unobserved heterogeneity.

### *5.2.1 Diagnostic Issues*

An important result found in Section 5.1.6 is that ML estimation can be employed to estimate for the non-recursive model with correlated disturbances. Therefore, similar techniques of ML estimation are also used to estimate the non-recursive model. Specifically, all equations in the model use year-clustered standard errors and firm dummies. To reiterate, the year clustering is used to control for time effects that were believed to vary over the years in the context of Vietnam's stock market. Firm dummies are used to absorb the unobserved firm fixed effects that make firms heterogeneous. In addition, the covariance structure of error terms across equations is set to be unstructured. That is, error terms are free to co-vary, and there is no constraint imposed on the error terms in different equations (Roodman, 2011).

Another problem is that the non-recursive model must be identified in order to be estimated. Unlike the recursive model, according to Kline (2010), the non-recursive model is not always identified. Two conditions are needed to determine whether or not this model is identified, the order condition and the rank condition. First, the order condition requires that the number of excluded variables for each endogenous variable is equal to or greater than the total number of endogenous variables minus 1. In the non-recursive model of this book, all dependent variables are assumed to be endogenous, including agency costs, corporate risk-taking, ROA, Q, lagged government ownership, lagged insider ownership and lagged foreign ownership. Thus, there are 6 endogenous variables, and so the number of excluded variables in each equation must equal or exceed 5. It can be seen that this condition is met in the non-recursive model. For example, in Equation 3.15, the excluded variables consist of firm age, firm growth, financial investment, lagged Q, SOE, industry and market dummies, which total more than 5.

Additionally, the rank condition requires that 'each variable in a feedback loop has a unique pattern of direct effects on it from variables outside the loop' (Kline, 2010). However, there is no feedback loop in this sense in the non-recursive model of this book because the feedback effect of lagged, not current, firm performance on current ownership structure is examined. Instead, this model has a bow-pattern of disturbance correlation, as already mentioned in Section 3.1.2.3. For such a non-recursive model, the rank condition does not apply (Kline, 2010). Hence, the order condition can be considered necessary and sufficient to claim that the non-recursive model is identified.

### *5.2.2 Empirical Results*

The empirical results of the non-recursive model are reported in Table 5.7. To highlight the results found for the non-recursive model, the results described below are compared directly, where they are relevant, with those found previously for the recursive model.

#### *5.2.2.1 Direct Effect of Ownership Structure on Agency Costs and Corporate Risk-Taking (Equations 3.13 and 3.14)*

As expected, it is found in Equation 3.13 that the effect of lagged government ownership on the asset utilisation ratio measure of agency costs is significantly positive at the 1% level. The effects of lagged insider ownership and lagged foreign ownership are not significant at all. The coefficients of both financial leverage and firm size are negative and significant at the 1% level, whereas the effect of firm age is significantly positive at the same level. To compare, the estimated effects of the explanatory variables of agency costs in Equation 3.13 are not much different from those found in the FE and ML estimations of the recursive model.

Regarding Equation 3.14, both lagged government ownership and lagged insider ownership are found to have significantly positive relationships with corporate risk-taking at the 10% level, whereas lagged foreign ownership is not associated with corporate risk-taking. The positive effects of lagged government ownership and lagged insider ownership on corporate risk-taking are consistent with the results previously found in both FE and ML estimations of the recursive model. Regarding the control variables, firm growth is estimated to have a significantly positive relationship with corporate risk-taking. The insignificant influence of the other control variables, including financial leverage, Big-4 audit company and financial investment, on corporate risk-taking are similar to those found in the recursive model.

*Table 5.7* Results for non-recursive model

| *Dependent variable* | *AC* | *RT* | *ROA* | *Q* | *GOV* | *INS* | *FOR* |
|---|---|---|---|---|---|---|---|
| *Equation* | *(3.13)* | *(3.14)* | *(3.15)* | *(3.16)* | *(3.17)* | *(3.18)* | *(3.19)* |
| **AC** | | | –22.235 | –2.319 | | | |
| | | | (3.783)*** | (0.297)*** | | | |
| **RT** | | | 10.589 | –0.431 | | | |
| | | | (4.959)** | (0.126)*** | | | |
| **GOV(–1)** | 0.003 | 0.017 | –0.094 | 0.015 | | | |
| | (0.001)*** | (0.009)* | (0.128) | (0.007)** | | | |
| **INS(–1)** | 0.002 | 0.012 | 0.022 | 0.015 | | | |
| | (0.003) | (0.007)* | (0.109) | (0.007)** | | | |
| **FOR(–1)** | –0.001 | 0.003 | –0.101 | –0.006 | | | |
| | (0.002) | (0.002) | (0.105) | (0.006) | | | |
| **LEV** | –0.003 | –0.003 | –0.155 | –0.007 | –0.013 | | –0.074 |
| | (0.001)*** | (0.003) | (0.027)*** | (0.004)* | (0.017) | | (0.036)** |
| **SIZE** | –0.360 | | –9.131 | –0.847 | –0.404 | –1.122 | 3.377 |
| | (0.052)*** | | (1.959)*** | (0.098)*** | (0.153)*** | (1.651) | (1.017)*** |
| **AGE** | 0.049 | | | | | –0.010 | |
| | (0.009)*** | | | | | (0.227) | |
| **BIG4** | | 0.055 | –2.647 | 0.045 | | | |
| | | (0.076) | (0.445)*** | (0.039) | | | |
| **GRO** | | 0.001 | | | | 0.014 | 0.004 |
| | | (0.000)*** | | | | (0.005)*** | (0.006) |
| **FIN** | | 0.001 | | | | | |
| | | (0.002) | | | | | |

| | | | | | | | |
|---|---|---|---|---|---|---|---|
| ROA(−1) | | | −0.002 | | −0.082 | −0.034 | 0.185 |
| | | | (0.066) | | (0.049)* | (0.071) | (0.057)*** |
| Q(−1) | | | | −0.056 | 3.189 | −1.342 | −3.210 |
| | | | | (0.105) | (0.504)*** | (1.070) | (2.205) |
| MARET | | | | | | | −1.725 |
| | | | | | | | (2.040) |
| SOE | | | | | 52.782 | | |
| | | | | | (0.738)*** | | |
| _cons | 8.184 | 1.251 | 209.448 | 21.004 | 5.386 | 26.225 | −61.290 |
| | (1.183)*** | (0.385)*** | (43.260)*** | (2.388)*** | (2.854)* | (34.732) | (18.576)*** |
| N | 380 | 380 | 380 | 380 | 380 | 380 | 380 |

Notes: This table reports the results for the non-recursive model of this research using ML estimation. It examines whether past ownership structure has mediated effects on current firm performance via agency costs and corporate risk-taking, and simultaneously whether past firm performance has any feedback effects on current ownership structure. Variables are denoted as follows. AC is agency costs. RT is corporate risk-taking. GOV is government ownership. GOV(−1) is lagged government ownership. INS is insider ownership. INS(−1) is lagged insider ownership. FOR is foreign ownership. FOR(−1) is lagged foreign ownership. LEV is financial leverage. SIZE is firm size. AGE is firm age. BIG4 is Big-4 auditing company. GRO is firm growth. FIN is financial investment. ROA is return on assets. ROA(−1) is prior return on assets. Q is Tobin's Q. Q(−1) is prior Tobin's Q. MARKET is listing market. SOE is formerly state-owned enterprise. All equations are estimated simultaneously. Year-clustered robust standard errors are presented in parentheses under the coefficients. Covariance structures of disturbances are specified as unstructured (i.e. disturbances are free to be correlated). Estimates of industry dummies and firm dummies in all equations are excluded for brevity. The individual coefficient is statistically significant a: the *10%, **5% or ***1% significant levels.

#### 5.2.2.2 *Direct Effect of Ownership Structure, Agency Costs and Corporate Risk-Taking on Firm Performance (Equations 3.15–3.16)*

In terms of Equation 3.15 for ROA, strikingly, the coefficient on the asset utilisation ratio measure of agency costs turns out to be negative and significant at the 1% level. Holding the other variables constant, a 1% increase in the asset utilisation ratio (a decrease in agency costs) in one year is found to be followed by a drop of more than 0.2% in ROA in the next year. In contrast, corporate risk-taking is found to have a significantly positive relationship with accounting firm performance at the 5% level. For a 1% increase in corporate risk-taking one year, ROA is estimated to increase by more than 0.1% in the next year, holding all other variables constant.[3]

To compare with the ML estimation for the recursive model, the signs of the coefficients on agency costs and corporate risk-taking are opposite in the non-recursive model. Also, the significant direct effect of lagged insider ownership on ROA found in both GMM and ML estimations disappears in Equation 3.15. As for the influence of the control variables in Equation 3.15, the significantly negative effect of financial leverage on ROA remains similar. The influence of firm size and Big4 auditing on ROA is significantly positive as expected, while current-year ROA is not affected by previous-year ROA.

With respect to Equation 3.16, for the effect of the two mediating variables, the direct link between the asset utilisation ratio measure of agency costs on Q is negative and significant at the 1% level. Holding the other variables constant, an increase of 1% in the asset utilisation ratio is followed by a reduction of about 2.3% in Q. While corporate risk-taking is estimated to have no connection with Q in Equation 3.12 of the recursive model, its effect on Q in Equation 3.16 is negative and significant at the 1% level. Precisely, for an increase of 1% in the corporate risk-taking level, Q is expected to decrease by over 0.4% in value.

Also, in Equation 3.16, the direct effects of both lagged government ownership and lagged insider ownership on Q are significantly positive at the 5% level. The coefficient on financial leverage is negative and significant at the 10% level in Equation 3.16, while the coefficient on firm size is negative and significant at the 1% level. BIG4 and lagged Q do not have explanatory power on Q.

#### 5.2.2.3 *Feedback Effects of Firm Performance on Ownership Structure (Equations 3.17–3.19)*

As already mentioned, Research question 3 of this book examines whether the non-contemporaneous feedback effect of firm performance exists in the ownership–performance relationship. The results of Equation 3.17

show that current-year government ownership is affected by both previous-year accounting and market firm performance (ROA and Q) in opposite directions: the impact of ROA is significantly negative at the 10% level, whereas that of Q is positive and significant at the 1% level. Firm size has a significantly negative relationship with government ownership at the 1% level. As indicated by the coefficient on SOE, government ownership is significantly higher in former SOEs.

Unlike government ownership, it is found in Equation 3.18 that the change in insider ownership is independent of changes in prior firm performance (for both ROA and Q). The only explanatory variable that has significant influence on insider ownership is firm growth, of which the effect is positive and significant at the 1% level.

In terms of foreign ownership, the results of Equation 3.19 show that current-year foreign ownership is influenced by prior accounting firm performance (ROA). Financial leverage has a significantly negative association with foreign ownership at the 5% level. The impact of firm size on foreign ownership is positive and significant at the 1% level.

To sum up, when the feedback effect of performance is considered in the non-recursive model, the empirical results confirm that both agency costs and corporate risk-taking are two potential mediators in the ownership structure and firm performance. This is because the constituent paths of the indirect effects of past ownership structure (lagged government ownership and lagged insider ownership) on firm performance (both ROA and Q) are found to be significant. In addition, the empirical results of the non-recursive model suggest that there are significant non-contemporaneous/dynamic feedback effects of firm performance on government ownership and foreign ownership, but insider ownership is found to be exogenous from prior firm performance. The estimated coefficients from these results for the non-recursive model will help apply the Sobel test to calculating the total effect, as well as the direct and indirect effects, of ownership structure on firm performance (reported in Section 5.2.4).

### *5.2.3 Robustness Tests of Non-Recursive Model*

As already mentioned, all the estimations conducted for the recursive model in Section 5.1 can be regarded as the tests for the robustness of the non-recursive model to the extent that the hypothesised paths are examined under different model specifications and estimation techniques. This section presents further robustness tests to confirm whether or not the results obtained from ML estimation for the non-recursive model are largely sensitive to a change in the use of a variable. If there are no substantial changes in the estimates for the non-recursive model under these tests, the results of this model, as reported in Table 5.7, are considered to be robust.

### *5.2.3.1 Dropping One Measure of Firm Performance*

The first robustness test is to estimate the non-recursive model without market firm performance (Q). Equation 3.16 is dropped from the model. Likewise, Q is excluded from the ownership structure equations (Equations 3.17, 3.18 and 3.19). As a result, firm performance in the non-recursive model is proxied by an accounting measure (ROA) only. This robustness test is focused on the estimates of the variables of interest, including ownership variables, agency costs, corporate risk-taking and ROA.

The non-recursive model is then retested by ML estimation with the same techniques (i.e. firm dummies to control for unobserved firm fixed effects, year clustering to control for time fixed effects and disturbances in different equations allowed to be correlated). The results of this test are reported in Table 5.8.

As shown in Table 5.8, there are no substantial changes, with a few exceptions, in the estimates of all equations as compared to the full non-recursive model, i.e. the model with both ROA and Q. Among the variables of interest, the coefficient on lagged government ownership in the agency costs equation (Equation 3.13) remains the same in terms of both magnitude and significance level. This is also the case for the coefficients of lagged government ownership and lagged insider ownership in the corporate risk-taking equation (Equation 3.14). The effect of lagged foreign ownership on corporate risk-taking is still positive, but it becomes significant at the 5% level. In contrast, this significance level is not confirmed in the full model.

The effect of the asset utilisation measure of agency costs on ROA in Equation 3.15 remains significantly negative at the 1% level, but the magnitude of the effect is slightly smaller. The estimated impact of corporate risk-taking on ROA is still positive, but the effect is no longer confirmed at the 10% significance level. In the government ownership equation (Equation 3.17), the effect of previous-year ROA on current government ownership is no longer significant at the 10% level. Nevertheless, the signs and significance levels for the effect of previous-year ROA on lagged insider ownership and lagged foreign ownership do not change in comparison with the results for the full non-recursive model.

Therefore, it is plausible to argue that the estimated parameters of the non-recursive model are robust in relation to a change in estimation techniques. Specifically, when the non-recursive model is estimated as a system, the removal of Q from this system does not cause any significant changes in the estimates of the non-recursive model. This reveals that whether or not both measures of firm performance (ROA and/or Q) are used collectively or separately does not matter in obtaining robust estimates for the non-recursive model.

*Table 5.8* Results for non-recursive model without Q

| *Dependent variable* *Equation* | *AC* *(3.13)* | *RT* *(3.14)* | *ROA* *(3.15)* | *GOV* *(3.17)* | *INS* *(3.18)* | *FOR* *(3.19)* |
|---|---|---|---|---|---|---|
| **AC** | | | –21.228 | | | |
| | | | (2.517)*** | | | |
| **RT** | | | 8.011 | | | |
| | | | (11.684) | | | |
| **GOV(–1)** | 0.003 | 0.017 | –0.065 | | | |
| | (0.001)*** | (0.009)* | (0.167) | | | |
| **INS(–1)** | 0.002 | 0.012 | 0.054 | | | |
| | (0.003) | (0.007)* | (0.139) | | | |
| **FOR(–1)** | –0.000 | 0.004 | –0.089 | | | |
| | (0.002) | (0.002)** | (0.090) | | | |
| **LEV** | –0.003 | –0.003 | –0.161 | –0.018 | | –0.067 |
| | (0.001)*** | (0.003) | (0.033)*** | (0.020) | | (0.031)** |
| **SIZE** | –0.361 | | –8.717 | –0.603 | –1.224 | 3.543 |
| | (0.048)*** | | (1.834)*** | (0.422) | (1.628) | (0.772)*** |
| **AGE** | 0.050 | | | | 0.067 | |
| | (0.009)*** | | | | (0.159) | |
| **BIG4** | | 0.065 | –2.599 | | | |
| | | (0.052) | (0.522)*** | | | |
| **GRO** | | 0.001 | | | 0.013 | 0.001 |
| | | (0.000)*** | | | (0.005)** | (0.005) |

*(Continued)*

*Table 5.8* (Continued)

| *Dependent variable*<br>*Equation* | *AC*<br>*(3.13)* | *RT*<br>*(3.14)* | *ROA*<br>*(3.15)* | *GOV*<br>*(3.17)* | *INS*<br>*(3.18)* | *FOR*<br>*(3.19)* |
|---|---|---|---|---|---|---|
| **FIN** | | 0.004<br>(0.010) | | | | |
| **ROA(–1)** | | | 0.044<br>(0.078) | –0.024<br>(0.046) | –0.061<br>(0.067) | 0.118<br>(0.035)*** |
| **MARET** | | | | | | –3.220<br>(1.627)** |
| **SOE** | | | | 53.518<br>(1.120)*** | | |
| _cons | 8.236<br>(1.114)*** | 1.217<br>(0.417)*** | 203.854<br>(41.093)*** | 11.209<br>(7.394) | 27.036<br>(34.752) | –66.595<br>(14.896)*** |
| N | 380 | 380 | 380 | 380 | 380 | 380 |

Notes: This table reports the results of robustness tests of the non-recursive model exclusive of market firm performance (Q) using ML estimation. It tests for the sensitivity of the non-recursive model to a change in the firm performance variable. Variables are denoted as follows. AC is agency costs. RT is corporate risk-taking. GOV is government ownership. GOV(–1) is lagged government ownership. INS is insider ownership. INS(–1) is lagged insider ownership. FOR is foreign ownership. FOR(–1) is lagged foreign ownership. LEV is financial leverage. SIZE is firm size. AGE is firm age. BIG4 is Big-4 auditing company. GRO is firm growth. FIN is financial investment. ROA is return on assets. ROA(–1) is prior return on assets. MARKET is listing market. SOE is formerly state-owned enterprise. Year-clustered robust standard errors are presented in parentheses under the coefficients. Covariance structures of errors are specified as unstructured (i.e. disturbances are free to be correlated). Estimates of year and industry dummies are excluded from the table for brevity. The individual coefficient is statistically significant at the *10%, **5% or ***1% significant levels.

### *5.2.3.2 Using an Alternative Measure of Agency Costs*

Similar to the robustness check for agency costs in the recursive model, the operating expenses ratio (AC2) is also used to check for the robustness of agency costs in the non-recursive model. It is expected that the sign of the coefficient on AC2 is opposite to that of AC. When this model is re-estimated with AC2 in place of AC, the estimated links between the variables of interest are quite consistent (see Appendix A5.3a for details). However, a sharp difference is found in Equation 7a: the association between AC2 and firm performance is significantly negative, which is not opposite to the sign of AC on firm performance as expected. While the estimate for AC2 indicates that lower operating expenses (lower agency costs) are associated with improved firm performance, that for AC suggests that a higher asset utilisation ratio (lower agency costs) is associated with lower firm performance. Therefore, it is not certain whether the asset utilisation ratio (AC) really reflects agency costs.

In addition, there are two small variations found in the re-estimation of the non-recursive model in terms of the significance levels:

1. the negative effect of lagged insider ownership and the positive effect of lagged foreign ownership on agency costs become significant with AC2; and
2. in contrast, the positive effect of corporate risk-taking on firm performance loses its significance in the regression with AC2.

In practice, the estimated parameters for the relationship between agency costs and other variables are not entirely consistent when agency costs are defined by different measures. For example, Davidson and Singh (2003) found a significant association between insider ownership and agency costs proxied by the asset utilisation ratio, but this relationship disappears when agency costs are defined by the discretionary ratio or expenses ratio. Therefore, it can be said that the abovementioned variations are justifiable, but the contradictory results of AC and AC2 in explaining firm performance need further discussion, in particular for the asset utilisation measure of agency costs.

### *5.2.3.3 Using an Alternative Measure of Firm Performance*

Return on equity (ROE) is used as an alternative proxy of accounting firm performance. Like ROA, ROE is also based on net profit before tax. While the former is scaled by total assets, the latter is scaled by common equity. Both of them have the same expected signs of effects.

When ROE is employed instead of ROA in ML estimation, almost all the results are consistent with those found with ROA. The exceptions are that the impact of corporate risk-taking on firm performance in Equation 7a and that of lagged ROE on government ownership in Equation 8b become statistically insignificant. However, the economic inference remains the same since the signs of these effects do not change.

#### *5.2.3.4 Using an Alternative Measure of Financial Leverage*

Financial leverage is an important control variable in this book, and it is employed in nearly all equations of the non-recursive model. Hence, using another measure of financial leverage could be an appropriate option to check for the robustness of the estimated results of the non-recursive model. Consistent with the robustness test for the corporate risk-taking equation (Equation 3.11; see Section 5.1.5.3), the ratio of total liabilities over book value of common equity, or LEV2, is also employed to proxy financial leverage. LEV2 has the same expected signs as the first proxy of financial leverage (total liabilities over book value of total assets).

When the non-recursive model is retested using ML estimation with LEV2, the results show that there are almost no significant changes in the signs and the magnitude of effects of all variables, in comparison with ML estimation with the first proxy of financial leverage. Notably, the result for the associations between agency costs and firm performance is still highly consistent: the asset utilisation ratio measure of agency costs is significantly negatively correlated with firm performance.

Some small variations in significance levels are found for the effect of past insider ownership on current corporate risk-taking, that of corporate risk-taking on both measures of firm performance and that of prior accounting firm performance on current government ownership. Precisely, these effects become insignificant at the 10% level. However, their economic and predictive meanings are consistent, given the signs and magnitude of effects (see Appendix A5.3b for estimated results in detail).

In short, the results of the above additional tests show that the estimates for the non-recursive model are robust. The only notable exception is that the association between agency costs and firm performance is sensitive to the change in the proxy of agency costs. This fact requires further discussion of the appropriate measurement of agency costs (to be presented in Section 6.1).

### *5.2.4 Decomposition of Effects of Ownership Structure on Firm Performance*

The results of the non-recursive model have revealed that the mediating roles of agency costs and corporate risk-taking in the relationship between ownership structure and firm performance are potential since the paths defining the indirect effects of past ownership structure on current firm performance are found to be significant. Specifically, for the mediating role of agency costs, the two significant pathways are: (1) lagged government ownership → agency costs; and (2) agency costs → firm performance. Similarly, the two significant pathways for the mediating role of corporate risk-taking are: (1) lagged government ownership/lagged insider ownership → corporate risk-taking; and (2) corporate risk-taking → firm performance.

As a result, it is plausible to assume that the specific indirect effects of ownership structure via agency costs and corporate risk-taking are also significant. Under the product-of-coefficients approach, it is worth reiterating that the specific indirect effects are calculated by multiplying the coefficients on the constituent direct paths as listed above. To confirm whether the mediating roles of agency costs and corporate risk-taking are significant, the Sobel test (Sobel, 1982) is conducted to test for the magnitudes and significance levels of the specific indirect effects via agency costs and corporate risk-taking channels. Moreover, the estimates for the total effect of ownership structure on firm performance can also be obtained with Sobel testing.

### *5.2.4.1 Results for the Sobel Test*

Table 5.9 presents all types of effects and the decomposition of effects of past ownership structure on current firm performance, including direct effects, specific indirect effects and total effects, as well as the significance levels of these effects. In particular, the last two columns of this table report the testing results for the total effect of ownership structure, which answer Research question 4 of this book. It should be noted that the total effect is equal to the direct effects plus the specific indirect effects; and the total effect is considered as the ultimate effect of ownership structure on firm performance.

Columns (1) and (2) of Table 5.9 present the coefficients and significance levels of the *direct effects* of ownership structure on agency costs and corporate risk-taking, and those of ownership structure, agency costs and corporate risk-taking collectively on ROA and Q. The results are that all the coefficients and significance levels are the same as estimated previously in ML estimation for the non-recursive model (see Section 5.2.2 for the results in detail).

In columns (3) and (4), with respect to *the first specific indirect effect* channel via agency costs, the Sobel test shows that lagged government ownership has a significantly negative indirect effect through current agency costs on current firm performance. Through the mediating role of the asset utilisation measure of agency costs, a 1% increase in last-year government ownership is respectively associated with decreases of 0.076% and 0.793% in ROA and Q in this year; these results are both significant at the 1% level. In contrast, the indirect effects of past insider

*Table 5.9* Decomposition of effects of ownership structure on firm performance

| *Outcome variables* | *Direct effect (1)* | *Sig. level (2)* | *Indirect effect via AC (3)* | *Sig. level (4)* | *Indirect effect via RT (5)* | *Sig. level (6)* | *Total effect (7)* | *Sig. level (8)* |
|---|---|---|---|---|---|---|---|---|
| **AC** | | | | | | | | |
| GOV(–1) → AC | 0.342 | *** | – | – | – | – | 0.342 | *** |
| INS(–1) → AC | 0.158 | – | – | – | – | – | 0.158 | – |
| FOR(–1) → AC | –0.076 | – | – | – | – | – | –0.076 | – |
| **RT** | | | | | | | | |
| GOV(–1) → RT | 1.702 | * | – | – | – | – | 1.702 | *** |
| INS(–1) → RT | 1.225 | * | – | – | – | – | 1.225 | * |
| FOR(–1) → RT | 0.308 | – | – | – | – | – | 0.308 | – |
| **ROA** | | | | | | | | |
| GOV(–1) → ROA | –0.094 | – | –0.076 | *** | 0.180 | – | 0.009 | – |
| INS(–1) → ROA | 0.021 | – | –0.035 | – | 0.129 | * | 0.116 | *** |
| FOR(–1) → ROA | –0.100 | – | 0.017 | – | 0.032 | – | –0.050 | – |
| AC → ROA | –0.222 | *** | – | – | – | – | –0.222 | *** |
| RT → ROA | 0.105 | ** | – | – | – | – | 0.105 | ** |
| **Q** | | | | | | | | |
| GOV(–1) → Q | 1.545 | ** | –0.793 | *** | –0.733 | – | 0.018 | – |
| INS(–1) → Q | 1.515 | * | –0.368 | – | –0.528 | *** | 0.619 | *** |
| FOR(–1) → Q | –0.620 | – | 0.177 | – | –0.132 | – | –0.575 | *** |
| AC → Q | –2.319 | *** | – | – | – | – | –2.319 | *** |
| RT → Q | –0.431 | *** | – | – | – | – | –0.431 | *** |

Notes: This table reports the calculation of direct effects, specific indirect effects and total effects of ownership structure on firm performance using Sobel tests (Sobel, 1982, 1986). The main purpose of these tests is to calculate the specific indirect effects and the total effects of ownership structure on firm performance. Variables are denoted as follows. AC is agency costs (asset utilization ratio). RT is corporate risk-taking. ROA is return on assets. Q is Tobin's Q. GOV(–1) is lagged government ownership. INS(–1) is lagged insider ownership. FOR(–1) is lagged foreign ownership. All coefficients are standardised into percentage values. The significance levels are *10%, **5% or ***1% respectively.

ownership and past foreign ownership on current firm performance are not significant, and these results are consistent with the estimation results for the non-recursive model. Overall, the above results confirm the estimation results for the non-recursive model reported in Section 5.2.2, that agency costs play a mediating role in the relationship between past government ownership and current firm performance. However, it is not clear whether this mediating role of agency costs is negative or positive, due to the opposite signs of the two proxies of agency costs on firm performance, as already discussed in Section 5.2.3.2.

In columns (5) and (6), for *the second specific indirect effect* channel via corporate risk-taking, the Sobel test result shows that past insider ownership has a significant indirect effect on current firm performance via current corporate risk-taking. Specifically, the indirect effect via the corporate risk-taking channel of last-year insider ownership on current-year ROA is significantly positive at the 10% level, while that on current-year Q is negative and significant at the 1% level (the magnitude of these effects are 0.129 and –0.528 respectively). Like the case of lagged government ownership in the first mediating channel, this result confirms the estimation results of the non-recursive model, that corporate risk-taking plays a mediating role in the relationship between past insider ownership and current firm performance.

However, the Sobel test result for the specific indirect effect of lagged government ownership through corporate risk-taking is not as expected: this indirect effect is not significant at the 10% level. As a result, the proposition mentioned in Section 5.2.2, that corporate risk-taking plays a mediating role in the relationship between lagged government ownership and firm performance, is not supported.

Likewise, lagged foreign ownership is reported to have no significant indirect effect via the corporate risk-taking channel on firm performance, and this indirect effect is the smallest among the three types of ownership structure employed in this book (as shown by the values of the coefficients). These results show signs of little or no contribution of foreign ownership to firm performance.

In the last two columns of Table 5.9 (column (7) and column (8)), it can be observed that lagged insider ownership has a significantly positive total effect on both measures of firm performance at the 1% level. A 1% increase in insider ownership in one year is respectively followed by increases of 0.116% in ROA and 0.619% in Q in the next year. Thus, the magnitude of this effect on market firm performance is about six times larger than that on accounting firm performance.

In contrast, the total effect of lagged government ownership on firm performance is weak and insignificant (0.009% and 0.018% on ROA and Q, respectively). Hence, even if these effects were statistically significant at the 10% level, the total effects of past government ownership on current firm performance would not be economically meaningful.

The coefficients for the total effect of lagged foreign ownership on both current ROA and current Q are negative, but only the negative effect on Q is significant (at the 1% level). A 1% increase in the shareholdings of foreign investors in one year results in a reduction of 0.575% in Q in the next year. Notably, although the specific indirect effects of lagged foreign ownership are not significant, the total effect of lagged foreign ownership on current Q is still significant.

The driver for the total effect of past insider ownership on current ROA is the indirect effect through the corporate risk-taking channel, whereas this channel constitutes a considerable impediment to the total effect of past insider ownership on current Q. Rather, the total effect of past insider ownership on current market performance is strongly driven by the direct effect of current insider ownership.

#### *5.2.4.2 Bootstrapped Standard Errors of the Total Effects of Ownership Structure*

With respect to the standard errors obtained in the Sobel tests, it is assumed that the sampling distributions of the total indirect effect and specific indirect effects are normal (Preacher and Hayes, 2008). This is because Sobel (1982) used large samples to derive the standard errors of the indirect effects (MacKinnon, 2012, Preacher and Hayes, 2008). Therefore, if this assumption is not met in reality, the reliability of the estimates of standard errors of the total effect of ownership structure reported in the previous section might be affected because the total effect includes the total indirect effect. A solution in case the total indirect effect is not normal in distribution is to apply the bootstrapping method (Shrout & Bolger, cited in Preacher and Hayes, 2008).

Therefore, the bootstrapping method is applied in this book to retest the standard errors, and hence the significance level, of the total effect of ownership structure on firm performance. Accordingly, the same command of the Sobel test to calculate the total effect of ownership structure on firm performance is used, but the difference is that the syntax to obtain the bootstrap standard error of this effect is added. It is expected that the significance levels obtained under this bootstrapping method will remain the same as those already reported in Table 5.9. This can be regarded as a test for the robustness of the significance levels of the total effect of ownership structure.

A matter of concern in bootstrapping is the number of replications. This is preferably selected at 1000 at least in many studies. If bootstrapping is used with maximum likelihood regression (ML), however, a smaller number of 100 replications is typically computed in real-world studies that employ the ML approach (Pattengale et al., 2010). These authors find that bootstrapping computations in ML typically stop after 100–500 replications, which is the *stopping criterion*. According to

Pattengale et al. (2010), ML inference is too computationally demanding and expensive, to assess the impact of the number of replications used in bootstrapping on the quality of the supporting values. Thus, under the abovementioned stopping range of 100–500 replications, robust bootstrapping under ML inference becomes computationally practical for most datasets.

In this book, therefore, the number of replications in bootstrapping is set at 100 when performing the robustness test for the significance levels of the total effect of ownership structure on firm performance.[4] The bootstrapping results show that all the coefficients and significance levels of ownership structure on firm performance are consistent with those calculated previously in Table 5.9, except for a slight variation in the value of the coefficients. The details are presented in Table 5.10.

As shown in Table 5.10, the significance levels of all three types of ownership structure on ROA and Q respectively remain the same as already reported in the previous Sobel tests. Therefore, the normality assumption of the standard errors of the total effect of ownership structure can be made in this study. Since the total effect includes the specific indirect effects, it is also plausible to assume that the standard errors of the specific indirect effects via agency costs and corporate risk-taking are also normally distributed. As a result, it can be said that the results of the effect decomposition reported in Table 5.9 are sufficiently reliable.

## 5.3 Summary and Conclusions

This chapter reports the estimation results for both the recursive and non-recursive mediation models developed in this book. The former model is first estimated by the causal-steps approach, where the individual paths of the relationship are tested separately and then by maximum likelihood estimation to check for robustness and to retest the recursive model with correlated error terms in different equations. A mediating role of agency costs is found for the relationship between previous-year government ownership and current-year firm performance. This result is robust across different model specifications of the recursive model. In addition, a mediating role of corporate risk-taking is confirmed when agency costs and corporate risk-taking are treated as endogenous. Specifically, corporate risk-taking is found to negatively mediate the effects of previous-year government ownership and previous-year insider ownership on current-year ROA. No mediating roles of agency costs and corporate risk-taking are found for the relationship between ownership structure and Q.

The non-recursive model is estimated simultaneously using the maximum likelihood method, which allows the cross-equation correlation of disturbances, and takes into account the non-contemporaneous interdependence between ownership structure and firm performance. A mediating role of agency costs is confirmed in the non-recursive model

*Table 5.10* Bootstrapping results for the total effect of ownership structure on firm performance

| *Outcome variables* | *Observed Coefficient* | *Bootstrapping SE* | *Significance level* | *Number of set–up replications* | *Number of complete replications* |
|---|---|---|---|---|---|
| **ROA** | | | | | |
| GOV(–1) → ROA | 0.010 | 0.103 | – | 100 | 79 |
| INS(–1) → ROA | 0.116 | 0.025 | *** | 100 | 79 |
| FOR(–1) → ROA | –0.050 | 0.042 | – | 100 | 79 |
| **Q** | | | | | |
| GOV(–1) → Q | 0.019 | 0.090 | – | 100 | 79 |
| INS(–1) → Q | 0.618 | 0.184 | *** | 100 | 80 |
| FOR(–1) → Q | –0.575 | 0.187 | *** | 100 | 80 |

Notes: This table presents the estimates of the total effect of ownership structure on firm performance using the bootstrapping method. The main purpose is to check for the robustness of the significance level of the total effect of ownership structure as reported previously in Table 5.9. The number of set-up replications is the number of bootstrap replicates assigned to the bootstrap command. The number of complete replications is the actual bootstrap replicates that are successfully performed via the bootstrap command. The estimates of standard errors are based on complete replications only.

for the relationship between previous-year government ownership and current-year firm performance. Although there is strong evidence that prior government ownership helps mitigate agency costs, it is not certain whether the mediating effect of agency costs is positive or negative, because the sign of the asset utilisation measure of agency costs is not consistent with that of the operating expenses measure of agency costs. However, a mediating role of corporate risk-taking is confirmed for the relationship between previous-year insider ownership and current-year firm performance.

Nevertheless, the results of the Sobel tests show that the total effect of prior government ownership on current firm performance is not significant at all. On the other hand, previous-year insider ownership is found to have a significantly positive effect on both current-year firm performance measures. The total effect for previous-year foreign ownership is not meaningful with ROA, but it is negative for Q in the current year. In addition, it is found that the positive effect of insider ownership on firm performance relies more on the corporate risk-taking channel than the agency costs channel.

It is concluded that this mediation and dynamic approach, which takes into account the non-contemporaneous interrelationship between ownership structure and firm performance, helps obtain a proper understanding of the underlying mechanisms through which the effects of the former are transmitted to the latter. Moreover, the decomposition of effects has provided clear insight into each type of effect that can be the drivers of or barriers to the total effect of ownership structure on firm performance.

## Notes

1 Due to space limitation, the results of this estimation are not reported in this book, but are available upon request to the first author. This is also applied to the estimates in Sections 5.1.5.3, 5.1.6.1 and 5.2.3.3.

2 Some estimates were not produced regardless of whether the *collapse* option was alternatively imposed on the transformed equation, level equation or both equations in the system dynamic GMM estimation.

3 The unit values in agency costs and corporate risk-taking are times and so an increase of 1 in agency costs or corporate risk-taking means a 100% increase; while those of ROA are in percentages.

4 In this study, with the number of replications set at 100, it takes from 4 to 5 consecutive days to complete the computation of the bootstrapping for only one total effect of ownership structure.

## References

Acock, A. C. 2013. *Discovering structural equation modeling using stata*, College Station, Texas: Stata Press.

Ang, J. S., Cole, R. A. & Lin, J. W. 2000. Agency costs and ownership structure. *The Journal of Finance*, 55, 81–106.

Antonakis, J., Bendahan, S., Jacquart, P. & Lalive, R. 2010. On making causal claims: A review and recommendations. *The Leadership Quarterly*, 21, 1086–1120.

Baron, R. M. & Kenny, D. A. 1986. The moderator-mediator variable distinction in social psychological research: Conceptual, strategic, and statistical considerations. *Journal of Personality and Social Psychology*, 51, 1173–1182.

Davidson, W. N. & Singh, M. 2003. Agency costs, ownership structure and corporate governance mechanisms. *Journal of Banking & Finance*, 27, 793–816.

De Hoyos, R. E. & Sarafidis, V. 2006. Testing for cross-sectional dependence in panel-data models. *Stata Journal*, 6, 482–496.

Hassan, H., Islam, S. M. N. & Rashid, K. 2018. *Corporate governance, agency theory and firm value: advanced econometric analysis and empirical evidence*, Nova Science Publishers.

Hu, Y. & Izumida, S. 2008. Ownership concentration and corporate performance: A causal analysis with Japanese panel data. *Corporate Governance: An International Review*, 16, 342–358.

Kline, R. B. 2010. *Principles and practice of structural equation modeling*, New York: Guilford Press.

MacKinnon, D. 2012. *Introduction to statistical mediation analysis*, Hoboken: Taylor and Francis.

Mcknight, P. J. & Weir, C. 2009. Agency costs, corporate governance mechanisms and ownership structure in large UK publicly quoted companies: A panel data analysis. *Quarterly Review of Economics and Finance*, 49, 139–158.

Pattengale, N. D., Alipour, M., Bininda-Emonds, O. R. P., Moret, B. M. E. & Stamatakis, A. 2010. How many bootstrap replicates are necessary? *Journal of Computational Biology*, 17, 337–354.

Preacher, K. J. & Hayes, A. F. 2008. Asymptotic and resampling strategies for assessing and comparing indirect effects in multiple mediator models. *Behavior Research Methods*, 40, 879–891.

Roodman, D. 2009. How to do xtabond2: An introduction to difference and system GMM in Stata. *Stata Journal*, 9, 86–136.

Roodman, D. 2011. Fitting fully observed recursive mixed-process models with cmp. *Stata Journal*, 11, 159–206.

Sobel, M. E. 1982. Asymptotic confidence intervals for indirect effects in structural equation models. *Sociological Methodology*. Washington DC: American Sociology Association, Jossey-Bass Publishers.

# 6 Discussion of Implications

## Ownership Structure, Agency Cost, Corporate Risk-Taking and Firm Performance

This discussion is based on the estimated results already reported in Chapter 5, which are summarised in Table 6.1.

### 6.1 Agency Costs in the Relationship between Ownership Structure and Firm Performance

It is well established in agency theory that agency costs are a consequence of the agency conflicts within firms (Fama and Jensen, 1983, Jensen and Meckling, 1976, Berle and Means, 1932) and a certain structure of ownership can be utilised to reduce these agency problems (Jensen and Meckling, 1976, Agrawal and Knoeber, 1996). Hence, it is implied in prior studies that there are robust links between equity ownership and agency costs. In turn, agency costs are related to firm performance (Davidson and Singh, 2003, Ang et al., 2000). Taken together, ownership structure may affect firm performance by determining the severity of agency conflicts within a firm (Brown et al., 2011). Therefore, it is plausible to hypothesise a mediating role of agency costs in the relationship between ownership and firm performance, as depicted in the out-of-equilibrium phenomenon/model (Tan, 2009, Hermalin and Weisbach, 2003).

Many empirical studies have been undertaken to examine the impact of agency costs on a range of finance-related choices such as 'capital structure, maturity structure, dividend policy and executive compensation' (Ang et al., 2000). However, few studies have investigated the intervening role of agency costs in the equity ownership–performance relationship, while others only investigate separately the individual relationships between ownership structure and agency costs, or between agency costs and firm performance.

While most of the relevant literature focuses on the direct link between equity ownership and agency costs, Le and Buck (2011) provide evidence that agency costs positively mediate the effect of government ownership on the accounting performance of Chinese listed firms, and hence government ownership is not a burden but a 'strategic asset' of firms.

DOI: 10.4324/9781003255741-6

*Table 6.1* Summary of main results for discussion

| *Outcome variables* | *Direct effect* | *Indirect effect via AC* | *Indirect effect via RT* | *Total effect* |
|---|---|---|---|---|
| **AC** | | | | |
| GOV(–1) → AC | 0.342*** | – | – | 0.342*** |
| INS(–1) → AC | 0.158 | – | – | 0.158 |
| FOR(–1) → AC | -0.076 | – | – | -0.076 |
| **RT** | | | | |
| GOV(–1) → RT | 1.702* | – | – | 1.702*** |
| INS(–1) → RT | 1.225* | – | – | 1.225* |
| FOR(–1) → RT | 0.308 | – | – | 0.308 |
| **ROA** | | | | |
| GOV(–1) → ROA | -0.094 | -0.076*** | 0.180 | 0.009 |
| INS(–1) → ROA | 0.021 | -0.035 | 0.129* | 0.116*** |
| FOR(–1) → ROA | -0.100 | 0.017 | 0.032 | -0.050 |
| AC → ROA | -0.222*** | – | – | -0.222*** |
| RT → ROA | 0.105** | – | – | 0.105** |
| **Q** | | | | |
| GOV(–1) → Q | 1.545** | -0.793*** | -0.733 | 0.018 |
| INS(–1) → Q | 1.515* | -0.368 | -0.528*** | 0.619*** |
| FOR(–1) → Q | -0.620 | 0.177 | -0.132 | -0.575*** |
| AC → Q | -2.319*** | – | – | -2.319*** |
| RT → Q | -0.431*** | – | – | -0.431*** |
| **GOV** | | | | |
| ROA(–1) → GOV | -0.082* | – | – | – |
| Q(–1) → GOV | 0.031*** | – | – | – |
| **INS** | | | – | – |
| ROA(–1) → INS | -0.034 | – | – | – |
| Q(–1) → INS | -0.013 | – | – | – |
| **FOR** | | | | |
| ROA(–1) → FOR | 0.185*** | – | – | – |
| Q(–1) → FOR | -0.032 | – | – | – |

Notes: This table summarises all the main results of this book, which are referred to for discussion of implications of the relationship among ownership structure, agency costs, corporate risk-taking and firm performance. Variables are denoted as follows. AC is agency costs (asset utilisation ratio). RT is corporate risk-taking. GOV is government ownership. GOV(–1) is lagged government ownership. INS is insider ownership. INS(–1) is lagged insider ownership. FOR is foreign ownership. FOR(–1) is lagged foreign ownership. ROA is return on assets. ROA(-1) is prior return on assets. Q is Tobin's Q. Q(–1) is prior Tobin's Q. All coefficients are standardised into percentage values. The significance levels are *10%, **5% or ***1%, respectively.

The authors believe that such an intervening role of agency costs can be tested for similar markets such as Vietnam and India.

In this book, a similar result is found *in the recursive model* for a positive mediating role of agency costs in the relationship between government ownership (but not insider ownership or foreign ownership) and the accounting performance of Vietnamese listed firms. Specifically, a higher percentage of government ownership in one year is followed by a lower level of agency costs in the next year, and lower agency costs are associated with an improved accounting firm performance level in the same year (whereas this mechanism is not found for market firm performance). This finding is consistent regardless of whether agency costs are treated as exogenous or endogenous, and it is robust for both proxies for agency costs.

Therefore, there is primary evidence to claim that agency costs mediate the positive effect of previous government ownership on the current performance of Vietnam's listed firms. While Le and Buck (2011) find a positive mediating role of agency costs in the government ownership–accounting firm performance relationship from a static point of view, this book obtains the same finding from a dynamic perspective. Therefore, it can be argued that government ownership, either in the past or the current period, can be employed as an effective mechanism to mitigate agency problems in listed firms in the current period, because government ownership helps reduce agency costs in these firms. However, this mechanism is confirmed only for the recursive model, where the non-contemporaneous feedback effect of firm performance is not yet considered.

*In the non-recursive model*, which accounts for the dynamic feedback effect of firm performance on ownership structure, a positive mediating role of agency costs in government ownership and firm performance is not completely verified, because the coefficients of the two proxies for agency costs in relation to firm performance have opposite signs. The asset utilisation ratio measure of agency costs is found to have a negative relationship with firm performance, indicating that a higher asset utilisation ratio (and presumably lower agency costs) is associated with lower firm performance, and vice versa. This logic appears to be unreasonable if we believe that the asset utilisation ratio truly reflects agency costs because it runs counter to the generally accepted perception in corporate governance literature that lower agency costs imply higher firm performance. On the contrary, it is found (as reported in Section 5.2.3.2) that the operating expense ratio measure of agency costs confirms this mechanism: lower agency costs (or a lower operating expense ratio) are associated with higher firm performance.

Hence, it is suggested from this study that the asset utilisation ratio may not be a good proxy for agency costs. As an indirect measure of agency costs, a higher asset utilisation ratio does not necessarily mean lower agency costs and hence higher firm performance. In fact, the asset utilisation ratio is also termed the *asset turnover ratio* in the corporate finance literature; this is a component of the return on assets (ROA) and calculated as the ratio of sales over assets (sales/assets). The other component is net profit margin, which is calculated as the ratio of net income over sales (net income/sales). Hence, the formula for ROA is: ROA = (net income/sales) × (sales/assets).

Therefore, it can be seen that ROA depends not only on the asset turnover ratio, but also on the net profit margin ratio. There are some scenarios where the former ratio and ROA have a negative relationship. For example, when holding constant the asset base of the firm, the above formula shows that an increase in sales increases the asset turnover ratio, but simultaneously decreases the profit margin ratio, if net income is also held constant. Consequently, an increase in the asset turnover tends to be offset by a simultaneous reduction in the net profit margin, which leads to no improvement in ROA.

Assuming further that the net profit is not enhanced but reduced over time, then a large reduction in the net profit margin ratio can occur along with an increase in sales; consequently, an improved asset turnover ratio would ultimately result in a decrease in ROA. On the contrary, if assets of the firm are expanded at a higher rate than an increase in sales in the same fiscal year, then the asset turnover ratio tends to be lower. But the values of ROA can remain positive if the net profit margin is improved more than enough to drive up ROA. This might be the case for Vietnamese listed firms, because expanding capital into new business areas was quite common in these firms in the period of study, as noted in Section 1.3.3, not to mention the excessive reliance of these firms on borrowings, as noted in Section 4.3.1. Thus, the important implication is that the expansion in assets should come along with effective asset management in order to enhance the profit margin of the firm.

Therefore, it is plausible to argue that a negative association between the asset utilisation measure of agency costs and firm performance can occur. The asset utilisation ratio is commonly understood as a measure of firm efficiency. However, as Sun et al. (2002) pointed out, a higher level of firm performance does not necessarily imply a higher level of firm efficiency. Consequently, it is possible that the mediating role of agency costs in the ownership–performance relationship is negative if agency costs are defined as the asset utilisation ratio, as found in this book.

This mismatch between the two measures of agency costs (i.e. the asset utilisation ratio and the operating expense ratio) is also reported in previous literature. For example, Davidson and Singh (2003) find that the asset utilisation ratio is significantly affected by insider ownership, but the operating expense ratio is not affected at all by insider ownership. Hence, an appropriate proxy for agency costs should be selected with due care in further research on corporate finance and corporate governance. A direct measure of agency costs, such as the operating expense ratio, could be a better option.

Relying on the direct measure of agency costs (i.e. the operating expense ratio), it can be claimed that agency costs positively mediate the effect of past government ownership on current firm performance in the context of a developing and transition economy like Vietnam. This is because the results with the operating expense ratio are robust in both the recursive and non-recursive models with different model specifications. Specifically, a higher level of previous-year government ownership is associated with a lower level of current-year operating expenses, and a lower level of current-year operating expenses in turn is associated with a higher level of current-year firm performance. As mentioned earlier, therefore, it is suggested that government ownership can be employed as an internal corporate governance mechanism to mitigate agency problems in listed firms.

In this regard, as already noted in Chapter 1, Vietnam's stock markets are characterised by weak investor protection and concentrated government ownership. Brown et al. (2011) mention that concentrated ownership is a mechanism that protects small investors. As a large shareholder in the firm, therefore, it is possible that government ownership plays an effective role in minimising the conflict of interests between small investors and top managers, resulting in lower agency costs and hence better firm performance. In addition, government may use its power to support firms' operations by manipulating administrative instruments such as market entry regulations, taxation and loans decisions, hence helping firms to increase revenues and reduce costs, thus improving firm performance (Lu, cited in Le and Buck, 2011).

Nevertheless, with respect to the indirect measure of agency costs (i.e. the asset utilisation ratio), the implication is that an increase in government ownership in the previous year can help increase the asset turnover of the firm; however, this in turn can result in lower firm performance, due to the negative association with the asset turnover ratio and firm performance, as discussed earlier. Consequently, the positive effect of government ownership on firm performance through mitigating operating expenses tends to be cancelled out by the negative effect of government ownership on firm performance through the asset turnover ratio channel. Therefore, an increase in the proportion of government ownership in one year might not ultimately lead to improved firm performance in the following year.

Taken together, it can be inferred from this study that the Vietnamese Government could play a role in mitigating the agency conflicts in listed firms by increasing its shareholding in these firms and/or retaining significant ownership in privatised SOEs. However, this action alone cannot guarantee an improvement in firm performance. The expansion in assets of the firms should be closely monitored and in reference to the increase in sales, so that the expanded assets are utilised efficiently. Meanwhile, it is indicated that board members (insiders) and foreign investors are not very helpful in reducing agency costs in listed firms, because the mediating role of agency costs is not found in the relationships between them and firm performance.

## 6.2 Corporate Risk-Taking in the Relationship between Ownership Structure and Firm Performance

As previously discussed, one of the agency problems is the difference in the risk preferences of shareholders, and it is well established in risk theories that there are three typical risk attitudes in this aspect: risk-averse, risk-neutral and risk-seeking (Mcguigan et al., 2005, Dias and Mroczkowski, 2012). For example, it is hypothesised in the literature that managers are risk-averse, since their human capital in firms is not diversified (Himmelberg et al., 1999). It is thus plausible to assume that these attitudes could have an impact on the risk-taking behaviours of the firm. In addition, the trade-off between risk and return is specified in corporate risk management theories, whereby higher risk might be associated with a higher return, and vice versa (Gordon et al., 2009, Drever et al., 2007). As a result, a continual link between equity ownership structure and corporate risk-taking and return can be conceptualised, where corporate risk-taking transmits the effect of ownership structure on firm performance.

However, knowledge of the mediating role of corporate risk-taking is quite limited in the literature. Almost all prior empirical studies under review in this book merely examine one side of the connection: between ownership structure and corporate risk-taking, such as in Guner and Kursat (2002) and Kim (2011); or between corporate risk-taking and firm performance, such as in John et al. (2008).

Despite an attempt to uncover this link, this book cannot confirm the mediating role of corporate risk-taking in the relationship between past government ownership and current firm performance. However, it is found that the relationship between lagged government ownership and corporate risk-taking is significantly positive and consistent across the different model specifications. An interpretation of this outcome is that government shareholders are risk-seeking in Vietnam's stock markets. The risk-seeking behaviour of government ownership is consistent with the results found by Guner and Kursat (2002) for Turkish listed firms. The underlying incentives for government shareholders to prefer risk may be that the government can administratively push firms to be profitable, to demonstrate the efficiency of economic reforms and to facilitate government selling of firms' shares at higher prices (Green & Liu, cited in Le & Buck 2011). However, the risk-seeking preference of government shareholders in the Vietnamese context does not enhance the performance of listed firms. Although the path between corporate risk-taking and firm performance is significant, the Sobel test results show that the indirect effect of government ownership on firm performance through corporate risk-taking is not meaningful at all.

However, a mediating role of corporate risk-taking is confirmed for the relationship between past insider ownership and current firm performance.

Higher insider ownership in one year is found to be associated with higher corporate risk-taking in the following year, which is contradictory to the common assumption in the literature that insider shareholders are risk-averse. Additionally, this finding is not consistent with the argument in John et al. (2008) that insiders tend to avoid corporate risk-taking in countries with low investor protection to protect their expected private benefits. In the conditions of a transition economy like Vietnam, on the contrary, the pressure on preserving the jobs of insider shareholders is perhaps high as a consequence of the ongoing privatisation programs and economic reforms. Thus, insiders may choose to take risks if their jobs are not secure (Tirole, 2006).

Interestingly, the risk-taking behaviour of insider ownership is found to enhance accounting performance, but to reduce the market performance of firms. Hence, the 'higher risk–higher return' assumption is valid for insider ownership in its relationship with accounting performance. In contrast, a higher level of risk undertaken by insiders leads to a lower market value of the firm. The 'higher risk – lower return' assumption is thus implied in the insider ownership–market performance relationship. This finding confirms the argument in Chapter 1 that the risk-seeking preference is quite common among Vietnam's listed firms, resulting in significant deterioration of the market values of corporations during the study period.

The above two contrasting interpretations of the role of corporate risk-taking in the relationship between insider ownership and firm performance are based on the opposite impacts of corporate risk-taking on firm performance: corporate risk-taking is beneficial to accounting firm performance, but it is detrimental to market firm performance. This fact may stem from the ability of insiders to control for risks. It can be argued that board members/insiders can effectively manage the firm-specific risks associated with the operating performance of their firm. For example, financial risk is a common type of this category that encompasses the risks associated with borrowed funds or leverage by a firm, which is subject to unexpected changes in interest rates. The use of debt makes the firm vulnerable to unexpected increases in interest rates. Thus, the higher the level of the debt ratio, the greater the financial risk due to the leverage effect, which can magnify 'the impact of variability of firm returns' (Hardaker et al., 2004). Managers can avoid this risk by issuing shares on stock markets instead of borrowing funds from banks, thus keeping the operating performance under control.

As for market performance, however, it is often hard to avoid market risk from the market price of assets. For instance, shares prices on stock markets are normally associated with unpredictable fluctuations over time. In practice, unexpected changes in market prices can be managed using hedging instruments or derivative securities such as stock options or futures. Unfortunately, these instruments as such have not yet been introduced on Vietnam's stock markets, and hence insiders lack the instruments to efficiently manage market risks. During the period of the study from 2008 to 2012, the Vietnamese stock market experienced a substantial downturn and volatility. As a result, without an efficient exercise of risk management, it is reasonable to conclude that greater involvement in risk by insider shareholders resulted in a negative effect on the market performance of firms.

Regarding foreign ownership, corporate risk-taking does not play any significant role in the relationship between past foreign ownership and current firm performance. Although foreign ownership is found to have a risk-seeking attitude in the recursive model under causal-steps regression, the path between corporate risk-taking and firm performance is not established in this model. The relationship between past foreign ownership and current corporate risk-taking disappears in the non-recursive model. This demonstrates that the risk-seeking behaviour of foreign ownership found in the recursive model is a spurious result, and the direct impact of foreign ownership on corporate risk-taking is strongly affected by dynamic endogeneity problems (i.e. when the dynamic feedback effect of firm performance is accounted for in the non-recursive model). Thus, foreign shareholders are likely to be risk-neutral investors in Vietnamese listed firms. This is perhaps because foreign shareholders have short-term investment perspectives in frontier stock markets like Vietnam, particularly when they do not have controlling stakes in the firm. Hence, they are not willing to take much risk. In a developed market like Korea, by contrast, the shareholding of foreign investors encourages risk-taking behaviour of firms (Kim, 2011).

Overall, it can be said that there are large differences in the mediating role of corporate risk-taking in the relationship between different forms of ownership structure and firm performance. Risk-taking behaviours are not helpful in transmitting any significant effect of previous-year government ownership on current-year firm performance. Also, foreign investors appear to be indifferent to risk, or risk-neutral, in Vietnam's stock markets. The only form of ownership structure investigated in this book that is significantly mediated by corporate risk-taking is lagged insider ownership. Once market risk management is efficiently implemented by board members, the corporate risk-taking channel may be a driver for improving firm performance in terms of both accounting-based and market-based indicators.

## 6.3 Non-Contemporaneous Feedback Effect of Firm Performance on Ownership Structure

As already discussed, it is indicated in the corporate and finance literature that ownership structure and firm performance are endogenously determined, implying that the feedback effect of the latter on the former should not be ignored (Bhagat and Bolton, 2008, Firth and Rui, 2012). In a broader sense, there is potential interdependence between the constructs of corporate governance, including ownership structure and firm performance (Brown et al., 2011, Bhagat and Jefferis, 2002). The endogeneity in the ownership–firm performance relationship results from three sources: simultaneity, unobserved heterogeneity, and dynamic nature, although the dynamic aspect of endogeneity is often ignored in prior studies (Wintoki et al., 2012). To put this another way, most prior studies have investigated the interdependence between ownership structure and firm performance from a static point of view, on the basis of the simultaneity and/or unobserved heterogeneity mentioned above. Under such an approach, a contemporaneous feedback effect of firm performance on some types of ownership structure is not found, such as ownership concentration in the Japanese context (Hu and Izumida, 2008) or government ownership and foreign ownership in Chinese listed firms (Tian and Estrin, 2008, Wei et al., 2005).

From a dynamic perspective and in the mediation context, this book finds that past firm performance has a significant relationship with current government ownership. Specifically, it is found that a lower level of accounting performance in one year is followed by a higher level of government ownership in the next year. One interpretation of this negative association is that government shareholders in Vietnam's stock markets tend to hold shares in less profitable firms. This might be due to political and social objectives, such that government shareholders need to be retained or invested in the 'bad' firms. For example, the government may also want to avoid the rise in unemployment that can occur if firms are bankrupted or dissolved. The government may also regard some firms as belonging to strategic industries; hence government ownership is protected or even expanded in such firms, regardless of poor performance recorded in previous years.

In contrast, an increase in current-year market performance is found to be followed by an increase in next-year government ownership. Notably, the feedback effect of market performance on government ownership is much stronger than that of accounting performance. It is likely that the Vietnamese Government is more interested in market performance when making decisions about the proportion of its shareholdings in listed firms. As mentioned in the previous section, government may have incentives to demonstrate the success of economic reforms by increasing share prices on stock markets. Hence, in the post-privatisation period (i.e. when privatised SOEs are listed), the primary goal of government shareholders might be to increase the market value of invested capital in listed firms. To compare, these findings are not similar to those reported by Tian and Estrin (2008) from a static viewpoint for China's listed firms, where both measures of prior firm performance are not significant determinants of government ownership.

Contrary to government ownership, current insider ownership in Vietnam's listed firms is not significantly determined by past firm performance. This shows that board members' decision to hold shares depends on other factors than firm performance recorded in the past. For example, controlling rights or a monitoring role may be more important than the past performance from the perspective of insiders. Therefore, it is plausible to argue that the dynamic aspect of endogeneity in the ownership–firm performance relationship is not present in the direction of the influence from past firm performance to current ownership structure, at least in Vietnam's listed firms.

In terms of foreign ownership, this study finds that past accounting firm performance has a significantly positive feedback effect on the current level of foreign ownership. This suggests that foreign investors in the Vietnamese stock markets prefer to invest in listed firms that have improved profits in the last fiscal year. This is perhaps due to the short-term investment view of foreign investors in Vietnamese listed firms, as argued earlier so that holding shares in profitable firms can offer them potential opportunities to reap quick returns on invested capital, dividend or capital gains, in comparison with poorly performing firms. However, the past market performance of a firm does not affect current foreign ownership in Vietnam's listed firms. This outcome is consistent with the finding of Wei et al. (2005) for Chinese listed firms. It suggests that from both static and dynamic perspectives, foreign investors in stock markets of transition economies like China and Vietnam do not rely on the market value of the firm to make decisions on shareholdings in domestic firms. This finding also supports the argument made in Section 6.2 that foreign investors refrain from taking too much risk in Vietnam's stock markets.

In the context of a transition economy like Vietnam, therefore, when the non-contemporaneous feedback effect of firm performance is addressed in parallel with the mediated effect of ownership structure on firm performance, this study finds that current-year government ownership is determined by both measures of previous-year firm performance, while current-year foreign ownership is affected only by previous-year accounting performance of the firm. Current-year insider ownership is exogenous in relation to a change in firm performance realised in the previous year. These outcomes reveal that a dynamic nature exists in the relationship between ownership structure and firm performance, which in part constitutes the endogeneity in this relationship. This also supports the argument that a lead–lag relationship (Hu and Izumida, 2008) is possible between ownership structure (at least for government ownership and foreign ownership) and firm performance. More generally, it is implied in this study that the current values of firm performance are functions of the past values of ownership structure and that the current values of ownership structure are functions of past firm performance.

## 6.4 Total Effect of Ownership Structure on Firm Performance

### *6.4.1. Government Ownership–Firm Performance*

As argued in Chapter 2, there exist in the literature two major propositions about the effect of government ownership on firm performance. On the one hand, an overwhelming viewpoint in the literature, such as in privatisation theory, is that government ownership is associated with inefficiency and bureaucracy; that is, the relationship between government ownership and firm performance is negative (Djankov and Murrell, 2002, Netter and Megginson, 2001, Thomsen and Pedersen, 2000). On the other hand, many authors argue that government ownership contributes to improving firm performance, which can happen either for a certain group of firms, or subject to country-specific contexts. For example, in China's stock market, Li et al. (2009) find that the negative effect of government ownership on firm performance is 'only among the more profitable firms'. Vaaler and Schrage (2009) claim that government ownership positively contributes to firm performance if the government holds no more than 50% ownership in a low policy stability country and no more than 25% of ownership in a low-to-mid policy stability country. Nevertheless, it should be noted that most of these results are obtained from static models.

This book finds that the total effect of previous-year government ownership on current-year firm performance is positive as expected, but it is not significant. Two conclusions in relation to government ownership have been drawn. On the one hand, as discussed in Section 6.1, government ownership in the last year is helpful in reducing agency conflict in firms in the current year. On the other hand, the total effect of government ownership on firm performance is dynamically not meaningful. This does not provide strong support for the common view in relation to Vietnam's stock markets (as mentioned in Section 1.3.2), that government ownership should be further reduced in Vietnamese listed firms.

In contrast to the negative or positive viewpoints in previous literature, the above conclusions for government ownership suggest an 'indifference hypothesis'; that is, government ownership is neither good nor bad for firm performance in newly developed stock markets like Vietnam's. Further research on the issue from similar contexts is needed to confirm that government ownership is indifferent with respect to firm performance.

Among the constituents of the total effect of previous-year government ownership on current-year firm performance, the indirect effect via agency costs is significantly negative and thus is a serious impediment to achieving a positive total effect of government ownership. It is worth reiterating that this negative indirect effect is reported when defining agency costs as the asset utilisation ratio. As already argued in Section 6.1, however, even when agency costs are otherwise defined as the operating expense ratio, the indirect effect of past government ownership via agency costs may still be not meaningful because of the cancelling effect due to the negative relationship between the asset utilisation ratio and firm performance. Moreover, this study has revealed the underlying factor (i.e. a specific indirect effect via agency costs) that is useful in explaining why and how government ownership does not significantly contribute to enhancing firm performance.

### *6.4.2. Insider Ownership–Firm Performance*

As already mentioned, there are two main streams of literature regarding the linear relationship between managerial/insider ownership and firm performance. The first is termed the 'alignment of interest effect' (Jensen and Meckling, 1976). It is argued that the separation of ownership from control reduces managers' incentive to pursue the goal of corporate profit maximisation, as a result of the conflict of interest between managers and shareholders or between majority and minority shareholders (Clacher et al., 2010). If interests are aligned between managers and shareholders, a higher proportion of managerial ownership can result in an improved firm performance level. This proposition is supported by empirical evidence from Bhagat et al. (2010) and Mehran (1995), who also claim that managerial equity ownership and firm performance are positively associated.

In contrast, the second stream postulates an 'entrenchment effect' so that, as the proportion of equity owned by managers increases, they have less incentive to pursue the goal of corporate profit maximisation. In other words, managerial ownership and firm performance are negatively related. According to Shleifer and Vishny (2008), managers are involved in non-profit-maximising behaviours when they hold up to a certain level of a firm's ownership.

In this book, the 'alignment of interest effect' hypothesis in agency theory is assumed for the relationship between insider ownership and firm performance, and the empirical finding supports this hypothesis. Specifically, the evidence is that a higher level of insider ownership in one year is followed by a higher level of firm performance in the next year. This mechanism is effective for both the accounting performance and market performance of firms. It suggests that an increase in the ratio of shareholding by insider ownership in one year can align the interests of insider ownership and other shareholders more closely, which subsequently leads to a significant increase in firm performance in the next year. In a static model, the positive total impact of insider ownership on firm performance is also found by Tian and Estrin (2008) for the Chinese market.

Interestingly, past insider ownership is found to contribute to improving both current accounting performance and current market performance of Vietnam's listed firms, where the total effect on the latter is stronger than on the former. It is likely that an increase in the shareholding of insiders in the last fiscal year is highly appreciated by outside investors, who may consider it a strong commitment of the board members to the firm, and this can be reflected in higher share prices in this year.

An empirical implication of the above finding is that further privatisation should be carried out for the privatised SOEs where retained government ownership is still high. This can be 'follow-up privatisation' programs to transfer more shares owned by the government to the members of the board of directors (insider ownership). This is because government ownership is not greatly beneficial to increasing firm performance, as discussed earlier, while insider ownership improves both accounting performance and market performance. Additionally, it should be noted that there is at least a one-year lag time for the performance of post-privatised SOEs to improve in response to an increase in the shareholding of insiders because the conclusion about the relationship between insider ownership and firm performance is obtained from a dynamic model in this study.

Of the two mediation channels, the indirect effect via corporate risk-taking is found to have a significant influence on the total effect of past insider ownership on current firm performance, while agency costs do not. Specifically, the driving force for insider ownership to improve accounting firm performance is the corporate risk-taking channel. In contrast, the indirect effect via corporate risk-taking is a barrier to market firm performance. It turns out that market firm performance is jeopardised by risk-seeking behaviour of insider shareholders. However, the direct effect of insider ownership is strong enough to compensate for the negative effect of corporate risk-taking on the market performance of the firm, even resulting in the improvement of market performance.

It is worth noting that the agency costs channel does not have a significant role in the total positive effect of past insider ownership on current firm performance. Hence, while the total positive effect of past insider ownership is consistent with the 'alignment of interest' hypothesis, the consideration of the two mediation channels in this study suggests that insiders can make their interests more aligned with those of other shareholders in the firm by taking more risks. As also argued by Downs and Sommer (1999), when managers own more shares in firms, they are perhaps involved in more corporate risk-taking because their interests are then more closely aligned with those of owners. Of course, the above arguments are based on the assumption that insiders/managers generally prefer less risk than owners. Therefore, this book indeed provides empirical evidence to explain and support the theoretical proposition that corporate risk-taking is a mechanism for insider shareholders to obtain 'alignment of interest' within a firm, and hence to bring about improved performance of the firm.

### *6.4.3. Foreign Ownership and Firm Performance*

As already reviewed in Chapter 2, there are mixed findings in the literature on the total effect of foreign ownership on firm performance. Both positive and negative viewpoints of the impact of foreign ownership on firm performance can be put forward. A greater number of prior studies support the value-enhancing role of foreign ownership in firms (Dwivedi and Jain, 2005, Sabur et al., 2012, Sarkar and Sarkar, 2000, Wei et al., 2005, Ferreira and Matos, 2008). In contrast, foreign ownership is found to have a significant negative impact on firm performance (Sulong and Nor, 2008, Phung and Le, 2013).

As expected, this book finds that past foreign ownership does not make any positive contribution to the current accounting performance of Vietnam's listed firms. Both the total effect and the direct effect of past foreign ownership on firm performance are negative, while the negative impact on market firm performance is significant. This result is consistent with the evidence found in Phung and Le (2013) that foreign investors have a negative impact on the performance of Vietnam's listed firms. It is worth noting that the detrimental effect of foreign ownership is identified from both the static approach (Phung and Le, 2013) and the dynamic approach used in this study.

The implication is that foreign investors may lack an effective monitoring role in Vietnamese listed firms because their ownership was restricted to 49% of the total common shares during the sample period. Since this threshold does not provide them with dominant voting rights, foreign investors are certainly not controlling shareholders to drive the decision-making of the firm. Hence, they may lack long-term commitment and treat themselves as short-term or speculative investors in Vietnam's stock markets. In order for foreign investors to contribute to enhancing firm performance, the government of Vietnam has opened up greater participation of foreign investors in listed firms as discussed in Section 1.3.2.

To sum up, among the three forms of equity ownership employed in this book, this study finds that previous-year government ownership does not enhance firm performance in the current year, although government ownership can be used as an internal governance mechanism to mitigate agency problems in listed firms. In contrast, the 'alignment of interest' is confirmed to be valid for the relationship between insider ownership and firm performance, since previous-year insider ownership is found to have a positive total effect on current-year firm performance. This finding can imply such that more shareholdings should be transferred from the government to board members. Theoretically, it is implied that corporate risk-taking can be a mechanism for insider ownership to achieve alignment of interest within firms. Finally, previous-year foreign ownership is even negative in relation to the current market value of listed firms. In the context of young stock markets like Vietnam's, it appears that a value-enhancing role of foreign ownership on firm performance has not been prominent.

## 6.5 Summary and Conclusions

Regarding the mediating roles of agency costs and corporate risk-taking, it is suggested from this study that agency costs and corporate risk-taking are the two 'missing link' mediating variables in the ownership structure–firm performance relationship. Thus, academic studies of this relationship should not ignore these two important factors. The study of both agency costs and corporate risk-taking as the two main channels of the indirect effects of ownership structure contributes to in-depth analysis of why and how ownership structure affects firm performance.

As for the non-contemporaneous feedback effect of firm performance, ownership structure in the last year is found to have an effect on agency costs and corporate risk-taking in the current year, which in turn affects current-year firm performance, while previous-year firm performance also has feedback effects on current-year ownership structure. Therefore, it is plausible that there is a non-contemporaneous or dynamic bidirectional relationship between ownership structure and firm performance. This also suggests that the dynamic nature contributes in part to the endogeneity in the ownership–performance relationship.

In terms of the total effect of ownership structure on firm performance, although results imply weak positive government ownership effects and negative foreign ownership effects to improving firm performance in Vietnam. Nevertheless, government ownership may be used as an effective instrument to mitigate agency costs in listed firms. Policymakers and stock-market regulators can advocate the stronger involvement of private shareholders like foreign owners and insider shareholders, because a higher level of these ownerships can make their interests more aligned with those of other shareholders, which ultimately enhances firm performance. Further studies are necessary to confirm the above findings and implications.

## References

Agrawal, A. & Knoeber, C. R. 1996. Firm performance and mechanisms to control agency problems between managers and shareholders. *Journal of Financial & Quantitative Analysis*, 31, 377–397.

Ang, J. S., Cole, R. A. & Lin, J. W. 2000. Agency costs and ownership structure. *The Journal of Finance*, 55, 81–106.

Berle, A. A. & Means, G. C. 1932. *The modern corporation and private property*. New York: Macmillan Co.

Bhagat, S. & Bolton, B. 2008. Corporate governance and firm performance. *Journal of Corporate Finance*, 14, 257–273.

Bhagat, S., Bolton, B. & Romano, R. 2010. The effect of corporate governance on performance. *In:* Kent, B. H. & Ronald, A. (eds.) *Corporate governance: A synthesis of theory, research, and practice*. Chichester: Wiley.

Bhagat, S. & Jefferis, R. H. 2002. *The econometrics of corporate governance studies*, Cambridge, Mass: MIT.

Brown, P., Beekes, W. & Verhoeven, P. 2011. Corporate governance, accounting and finance: A review. *Accounting and Finance*, 51, 96–172.

Clacher, I., Hillier, D. & Mccolgan, P. 2010. Agency theory: Incomplete contracting and ownership structure. *In:* Kent, B. H. & Ronald, A. (eds.) *Corporate governance: A synthesis of theory, research, and practice*. Chichester: Wiley.

Davidson, W. N. & Singh, M. 2003. Agency costs, ownership structure and corporate governance mechanisms. *Journal of Banking & Finance*, 27, 793–816.

Dias, R. & Mroczkowski, N. A. 2012. Do banks use credit default swaps to hedge or speculate? An agency theoretic perspective. *International Journal of Critical Accounting*, 4, 283.

Djankov, S. & Murrell, P. 2002. Enterprise restructuring in transition: A quantitative survey. *Journal of Economic Literature*, 40, 739–792.

Downs, D. H. & Sommer, D. W. 1999. Monitoring, ownership, and risk-taking: The impact of guaranty funds. *The Journal of Risk and Insurance*, 66, 477–479.

Drever, M., Stanton, P. A. & McGowan, S. 2007. *Contemporary issues in accounting*, Milton, Qld: John Wiley & Sons Australia.

Dwivedi, N. & Jain, A. K. 2005. Corporate governance and performance of Indian firms: The effect of board size and ownership. *Employee Responsibilities and Rights Journal*, 17, 161–172.

Fama, E. F. & Jensen, M. C. 1983. Separation of ownership and control. *Journal of Law and Economics*, 26, 301–325.

Ferreira, M. A. & Matos, P. 2008. The colors of investors' money: The role of institutional investors around the world. *Journal of Financial Economics*, 88, 499–533.

Firth, M. A. & Rui, O. M. 2012. Does one size fit all? A study of the simultaneous relations among ownership, corporate governance mechanisms, and the financial performance of firms in China. *In:* Boubaker, S., Nguyen, B. D. & Nguyen, D. K. (eds.) *Corporate governance: Recent developments and new trends*. Berlin Heidelberg: Springer-Verlag.

Gordon, L. A., Loeb, M. P. & Tseng, C.-Y. 2009. Enterprise risk management and firm performance: A contingency perspective. *Journal of Accounting and Public Policy*, 28, 301–327.

Guner, G. & Kursat, A. 2002. Equity ownership structure, risk taking, and performance. *Emerging Markets, Finance & Trade*, 38, 6.

Hardaker, J. B., Huirne, R. B. M., Anderson, J. R., Ebooks Corporation, L. & International, C. A. B. 2004. *Coping with risk in agriculture*, Wallingford (U.K.): CABI Pub.

Hermalin, B. E. & Weisbach, M. S. 2003. Boards of directors as an endogenously determined institution: A survey of the economic literature. *Economic policy review*, 9, 7–26.

Himmelberg, C. P., Hubbard, R. G. & Palia, D. 1999. Understanding the determinants of managerial ownership and the link between ownership and performance. *Journal of Financial Economics*, 53, 353–384.

Hu, Y. & Izumida, S. 2008. Ownership concentration and corporate performance: A causal analysis with Japanese panel data. *Corporate Governance: An International Review*, 16, 342–358.

Jensen, M. C. & Meckling, W. H. 1976. Theory of the firm: Managerial behavior, agency costs and ownership structure. *Journal of Financial Economics*, 3, 305–360.

John, K., Litov, L. & Yeung, B. 2008. Corporate governance and risk-taking. *The Journal of Finance*, 63, 1679–1728.

Kim, B. 2011. Do foreign investors encourage value-enhancing corporate risk taking? *Emerging Markets Finance & Trade*, 47, 88–110.

Le, T. V. & Buck, T. 2011. State ownership and listed firm performance: A universally negative governance relationship? *Journal of Management and Governance*, 15, 227–248.

Li, T., Sun, L. & Zou, L. 2009. State ownership and corporate performance: A quantile regression analysis of Chinese listed companies. *China Economic Review*, 20, 703–716.

Mcguigan, J. R., Moyer, R. C. & Harris, F. H. D. 2005. *Managerial economics: Applications, strategy, and tactics*, Mason, Ohio: Thomson / South-Western, 10th ed.

Mehran, H. 1995. Executive compensation structure, ownership, and firm performance. *Journal of Financial Economics*, 38, 163–184.

Netter, J. & Megginson, W. L. 2001. From state to market: A survey of empirical studies on privatisation. *Journal of Economic Literature*, 39, 321–389.

Phung, D. N. & Le, T. P. V. 2013. Foreign ownership, capital structure and firm value: Empirical evidence from Vietnamese listed firms. *The IUP Journal of Corporate Governance*, 12, 40–58.

Sabur, M., Omar Al, F. & Wares, K. 2012. Ownership structure, corporate governance and firm performance. *Studies in Economics and Finance*, 29, 301–319.

Sarkar, J. & Sarkar, S. 2000. Large shareholder activism in corporate governance in developing countries: Evidence from India. *International Review of Finance*, 1, 161–194.

Shleifer, A. & Vishny, R. W. 2008. Large shareholders and corporate control. *In*: Ricketts, M. (ed.) *The economics of modern business enterprise. Elgar reference collection. International Library of Critical Writings in Economics*, vol. 214. Cheltenham, U.K. and Northampton, Mass.: Elgar.

Sulong, Z. & Nor, F. M. 2008. Dividends, ownership structure and board governance on firm value: Empirical evidence from Malaysian listed firms. *Malaysian Accounting Review*, 7, 55–94.

Sun, Q., Tong, W. H. S. & Tong, J. 2002. How does government ownership affect firm performance? Evidence from China's privatisation experience. *Journal of Business Finance & Accounting*, 29, 1–27.

Tan, D. T. 2009. *Corporate governance and firm outcomes: Causation or spurious correlations?* PhD, University of New South Wales.

Thomsen, S. & Pedersen, T. 2000. Ownership structure and economic performance in the largest European companies. *Strategic Management Journal*, 21, 689–705.

Tian, L. & Estrin, S. 2008. Retained state shareholding in Chinese PLCs: Does government ownership always reduce corporate value? *Journal of Comparative Economics*, 36, 74–89.

Tirole, J. 2006. *The theory of corporate finance*, Princeton, NJ: Princeton University Press.

Vaaler, P. M. & Schrage, B. N. 2009. Residual state ownership, policy stability and financial performance following strategic decisions by privatising telecoms. *Journal of International Business Studies*, 40, 621–641.

Wei, Z., Xie, F. & Zhang, S. 2005. Ownership structure and firm value in China's privatised firms: 1991-2001. *Journal of Financial & Quantitative Analysis*, 40, 87–108.

Wintoki, M. B., Linck, J. S. & Netter, J. M. 2012. Endogeneity and the dynamics of internal corporate governance. *Journal of Financial Economics*, 105, 581–606.

# 7 Corporate Governance, Ownership Structure and Firm Performance

## Summary and Conclusions

### 7.1 Summary of Research Problems and Research Questions

A mediated and dynamic relationship between ownership structure and firm performance has been recognised as a new approach in corporate governance and corporate finance literature. This approach is helpful to further understanding of the nature of the ownership–firm performance relationship, which is otherwise limited within the traditional approach that treats ownership structure and firm performance as directly and contemporaneously related. Specifically, the mediation approach to the issue helps to uncover the 'missing links' that can explain why and how the effect of ownership structure is transmitted to firm performance, and hence this approach also suggests the underlying mechanisms by which the former improves the latter. Meanwhile, the dynamic or non-contemporaneous perspective reflects the dynamic nature of this relationship. The dynamic specification is also well-suited in a mediation context, where temporal order change is necessary for mediation effects to occur effectively.

Building on the theoretical implications of agency theory, corporate risk management theory and endogeneity in the ownership–performance relationship, as well as on empirical implications in the existing work (Antonakis et al., 2010; MacKinnon, 2012; Le and Buck, 2011; Hu and Izumida, 2008; Preacher and Hayes, 2008; Wintoki et al., 2012), this study has set out to primarily investigate the effects (including mediated effects, direct effects and total effects) of previous-year ownership structure on current-year firm performance in the context of Vietnam's stock markets. In this connection, agency costs and corporate risk-taking are argued to be the two main mediators that transmit the effect of ownership structure on firm performance. Furthermore, such a mediation mechanism has been examined within the framework of the bidirectional non-contemporaneous relationship between ownership structure and firm performance. Therefore, this book sought to answer four research questions, as below:

DOI: 10.4324/9781003255741-7

1. Do agency costs and corporate risk-taking mediate the effect of ownership structure on the performance of listed firms, assuming that agency costs and corporate risk-taking are exogenous?
2. Is there any variation in the mediating roles of agency costs and corporate risk-taking in the ownership structure–firm performance relationship, assuming that agency costs and corporate risk-taking are endogenous covariates?
3. Is there any non-contemporaneous feedback effect of firm performance on ownership structure in the mediation context?
4.
    i. What is the total effect of ownership structure on firm performance when the non-contemporaneous interrelationship is accounted for?
    ii. Which mediation channel is more important in determining the improvement in the performance of Vietnamese listed firms?

## 7.2 Summary of Findings Concerning Research Questions

The detailed findings of this study are summarised in Chapter 5. This section synthesises these findings with respect to the four research questions.

> ***Research question 1:*** *Do agency costs and corporate risk-taking mediate the effect of ownership structure on the performance of listed firms, assuming that agency costs and corporate risk-taking are exogenous?*

When agency costs and corporate risk-taking are treated as exogenous, the causal-steps regressions for the recursive model of Baron and Kenny (1986) reveal that only the mediating role of agency costs is significant, whereas a mediating role of corporate risk-taking is not found. Specifically, agency costs positively mediate the effect of past government ownership on current accounting-based performance in listed firms. That is, a higher proportion of government ownership in one year is followed by a lower level of agency costs in the next year, and the lower agency costs are associated with an improved accounting-based performance level. This is new empirical evidence in the literature since a mediating role of agency costs is found for the non-contemporaneous relationship between ownership structure and firm performance.

> ***Research question 2:*** *Is there any variation in the mediating roles of agency costs and corporate risk-taking in the ownership structure–firm performance relationship, assuming that agency costs and corporate risk-taking are endogenous covariates?*

When agency costs and corporate risk-taking are treated as endogenous covariates, the recursive model has been estimated simultaneously using the ML method so that the disturbances across equations were permitted to co-vary. The results are that the positive mediating role of agency costs remains robust in the relationship between past government ownership and current accounting-based firm performance. Nevertheless, a significant variation is that a negative mediating role of corporate risk-taking is confirmed for the links between past government ownership and current accounting-based firm performance, as well as between past insider ownership and current accounting-based firm performance.

While the above findings demonstrate that the positive influence of past government ownership on current firm performance is consistent, they also indicate that the absence of the mediating role of corporate risk-taking in causal-steps regression might be a spurious result. It is thus implied that there are unobserved common causes of the two mediators and, hence, an approach that considers one mediator at a time will not yield robust estimates (Vanderweele and Vansteelandt, 2014). This is empirical evidence from Vietnam to validate the claim that allowing the correlation of mediator disturbances is necessary in two-mediator mediation models, as recommended by Acock (2013), Antonakis et al. (2010) and Preacher and Hayes (2008).

> ***Research question 3:*** *Is there any non-contemporaneous feedback effect of firm performance on ownership structure in the mediation context?*

When the non-contemporaneous interrelationship between ownership structure and firm performance is taken into consideration, the mediated effect of ownership structure has been examined in the non-recursive model with the feedback effects of firm performance on ownership structure. It is found that prior firm performance has a significant direct effect on current government ownership. While a similar feedback effect of firm performance on government ownership is not found in prior research, such as that of Tian and Estrin (2008), this book suggests that such a dynamic feedback effect can be uncovered in the mediation context. However, a non-contemporaneous feedback effect of firm performance on insider ownership is not found.

In contrast, this study found that current foreign ownership is significantly determined by prior accounting-based firm performance but not prior market-based firm performance. This finding is consistent with that of Wei et al. (2005), suggesting that foreign ownership is not affected by market-based firm performance for both contemporaneous and non-contemporaneous dimensions.

***Research question 4:***

i. *What is the total effect of ownership structure on firm performance when the non-contemporaneous interrelationship is accounted for?*

   In the non-recursive model, which considers the non-contemporaneous interrelationship between ownership structure and firm performance, it is found that past insider ownership has a significantly positive total effect on current firm performance, where the effect on accounting performance is stronger than on market performance. The total effect of past government ownership on current firm performance is weak and insignificant, while that of past foreign ownership on current market performance is significantly negative. From the mediation and dynamic approach, therefore, this study provides empirical evidence supporting the proposition in privatisation theory that government ownership is not efficient, while the private sector (e.g. insider ownership) can contribute positively to firm performance. The finding of a negative role of foreign ownership in Vietnamese listed firms is also similar to those of prior studies on this market, such as that of Phung and Le (2013).

ii. *Which mediation channel is more important in determining the improvement in the performance of Vietnamese listed firms?*

The mediation channel via corporate risk-taking has been demonstrated to be more important in comparison with that via agency costs in terms of determining the positive total effect of ownership structure on firm performance. Since insider ownership, but not government ownership or foreign ownership, is found to have a positive total effect on firm performance, the assessment of the importance of the mediating variables as mentioned above is confined to considering which mediation channel is more important in determining the positive total effect of insider ownership on firm performance.

There are two main reasons that corporate risk-taking has been judged as more important than agency costs in this regard. First, there are significant associations between both forms of ownership structure, namely, past government ownership and past insider ownership, and current corporate risk-taking, while only past government ownership is found to have a significant relationship with current agency costs. Notably, this result is consistent throughout both the recursive and non-recursive models with different estimation techniques. Second, the specific indirect effect of past insider ownership through corporate risk-taking on both measures of firm performance is significant. This finding provides new insights to the literature in postulating that corporate risk-taking is an important link but often ignored in the ownership–firm performance relationship.

## 7.3 Key Contributions of the Study

### *7.3.1 Theoretical and Methodological Contributions*

Firstly, this book provides new theoretical arguments for the ownership–performance relationship. As summarised by Brown et al. (2011), it is generally implied in the literature that the ownership structure of a firm may affect its performance, whereas firm performance can also have an impact on its ownership structure. There is also the endogenous and dynamic nature of the relationship between ownership structure and firm performance (Hu and Izumida, 2008). In addition to the existing literature, this book argues that ownership structure does not directly affect firm performance, and this insight has been uncovered by considering its endogenous nature in a non-contemporaneous interrelationship and mediation framework. Specifically, this study demonstrates that the impact of ownership structure on firm performance can be effectively transmitted through two indirect links, namely, agency costs and corporate risk-taking; where the corporate risk-taking channel is more important than agency costs in determining firm performance. It is thus suggested that ownership structure and firm performance may have a mediated and dynamic interdependence.

Secondly, this is the first study that adopts both mediation and dynamic approaches to investigate the mediated effect of ownership structure on firm performance and the non-contemporaneous interdependence between them. The ownership structure–firm performance relationship has been extensively examined in the literature, but the existence of indirect links between them has been neglected, and the dynamic interrelationship between ownership structure and firm performance has not been adequately explored. By studying the effect of past ownership structure on current firm performance and vice versa (i.e. past firm performance on current ownership structure), this study combines a dynamic perspective and a mediation approach. This combination is appropriate, as it is suggested by MacKinnon (2012) that the mediation effect needs time to take place.

In terms of the mediation approach, this book extends the work of Le and Buck (2011) on uncovering the indirect effects of multiple types of ownership structure on firm performance, exploring the second mediation channel via corporate risk-taking and furthermore examining the mediated effects associated with the non-contemporaneous interdependence between them. With respect to the dynamic perspective, unlike prior studies that examine the contemporaneous or static ownership–performance relationship, this book endorses the recommendations of Hu and Izumida (2008) and Wintoki et al. (2012) that empirical research should consider the non-contemporaneous or dynamic interrelationship between ownership structure and firm performance, to obtain an enhanced understanding of the ownership–performance relationship.

Thirdly, this book provides an original contribution to the literature by developing two-mediator models (a recursive and a non-recursive model) where agency costs and corporate risk-taking play the mediating roles in the bidirectional relationship between ownership structure and firm performance. These theoretical models are new contributions to corporate governance and corporate finance theory because they are innovated on the combination of agency theory, corporate risk management theory and the dynamic aspect of endogeneity in the ownership–performance relationship, the last of which has not yet been addressed in previous literature on the issue. On the one hand, agency theory (Fama and Jensen, 1983; Jensen and Meckling, 1976; Berle and Means, 1932) suggests a link from ownership structure via agency costs to firm performance. On the other hand, this theory also suggests a link between ownership structure and corporate risk-taking. However, agency theory alone is not sufficient to explain why corporate risk-taking results in variation in firm performance. This book bridges this gap by incorporating corporate risk management theory into the model, where the association between corporate risk-taking and firm performance is explained by the practice of risk management that helps in creating firm value (Léautier, 2007). In addition to considering the second mediating variable, this book advances prior mediation research on the issue, such as that of Le and Buck (2011), in terms of accounting for the feedback effect of firm performance on ownership structure.

Fourthly, this book supports a new consideration that using the asset utilisation ratio to define agency costs is perhaps a mistake, at least in the context of a developing country. As discussed earlier, there is good reason to suspect that this ratio does not necessarily reflect the efficiency in asset utilisation or improved firm performance. Indeed, this position contradicts previous research in the field, such as studies by Chen and Yur-Austin (2007), Davidson and Singh (2003) and Mcknight and Weir (2009). As Ang et al. (2000) point out, this ratio and the operating expense ratio are the two most frequently used proxies for agency costs in the literature. A common understanding is that the asset utilisation ratio is an indirect measure of agency costs in the sense that a higher value of this ratio reflects a lower level of agency costs because the firm is more efficient in asset utilisation. This mechanism was confirmed for the recursive model of this book, but the results for the non-recursive model (Section 5.2.2) show that a higher asset utilisation ratio is associated with a lower level of firm performance. Thus, it can be argued that the asset utilisation ratio may not properly reflect agency costs. Nevertheless, the direct measure of agency costs, the operating expense ratio, still indicates the expected correlation between agency costs and firm performance. Therefore, the employment of the asset utilisation ratio to proxy agency costs should be considered with due care in corporate governance literature.

Lastly, an interesting contribution to econometrics applications is that fixed-effects estimation with Driscoll-Kraay standard errors (Hoechle, 2007) can be best fitted by full-information maximum likelihood estimation (Roodman, 2011).[1] As shown in Section 5.1.6, maximum likelihood estimation, after controlling for cross-sectional dependence and unobserved firm fixed effects, can produce nearly identical parameters as obtained in fixed-effects estimation, in terms of both the magnitude and significance level of effects. Of course, it is necessary that maximum likelihood estimation is performed with independent cross-equation disturbances because fixed-effects estimation is conducted for an individual equation each time. It is equally important to select the appropriate clustering of the panel and/or time variables. Maximum likelihood estimation also performs well as an alternative to the generalised method of moment estimation, but it does not appear to be the best fit. Therefore, it is plausible that maximum likelihood estimation can replace fixed-effects estimation in panel regressions with cross-sectional dependence, and this outcome is an addition to Hoechle (2007) in terms of the econometrics techniques to deal with panel models in order to obtain robust standard errors.

### 7.3.2 *Practical and Policy Contributions*

The results of this study contribute to an enhanced understanding of the general mediated and dynamic relationship between ownership structure and firm performance in general, which are helpful to formulate some policies for reforms. However, more comprehensive studies on the relationship are essential to draw conclusions regarding the impacts of ownership structure on firm performance, and formulating policy and reform agenda for SOEs and corporate governance for Vietnam and other similar countries. Some of the findings of this study, which have policy and reform implications, are summarised as below:

Firstly, the results of this book imply that government ownership can be used as an internal corporate governance mechanism to mitigate agency costs in listed firms, at least in the context of a developing country like Vietnam. There is strong evidence that past government ownership helps mitigate current agency costs, as discussed in Section 6.1 because this negative relationship is robust in relation to various econometric estimation techniques. The mitigating power of government ownership towards agency costs from a dynamic perspective is new evidence found in this book. It helps enrich the current understanding of the government ownership–agency costs relationship in the literature. While Le and Buck (2011) conclude, from a static viewpoint, that government ownership helps reduce agency costs in the Chinese context, this book supports this position from a dynamic perspective for the Vietnamese stock market. Therefore, a positive view of government ownership in relation to agency problems within listed firms is found in this study. However, the total effect of government ownership is not relatively statistically significant as compared to the effects of other types of ownership.

Secondly, this study develops the understanding of the underlying mechanism through which insider ownership affects firm performance in Vietnam's stock markets. Unlike the common assumption in the literature that insiders are risk-averse (Himmelberg et al., 1999), this book finds that insiders are actually risk-seeking in Vietnamese listed firms. A possible justification for this is that their jobs are not secure (Tirole, 2006). Interestingly, the risk-seeking behaviour of insider ownership has two opposite effects, namely: a positive effect on firm accounting performance but a negative effect on firm market performance. It is plausible to argue that the negative relationship between corporate risk-taking and market performance is due to the lack of efficient risk management in listed firms, particularly against the downside risk in stock markets. These insights are useful to explain why it was a common phenomenon in Vietnam's stock markets that listed firms engaged actively in financial investment during the period of study and so suffered from huge losses in market values of invested capital due to the downturn in the stock markets. Since it has been found that the positive total effect of insider ownership on firm performance is more influenced by corporate risk-taking than by the agency costs channel, corporate risk management should be regarded as one of the top business priorities in listed firms for avoiding deterioration in the market value of the firm.

Thirdly, the results show a negative role of foreign investors in Vietnam's stock markets. This result is possibly caused by the limitations of the foreign ownership data. This data has a restriction that foreign ownership was restricted at 49% of common shares in Vietnamese listed firms during the sample period. The policy of the Vietnamese Government to remove the previous threshold of 49% of foreign ownership in Vietnam's stock markets (as already mentioned in Section 1.3.2) is expected to bring about a significantly positive contribution of foreign shareholders in listed firms. This might be a way for foreign ownership to play a positive role in enhancing the performance of local firms. It is likely that under this new policy, foreign ownership will be more concentrated, hence generating more voting rights and a stronger monitoring role for foreign investors to influence firm performance positively.

Fourthly, this book can provide implications for the role of private ownership in developing and transition economies. By examining both public (government ownership) and private (insider and foreign ownership) types of equity ownership in listed firms, this study points out that insider ownership is beneficial for firm performance. Specifically, higher private ownership of insider shareholders is associated with improved firm performance (in relation to both profit-based and market-based measures). Since insider ownership includes managerial ownership in this study, this finding is consistent with the 'alignment of interests' hypothesis (Jensen and Meckling, 1976). To some extent, this evidence supports the positive view of private ownership. It implies that more shares are transferred to the private sector to achieve better performance of firms in particular and improved economic efficiency of the economy as a whole.

Fifthly, an array of meaningful conclusions can be drawn from this study for corporate governance reform in developing countries in terms of an appropriate structure of equity ownership. As an internal mechanism of corporate governance, a well-designed ownership structure in listed firms is expected to enable the firms to achieve better financial outcomes following the reform. Thus, the proportion of equity held by one type of shareholders should be set out relative to that of others and from the outset of the reform agenda of corporate governance. In the context of a transition economy like Vietnam, government ownership can be retained at a significant level in listed firms as a mechanism to protect small investors and to mitigate agency problems in listed firms. Meanwhile, insider shareholders are encouraged to increase their shares in listed firms so as to create the 'alignment of interest effect', which results in improved firm performance. Corporate governance reform in developing economies is also better off aiming at increasing the shareholding of boards of directors (insider ownership) to enhance firm performance.

Lastly, this book is the first study that examines the mediated and dynamic interrelationship between ownership structure and firm performance in the Vietnamese context. The findings of the study add to the current understanding of the listed firms of Vietnam. In particular, this study has provided new insights about agency costs and risk-taking behaviours associated with shareholders in Vietnamese listed firms, opening up new areas for further research.

## 7.4 Limitations and Recommendations for Further Research

There are several limitations in this book. Firstly, the findings can only be generalised to listed firms, because the sample data does not contain unlisted firms. Since the stocks of unlisted companies are not traded on stock exchanges, there is no reliable market-based measure of firm performance like Q (in fact, these stocks can still be exchanged on over-the counter (OTC) markets). Hence, the findings and conclusions about the relationship between ownership structure and Q may not be applicable to unlisted firms outside stock exchanges. Therefore, further research could explore the issue for a separate panel of unlisted firms and compare this with a panel of listed firms, so that the understanding of the mediated and dynamic relationship between ownership structure and firm performance could be enriched.

Secondly, since this book uses data for Vietnamese listed firms, the empirical results provide evidence from a single country only. If data from other markets is employed, then a comparison of empirical evidence on a multiple-country basis could be made in later studies, thus verifying and enhancing the generalisation of the findings of this book. In addition, the sample dataset for the research, consisting of 95 firms over five years from 2008 to 2012, is relatively small. However, before conducting several data cleansing procedures as discussed in Section 4.2.2, this book employed a population of all listed companies on Vietnam's stock market in 2008 (288 firms). It is worth noting that the mainboard and second board of the Vietnamese stock markets were operational since 2000 and 2005 only. There have not been major changes on the markets in terms of policy and regulations following the passage of the Securities Law of 2007. Thus, it is expected that this dataset reflects properly the scope and nature of Vietnam's capital market.

Thirdly, the time dimension of the data panel in this book is only five years due to the condition of new stock markets in Vietnam. Hence, there are only four clusters in the ML estimation, which may be a small number. While there are no generally accepted guidelines in the literature on how many clusters are sufficient for a particular panel data sample, the consistency of estimated standard errors may be influenced by the size of the clusters (Petersen, 2009). To account for this, this book has used different estimation methods, namely FE and GMM versus ML, and compared them for robustness. For further research, another solution would be that a longer period of time series data is collected from Vietnamese listed firms to check the consistency of the estimated results in this study.

Fourthly, this book does not take into account the feedback effects of the outcome variable (firm performance) on the two mediating variables (agency costs and corporate risk-taking). If further research could verify whether these are contemporaneously or non-contemporaneously related, then new insights about the mediated ownership–performance relationship could be obtained.

Lastly, like most prior studies on mediation analysis, this book assumes that all the paths among the variables of interest are linear. Further research could explore whether non-linear relationships between ownership structure and firm performance can be tested in the mediation context using panel data. This could be performed in light of the estimation methods and techniques for mediation models with non-linear paths proposed in recent studies, such as those of Hayes and Preacher (2010), Loeys et al. (2013) and Vanderweele and Vansteelandt (2014).

## 7.5 Conclusions

The main finding of this study is that agency costs and corporate risk-taking are the mediating variables in the relationship between ownership structure and firm performance and that this result is robust across different model specifications and estimation techniques. Additionally, there is non-contemporaneous interdependence between government ownership and firm performance. Ultimately, previous-year insider ownership has a significantly positive total impact on current-year firm performance, and this effect is influenced more by corporate risk-taking than by the agency costs channel.

This study has also provided important contributions to the literature in terms of theoretical, methodological and practical aspects, together with implications for policymaking at both regulator and firm levels. In particular, a key contribution at the top of this list is the mediation and dynamic research approach to the issue, within which two-mediator mediation models are innovated for the ownership–performance relationship. Nevertheless, this book is not without limitations. Several directions for further research on the issue are recommended. Overall, the use of combined mediation and dynamic approaches produces the novelty of this study in terms of providing new insights into the nature of the relationship between ownership and firm performance and shedding light on the underlying mechanisms for explaining why and how ownership structure and firm performance are related.

## Note

1 Stata's *cmp* and *xtscc* command, respectively.

## References

Acock, A. C. 2013. *Discovering structural equation modeling using stata*, College Station, Texas: Stata Press.

Ang, J. S., Cole, R. A. & Lin, J. W. 2000. Agency costs and ownership structure. *The Journal of Finance*, 55, 81–106.

Antonakis, J., Bendahan, S., Jacquart, P. & Lalive, R. 2010. On making causal claims: A review and recommendations. *The Leadership Quarterly*, 21, 1086–1120.

Baron, R. M. & Kenny, D. A. 1986. The moderator-mediator variable distinction in social psychological research: Conceptual, strategic, and statistical considerations. *Journal of Personality and Social Psychology*, 51, 1173–1182.

Berle, A. A. & Means, G. C. 1932. *The modern corporation and private property*. New York: The Macmillan Co.

Brown, P., Beekes, W. & Verhoeven, P. 2011. Corporate governance, accounting and finance: A review. *Accounting and Finance*, 51, 96–172.

Chen, X. & Yur-Austin, J. 2007. Re-measuring agency costs: The effectiveness of blockholders. *Quarterly Review of Economics and Finance*, 47, 588–601.

Davidson, W. N. & Singh, M. 2003. Agency costs, ownership structure and corporate governance mechanisms. *Journal of Banking & Finance*, 27, 793–816.

Djankov, S. & Murrell, P. 2002. Enterprise restructuring in transition: A quantitative survey. *Journal of Economic Literature*, 40, 739–792.

Fama, E. F. & Jensen, M. C. 1983. Separation of ownership and control. *Journal of Law and Economics*, 26, 301–325.

Hayes, A. F. & Preacher, K. J. 2010. Quantifying and testing indirect effects in simple mediation models when the constituent paths are non-linear. *Multivariate Behavioral Research*, 45, 627–660.

Himmelberg, C. P., Hubbard, R. G. & Palia, D. 1999. Understanding the determinants of managerial ownership and the link between ownership and performance. *Journal of Financial Economics*, 53, 353–384.

Hoechle, D. 2007. Robust standard errors for panel regressions with cross-sectional dependence. *Stata Journal*, 7, 281–312.

Hu, Y. & Izumida, S. 2008. Ownership concentration and corporate performance: A causal analysis with Japanese panel data. *Corporate Governance: An International Review*, 16, 342–358.

Jensen, M. C. & Meckling, W. H. 1976. Theory of the firm: Managerial behavior, agency costs and ownership structure. *Journal of Financial Economics*, 3, 305–360.

Le, T. V. & Buck, T. 2011. State ownership and listed firm performance: A universally negative governance relationship? *Journal of Management and Governance*, 15, 227–248.

Léautier, T.-O. 2007. *Corporate risk management for value creation: A guide to real-life applications*, London: Risk.

Loeys, T., Moerkerke, B., De Smet, O., Buysse, A., Steen, J. & Vansteelandt, S. 2013. Flexible mediation analysis in the presence of non-linear relations: Beyond the mediation formula. *Multivariate Behavioral Research*, 48, 871–894.

MacKinnon, D. 2012. *Introduction to statistical mediation analysis*, Hoboken: Taylor and Francis.

Mcknight, P. J. & Weir, C. 2009. Agency costs, corporate governance mechanisms and ownership structure in large UK publicly quoted companies: A panel data analysis. *Quarterly Review of Economics and Finance*, 49, 139–158.

Netter, J. & Megginson, W. L. 2001. From state to market: A survey of empirical studies on privatisation. *Journal of Economic Literature*, 39, 321–389.

Petersen, M. A. 2009. Estimating standard errors in finance panel data sets: Comparing approaches. *Review of Financial Studies*, 22, 435–480.

Phung, D. N. & Le, T. P. V. 2013. Foreign ownership, capital structure and firm value: Empirical evidence from Vietnamese listed firms. *The IUP Journal of Corporate Governance*, 12, 40–58.

Preacher, K. J. & Hayes, A. F. 2008. Asymptotic and resampling strategies for assessing and comparing indirect effects in multiple mediator models. *Behavior Research Methods*, 40, 879–891.

Roodman, D. 2011. Fitting fully observed recursive mixed-process models with cmp. *Stata Journal*, 11, 159–206.

Thomsen, S. & Pedersen, T. 2000. Ownership structure and economic performance in the largest European companies. *Strategic Management Journal*, 21, 689–705.

Tian, L. & Estrin, S. 2008. Retained state shareholding in Chinese PLCs: Does government ownership always reduce corporate value? *Journal of Comparative Economics*, 36, 74–89.

Tirole, J. 2006. *The theory of corporate finance*, Princeton, NJ: Princeton University Press.

Vanderweele, T. & Vansteelandt, S. 2014. Mediation analysis with multiple mediators. *Epidemiologic methods*, 2, 95–115.

Wei, Z., Xie, F. & Zhang, S. 2005. Ownership structure and firm value in China's privatised firms: 1991-2001. *Journal of Financial & Quantitative Analysis*, 40, 87–108.

Wintoki, M. B., Linck, J. S. & Netter, J. M. 2012. Endogeneity and the dynamics of internal corporate governance. *Journal of Financial Economics*, 105, 581–606.

# Appendices

*Appendix A5.2a* Robustness tests of Equations 3.9 and 3.12 of recursive model (using an alternative measure of firm size – SIZE2)

| *Dependent variable* | *ROA* | |
|---|---|---|
| *Equation* | *(3.9)* | *(3.12)* |
| AC | | 5.753 |
| | | (2.351)** |
| RT | | 0.157 |
| | | (0.464) |
| GOV(–1) | 0.116 | 0.001 |
| | (0.058)** | (0.073) |
| INS(–1) | 0.264 | 0.156 |
| | (0.107)** | (0.121) |
| FOR(–1) | 0.186 | 0.010 |
| | (0.115) | (0.122) |
| LEV | –0.207 | –0.190 |
| | (0.042)*** | (0.054)*** |
| SIZE2 | 2.717 | 1.954 |
| | (1.039)** | (1.096)* |
| BIG4 | –5.813 | –2.472 |
| | (2.413)** | (2.210) |
| ROA(–1) | 0.206 | 0.195 |
| | (0.110)* | (0.146) |
| | (25.996)* | (14.680) |
| _cons | –15.233 | –19.164 |
| | (28.747) | (26.755) |
| Observations | 380 | 380 |
| Number of instruments | 50 | 64 |
| Number of groups | 95 | 95 |
| AR(1) | –2.82 | –2.44 |
| [P-value] | [0.005] | [0.015] |
| AR(2) | –1.61 | –1.58 |
| [P-value] | [0.108] | [0.114] |

(*Continued*)

*Appendix A5.2a* (Continued)

| *Dependent variable* | *ROA* | |
|---|---|---|
| *Equation* | *(3.9)* | *(3.12)* |
| **Hansen test** | 25.54 | 41.84 |
| **[P-value]** | [0.489] | [0.308] |
| **Difference-in-Hansen test** | 20.01 | 30.91 |
| **[P-value]** | [0.274] | [0.192] |
| **F-statistics** | 12.79 | 75.47 |
| **[P-value]** | [0.000] | [0.000] |
| **Time effects** | Included | Included |
| **Industry effects** | Included | Included |

Notes: This table reports the results of dynamic system GMM regression of Equation 1.1 and Equation 1.4. The purpose is to check for the robustness of these two equations when the same GMM estimation techniques are employed with an alternative measure of firm size (SIZE2). Variables are denoted as follows. ROA is return on assets. AC is agency costs. RT is corporate risk-taking. GOV(–1) is lagged government ownership. INS(–1) is lagged insider ownership. FOR(–1) is lagged foreign ownership. LEV is financial leverage. SIZE2 is firm size (natural logarithm of market capitalisation). BIG4 is Big-4 audit company. ROA(–1) is prior return on assets. Endogenous variables are GOV(–1), INS (–1) and FOR(–1). Predetermined variables are AC, RT, LEV, SIZE2 and ROA(-1). Exogenous variables are BIG4, time dummies and industry dummies. The parameters were estimated using two-step procedures for dynamic system GMM. The robust standard errors using the Windmeijer correction for small-sample are included in parentheses under the coefficients. The estimates of year and industry dummies were excluded from the table for brevity. The individual coefficient is statistically significant at the *10%, **5% or ***1% significance level.

*Appendix A5.2b* Robustness tests of Equation 3.10 of recursive model (using an alternative measure of agency costs - AC2)

| *Dependent variable*<br>*Equation* | *AC2*<br>*(3.10)* |
|---|---|
| **GOV(–1)** | –0.040<br>(0.006)*** |
| **INS(–1)** | –0.071<br>(0.009)*** |
| **FOR(–1)** | 0.057<br>(0.003)*** |
| **LEV** | 0.014<br>(0.011) |
| **SIZE** | –2.159<br>(0.491)*** |
| **AGE** | 0.732<br>(0.089)*** |
| **_cons** | 50.046<br>(9.141)*** |
| **Observations** | 380 |
| **Number of groups** | 95 |
| **F-statistic** | 261.50 |
| **Within R-squared** | 0.1254 |

Notes: This table reports the results for the robustness test of Equation 1.2 using fixed-effects regression with Driscoll–Kraay standard error. The purpose is to check for the robustness of the effects of ownership structure variables on the agency costs when operating expense ratio is employed to proxy agency costs (AC2). Variables are denoted as follows. AC2 is the operating expense measure of agency costs. GOV(–1) is lagged government ownership. INS(–1) is lagged insider ownership. FOR(–1) is lagged foreign ownership. LEV is financial leverage. SIZE is firm size. AGE is firm age. Robust standard errors are reported in parentheses under the coefficients. The individual coefficient is statistically significant at the *10%, **5% or ***1% significance level.

*Appendix A5.3a* Robustness tests of non-recursive model using AC2

| *Dependent variable*<br>*Equation* | *AC2*<br>*(3.13)* | *RT*<br>*(3.14)* | *ROA*<br>*(3.15)* | *Q*<br>*(3.16)* | *GOV*<br>*(3.17)* | *INS*<br>*(3.18)* | *FOR*<br>*(3.19)* |
|---|---|---|---|---|---|---|---|
| **AC2** | | | –1.435 | –0.156 | | | |
| | | | (0.200)*** | (0.019)*** | | | |
| **RT** | | | 14.867 | –0.697 | | | |
| | | | (9.873) | (0.698) | | | |
| **GOV(–1)** | –0.054 | 0.017 | –0.323 | 0.003 | | | |
| | (0.007)*** | (0.009)* | (0.227) | (0.018) | | | |
| **INS(–1)** | –0.068 | 0.012 | –0.170 | 0.004 | | | |
| | (0.013)*** | (0.007)* | (0.134) | (0.007) | | | |
| **FOR(–1)** | 0.054 | 0.003 | –0.011 | 0.005 | | | |
| | (0.006)*** | (0.002) | (0.084) | (0.003) | | | |
| **LEV** | 0.014 | –0.003 | –0.056 | 0.002 | –0.012 | | –0.075 |
| | (0.014) | (0.003) | (0.053) | (0.002) | (0.017) | | (0.037)** |
| **SIZE** | –2.203 | | –4.438 | –0.354 | –0.388 | –1.020 | 3.362 |
| | (0.606)*** | | (0.343)*** | (0.100)*** | (0.176)** | (1.589) | –0.075 |
| **AGE** | 0.746 | | | | | –0.049 | |
| | (0.131)*** | | | | | (0.232) | |
| **BIG4** | | 0.056 | –2.813 | 0.066 | | | |
| | | (0.087) | (0.878)*** | (0.065) | | | |
| **GRO** | | 0.001 | | | | 0.009 | 0.008 |
| | | (0.001)* | | | | (0.004)** | (0.006) |

(*Continued*)

*Appendix A5.3a* (Continued)

| *Dependent variable*<br>*Equation* | *AC2*<br>*(3.13)* | *RT*<br>*(3.14)* | *ROA*<br>*(3.15)* | *Q*<br>*(3.16)* | *GOV*<br>*(3.17)* | *INS*<br>*(3.18)* | *FOR*<br>*(3.19)* |
|---|---|---|---|---|---|---|---|
| FIN | | 0.000<br>(0.002) | | | | | |
| ROA(–1) | | | 0.007<br>(0.073) | | –0.085<br>(0.052) | –0.038<br>(0.067) | 0.189<br>(0.055)*** |
| Q(–1) | | | | –0.064<br>(0.102) | 3.574<br>(0.475)*** | –1.497<br>(0.980) | –3.153<br>(2.037) |
| MARET | | | | | | | –1.502<br>(2.028) |
| SOE | | | | | 52.595<br>(0.792)*** | | |
| _cons | 49.359<br>(12.427)*** | 1.267<br>(0.355)*** | 95.534<br>(13.416)*** | 10.021<br>(2.677)*** | 4.910<br>(3.388) | 24.367<br>(33.485) | –61.236<br>(17.803)*** |
| N | 380 | 380 | 380 | 380 | 380 | 380 | 380 |

Notes: This table presents the results of ML estimation for the robustness tests of the non-recursive model using the second proxy of agency costs namely operating expense ratio (AC2). Variables are denoted as follows. AC2 is agency costs (operating expense ratio). RT is corporate risk-taking. GOV is government ownership. GOV(–1) is lagged government ownership. INS is insider ownership. INS(–1) is lagged insider ownership. FOR is foreign ownership. FOR(–1) is lagged foreign ownership. LEV is financial leverage. SIZE is firm size. AGE is firm age. BIG4 is Big-4 auditing company. GRO is firm growth. FIN is financial investment. ROA is return on assets. ROA(–1) is prior return on assets. Q is Tobin's Q. Q(–1) is prior Tobin's Q. MARKET is listing market. SOE is formerly state-owned enterprises. All equations are estimated simultaneously. Year-clustered robust standard errors are presented in parentheses under the coefficients. Covariance structures of disturbances are specified as unstructured (i.e. disturbances are freed to be correlated). Estimates of industry dummies and firm dummies are excluded for brevity. The individual coefficient is statistically significant at the *10%, **5% or ***1% significant level.

*Appendix A5.3b* Robustness tests of non-recursive model using LEV2

| *Dependent variable*<br>*Equation* | *AC*<br>*(3.13)* | *RT*<br>*(3.14)* | *ROA*<br>*(3.15)* | *Q*<br>*(3.16)* | *GOV*<br>*(3.17)* | *INS*<br>*(3.18)* | *FOR*<br>*(3.19)* |
|---|---|---|---|---|---|---|---|
| **AC** | | | –24.238<br>(3.167)*** | –2.342<br>(0.220)*** | | | |
| **RT** | | | 10.619<br>(10.933) | –0.458<br>(0.467) | | | |
| **GOV(–1)** | 0.003<br>(0.001)*** | 0.017<br>(0.009)* | –0.094<br>(0.206) | 0.016<br>(0.011) | | | |
| **INS(–1)** | 0.001<br>(0.003) | 0.013<br>(0.006)** | 0.010<br>(0.150) | 0.015<br>(0.008)* | | | |
| **FOR(–1)** | –0.001<br>(0.002) | 0.004<br>(0.002)** | –0.120<br>(0.103) | –0.007<br>(0.006) | | | |
| **LEV2** | –0.001<br>(0.000)*** | 0.001<br>(0.001) | –0.041<br>(0.012)*** | –0.001<br>(0.000)*** | –0.001<br>(0.003) | | –0.010<br>(0.006) |
| **SIZE** | –0.312<br>(0.043)*** | | –8.018<br>(1.699)*** | –0.762<br>(0.075)*** | –0.518<br>(0.253)** | –1.169<br>(1.621) | 3.637<br>(1.079)*** |
| **AGE** | 0.048<br>(0.009)*** | | | | | –0.013<br>(0.225) | |
| **BIG4** | | 0.023<br>(0.069) | –2.404<br>(0.264)*** | 0.030<br>(0.046) | | | |
| **GRO** | | 0.001<br>(0.001)* | | | | 0.014<br>(0.005)*** | 0.004<br>(0.006) |

(*Continued*)

*Appendix A5.3b* (Continued)

| *Dependent variable* *Equation* | *AC* *(3.13)* | *RT* *(3.14)* | *ROA* *(3.15)* | *Q* *(3.16)* | *GOV* *(3.17)* | *INS* *(3.18)* | *FOR* *(3.19)* |
|---|---|---|---|---|---|---|---|
| **FIN** | | 0.001 (0.003) | | | | | |
| **ROA(–1)** | | | –0.018 (0.066) | | –0.083 (0.051) | –0.035 (0.071) | 0.175 (0.050)*** |
| **Q(–1)** | | | | –0.050 (0.107) | 3.253 (0.498)*** | –1.336 (1.072) | –3.164 (2.197) |
| **MARET** | | | | | | | –3.861 (1.278)*** |
| **SOE** | | | | | 52.439 (0.561)*** | | |
| **_cons** | 7.127 (1.006)*** | 0.969 (0.327)*** | 184.141 (41.179)*** | 19.044 (1.828)*** | 7.354 (5.010) | 27.236 (34.093) | –67.675 (19.975)*** |
| **N** | 380 | 380 | 380 | 380 | 380 | 380 | 380 |

Notes: This table presents the results of ML estimation for the robustness tests of the non-recursive model using another measure of financial leverage (LEV2). Variables are denoted as follows. AC is agency costs. RT is corporate risk-taking. GOV is government ownership. GOV(–1) is lagged government ownership. INS is insider ownership. INS(–1) is lagged insider ownership. FOR is foreign ownership. FOR(–1) is lagged foreign ownership. LEV2 is financial leverage (the ratio of total liabilities over total common equity). SIZE is firm size. AGE is firm age. BIG4 is Big-4 auditing company. GRO is firm growth. FIN is financial investment. ROE is return on equity. ROE(–1) is lagged return on equity. Q is Tobin's Q. Q(–1) is prior Tobin's Q. MARKET is listing market. SOE is formerly state-owned enterprises. All equations are estimated simultaneously. Year-clustered robust standard errors are presented in parentheses under the coefficients. Covariance structures of disturbances are specified as unstructured (i.e. disturbances are freed to be correlated). Estimates of industry dummies and firm dummies are excluded for brevity. The individual coefficient is statistically significant at the *10%, **5% or ***1% significant level.

# Index

Note: *Italic* page numbers refer to figures; **Bold** page numbers refer to tables and page numbers followed by "n" indicate notes.

For Product Safety Concerns and Information please contact our EU
representative GPSR@taylorandfrancis.com
Taylor & Francis Verlag GmbH, Kaufingerstraße 24, 80331 München, Germany

www.ingramcontent.com/pod-product-compliance
Ingram Content Group UK Ltd.
Pitfield, Milton Keynes, MK11 3LW, UK
UKHW022354190926
475702UK00015B/2289
* 9 7 8 1 0 3 2 1 8 6 9 0 0 *